MW01260054

The Essential I Ching

360 Degrees of Wisdom

Also by the same author:

The Mind's Mirror: Dream Dictionary ~ Translation Guide
Nothing Bad Happens in Life: Nature's Way of Success
Tao te Ching: The Poetry of Nature
The Mythology of Sleep: The Waking Power of Dreams
The Common Archetypes of Tarot: Dreams and Myths

The Essential I Ching
360 Degrees of Wisdom

By Kari Hohne

Published by Way of Tao Books.
P.O. Box 1753 Carnelian Bay, Ca 96140
PaperBird is a division of Way of Tao Books.
www.wayoftao.com
Printed in the United States of America

ISBN 978-0-9819779-4-2

For Ryan

In the great circle
the light is timeless

and the earth
incomplete.

What lasts forever
is a movement
without a rest.

All that opposes,
is also complimentary.
The art of yielding
surrenders the past.

We live the questions
because uncertainty
is the only answer.

"Changes is a book
from which one may not hold aloof.
Its Tao is forever changing;
alteration, movement without rest.

Flowing through
the six empty places;
rising and sinking
without fixed law,
Firm and yielding
transform each other.

They cannot be confined
within a rule;
it is only change
that is at work here."

The I Ching or Book of Changes is one of the world's oldest works of literature. It is based on the ancient idea of Yin as a magnetic field and Yang as the active force of creation. Together, they complete each other because one cannot exist without the other.

The creation of the eight Pa Kua or trigrams at the root of the sixty-four principles are ascribed to the legendary Fu-hsi, who ruled during the third millennium BC. Each hexagram is composed of four trigrams: upper, lower and two nuclear trigrams.

Each of the sixty-four hexagrams embodies principles active in nature as it seeks to transform. Since nature is in a continuous movement toward change, the Book of

Changes allows one to examine what nature can reveal about the human journey.

The I Ching presents a flowing and well ordered universe moving through sixty-four transformative principles as a pathway to empowerment. By observing natural forces active in the world, each portrays an evolutionary principle in a way that will allow you to understand life's pursuit of growth applied to your current situation.

Over the centuries, the I Ching evolved as a popular oracle. Its roots, however, show it to be a profound philosophical work with a great influence on Taoism, Confucianism, Buddhism and Zen. Virtually all of the ancient Chinese philosophers were inspired by its basic principles and the interpretations in this book include many of their quotes.

"As a book, the I Ching is vast and comprehensive: by following the principles of essence and life, understanding the reasons of the obscure and the obvious, and comprehending the conditions of things and beings, it shows the way to enlighten people and accomplish tasks." Ch'eng I 11th century AD

Founded upon the ancient concept of Yin and Yang, and captured in the images of changing lines, each of the sixty four principles is constructed by six variations of either solid (Yang) or broken (Yin) lines. The idea of Yin and Yang literally means the dark and sunny side of a hill. While it is the same hill, there is a natural ebbing and flowing of phenomena that has the effect of changing its appearance.

"Tao is the One, which emerges as the Two." Tao is portrayed in the joining of negative Yin and positive Yang. In science we observe a pushing and pulling phenomena in force and field although they are interdependent.. "The Three emanate to become the many," called the "ten thousand things." Science also describes the interaction of the negatively charged electron and positive nuclei as the building blocks of the many manifestations that we observe.

Legend describes how Fu-hsi looked upward to contemplate the images of heaven, and looked downward to contemplate its manifestation on the earth. On the back of a tortoise shell, he discovered the arrangement of the eight trigrams that defined the order of change in the cosmos. It was these basic ideas that gave birth to this ancient philosophical text and even Confucius was known to have a well-thumbed copy of the I Ching.

Other legends describe King Wen, founder of the Chou Dynasty as the author of the sixty-four principles. Forced to remain in prison by a warring rival, he saw the sixty-four images on the wall of his cell. Representing the forces of change inherent in the universe, he translated these images into words.

"Without going anywhere, one can see the way of heaven."

Regardless of where this philosophical treatise originated, it became a philosophy of change that greatly influenced Taoism. This return to nature philosophy presented a universe that is in constant change. Augmented by the many philosophers of ancient China, the I Ching developed as a text that interprets how situations change and evolve. The Tao te Ching is also a compilation of many philosophers and presents a book that cultivates te as one comes to follow the mysterious Way of Tao. In this way, the history of Taoism demonstrates how nature moves us powerfully toward regeneration.

> What need has nature
> of thought or care?
> When the sun goes,
> the moon comes.
>
> Cold and heat alternate.
> The past contracts,
> the future expands.
>
> When you can understand
> the transformations,
> you lift your nature
> to the level
> of the miraculous."
>
> --I Ching

The I Ching Oracle

In ancient times, rulers consulted oracles where characters were engraved onto tortoise shells or bones. Inserting a heated bronze pin, cracks would form on the reverse side. By analyzing the cracks in relation to the characters, important decisions were made. From the characters carved onto shells and bones, the original Chinese language of pictographs emerged. While other civilizations developed letters and a phonetic system of language, Chinese would remain a language based largely on picture images.

Those who could read the oracles were called shih and developed as the scholarly-gentry class who roamed the countryside, advising rulers. While the decaying Chou Empire was giving way to the Warring States Period, speculation and philosophical thought turned toward exploring the foundation for proper government and ethics. It was in this environment of practical concerns that the Hundred Schools arose and Chinese thought entered its Golden Era. As scholars traveled from one feudal state to another, they became government officials and offered rulers ideas for social reform.

Through experience and study, the Great Masters recognized nature as a teacher. They observed the effects of the sun, wind, rain and other elements apparent in the natural world. Eight Primary principles (Pa Gua) would emerge, describing the forces inherent in change, and they applied these ideas to the human condition. They used these principles as a guide in promoting an understanding of how rulers and their people could practice the way of nature.

Each of the sixty four principles is composed of variations of Yin and Yang lines. Four trigrams emerge in each composition and their changing positions describe the current environment and how one can equip themselves to approach it. "Knowing that which is to come can make you the master of your experiences."

"The beginning line is difficult to understand.
The top line is easy to understand.
For they stand in the relationship to cause and effect."

The beginning line represents the unknown elements at play as something new emerges to set the stage for change. The top line "is easy to understand" because it represents all that has become familiar and the aspect of the situation, which has run its course as one hexagram transforms into the next one. The upper and lower trigrams describe the current situation as portrayed by the successive movement of the eight Pa Kua. Inside of each principle are two additional nuclear trigrams, which suggest a proper approach in meeting changing events: what not to do and what is attempting to manifest.

Each trigram suggests an image and in some cases, the hexagram is unchanging. In this case, one is asked to appreciate the deeper aspects of this message. At other times, the first situation will be described as changing

(First Hexagram) into a second image (Second Hexagram). Both images need to be considered as a pathway to enlightenment.

Observing conflict as a pathway to return to Tao a cycle of interpretations result in sixty-four possible combinations of Yin and Yang lines. The lower and upper trigrams represent nature in a state of transformation and how they interact. As these natural forces move toward or away from each other, they embody the different types of situations you may encounter. The nuclear trigrams suggest how best to approach the changes. When you emulate nature, these active principles will teach you how to achieve success, using every opportunity as a way to manifest your Tao.

The interpretations in the Essential I Ching are based on the 64 principles from the Book of Changes with interpretations inspired by the elements of nature.

Throwing the Coins

By throwing three coins six times, a primary hexagram will be built from the bottom up based upon the lines created by the coin toss. Coins are determined to be either heads or tails where the head side is Yang and the tail side is Yin. Traditional I Ching coins show four figures on a coin as Yin and two figures as Yang. Three of the same side will lead to an Old Yang, Old Yin or what is called a changing line.

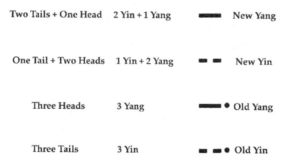

Two Tails + One Head	2 Yin + 1 Yang	▬▬	New Yang
One Tail + Two Heads	1 Yin + 2 Yang	▬ ▬	New Yin
Three Heads	3 Yang	▬▬●	Old Yang
Three Tails	3 Yin	▬ ▬●	Old Yin

How Hexagrams are Created

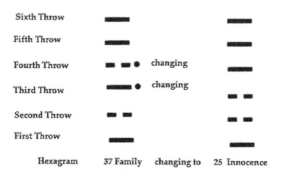

Sixth Throw	▬▬		▬▬
Fifth Throw	▬▬		▬▬
Fourth Throw	▬ ▬●	changing	▬▬
Third Throw	▬▬●	changing	▬ ▬
Second Throw	▬ ▬		▬ ▬
First Throw	▬▬		▬▬
Hexagram	37 Family	changing to	25 Innocence

The Changing Lines

There are four types of lines that can be generated by throwing the coins: Yang (solid) Yin (broken) Old Yang (changing Solid) and Old Yin (changing Broken.) Any changing or old lines will create a secondary hexagram which reveals both the basis of your question and the changes that are at play. Consider both hexagrams and any changing lines as an answer to your question. You will find a trigram chart at end of this book.

No Changing Lines: If you receive a hexagram with no changing lines, read the interpretation for the Unchanging hexagram. Unchanging hexagrams are observed to be in a static condition and require careful examination in order to understand why the situation might be at an impasse or unchanging.

Primary and Secondary Hexagrams

The secondary or relating hexagram can show both the foundation of your question and the potential outcome. In many cases, the transformed hexagram will show the lingering atmosphere or longer influence at play while the first hexagram is revealing your current mindset. For example, (64) Before Completion, line 3 changing to become (50) Cauldron would suggest that a situation requiring patience to 'simmer in the pot' (50) to define itself more completely is meeting your current mindset that it should be reaching completion already. So line 3 of hexagram (64) warns you about moving too hastily on past assumptions and the need for patience to examine other possible outcomes.

The lines will offer advice about how to transcend any misunderstandings about the principles at work in both hexagrams. This is important because many people use the wrong approach in assuming the first hexagram always changes to become the second. Change is not linear ~ it is usually circular. In this way the primary and secondary hexagrams are interacting and influencing each other ~ one is not always destined to become the other. The hidden influence or Nuclear

Hexagram of (64) Before Completion is (63) After Completion. Hexagram (63) can feel like a missed opportunity when we fail to prepare for the inevitable cycle of change. That is the lesson of (64) Before Completion too, because its message is about preparation. Looking too far ahead, or operating with impatience and hard line assumptions would lead (64) Expecting Completion to feel more like the initiation/testing or challenge presented by (50) Cauldron. Any disappointment or 'dark night of the soul' testing (50) Cauldron can occur because you failed to heed the warning of line 3 to do things differently.

The Most Comprehensive I Ching Reading

For deeper insight into the meaning of a changing line, all line interpretations include the resulting hexagram that would have been generated if that were the only line changing. For example (31) Wooing with line 2 changing would become (28) Critical Mass. Line 2 is a warning about the same excess that (28) Critical Mass describes so the message of (31) Wooing line 2 suggests Wooing requires a strong foundation. The roof of your aspirations with a weak foundation and aggressive response won't work because (28) offers a message: too much. Add line 5 which would have changed to become (62) Small Exceeding and we are warned to honor the small and less significant aspects and not be too rigid. When both lines are changing (31) Wooing leads to (32) Duration because we establish a strong foundation (line 2) with flexibility, consistency and honor the small things (line 5.)

10

Hexagram interpretations also include the Hu Gua or nuclear hexagram as a secondary influence and the Zong Gua or reversed hexagram which shows the opposite condition.

The Hu Gua gives added insight into the meaning of a hexagram because it shows the base motivation that is trying to manifest within the core hexagram. For example, the Hu Gua of (6) Conflict shows (7) Family as both the dynamics that can create conflict and how establishing clarity in expectations (like the Family) can solve it.

The Zong Gua of (6) Conflict would be (36) Brightness Hiding which is the opposite of what should be done in this situation. In Brightness Hiding we would have assumed nothing needed rectification and merely held to our inner light.

Which Line Prevails in an I Ching Reading?

Often there can be conflicting information in the interpretations when multiple lines are changing. Some oracle readers view the progression from bottom to top and consider the topmost line as the prevailing line. Others observe Line 5 as the highest expression in activating the message of the hexagram. Line 6 can show how the hexagram's message gets exhausted or is overdone. When line 1 and 6 are the only changing lines, many feel that the Hexagram's message is especially auspicious in that a line by line examination will need to be explored to make its message more clear. In (31) Wooing line 1, we are not inspired enough to act and in line 6 any action is superficial. When both lines change it leads to (13) Fellowship which is a superficial connection without intimacy. We would need to explore each line of (31) Wooing if we want to understand the law of attraction, especially when the heart is involved. In (12) Standstill we get stuck. This is where the transforming lines mentioned above become important. Line 1 associates with (25) Innocence so we open our perspective. Line 6 associates with (45) Gathering Together or networking. If both lines change it leads to (17) Following. If we are stuck, an innocent outlook and networking incorporates the needs or vision of others in a way that others follow. (12) Standstill with only line 5 changing (hexagrams highest expression) leads to (35) Progress. In line 5 we see that the only obstacle is fear or clinging to the past. We recommend that you take all lines into consideration because intuitively you will be able to see beyond any conflicting line interpretations.

Below are additional guidelines from ancient texts that can be used to determine which line prevails:

No lines are changing: Read the unchanging interpretation for that Hexagram.
One line is changing: Read the advice of that line interpretation.
Two lines are changing: If the lines are the same (changing broken or changing solid) the changing line closest to the top prevails. If there is one of each, read only the changing broken (Yin) line.

Three lines are changing: Read the middle line.
Four lines are changing: Read the uppermost line that is
not changing.
Five lines are changing: Read the only non changing
line.
Six lines are changing: Read only the transformed
hexagram as the first hexagram has been exhausted.

By examining all possible ancient and modern
interpretations we strive to bring you the most
comprehensive I Ching translation. All interpretations
include quotes from the ancient masters of Chinese
philosophy as well as being based on the power of
nature which originally inspired the Book of Changes.

To get the most out of the I Ching oracle, approach it
with an open mind and as a Teacher. The I Ching was
originally composed by Taoist masters who had an
understanding of life which matches to how modern
physics describes it. Additionally, they were inspired by
natural processes where only now we are recognizing
how nature can be a teacher. Think of the answer as a
koan or riddle - this is not an oracle with random
messages to be rushed through. Contemplate the Hu
Gua, Zong Gua, lines and changing hexagrams until
you understand the message prior to asking more
questions.

Hexagram #1
Qián The Creative

Action: Initiate
Hu Gua (secondary influence) 1 Creative: Initiate
Zong Gua (underlying cause) 2 Receptive: Yield
Received as 2nd Hexagram: Empowerment is at the core of your question.

Life shows its harmony,
when you discover your connection to what unfolds.

A little kingdom I possess, where thoughts and feelings dwell;
and very hard, the task I find of governing it well. – L.M.
Alcott

Reading at a glance: The Creative embodies the active principle in the universe and represents initiating action. The lines in this hexagram refer to the Dragon which in China is honored as a benevolent and powerful creature. When this energy of empowerment remains dormant in the psyche we can give our power away. We can operate with the undermining or self gratifying and fearful behavior of the ego. This suppressed energy funds the Shadow in dreams, a great source of our original power. We therefore project and encounter it in others until we can own it and become fully empowered. An opportunity for expansion and authentic empowerment emerges which requires assertiveness and persistence. If you currently feel held back or victimized, remove the shackles because they are merely self limiting beliefs. Initiative is required to succeed, although it is important to move in sync with the time and respond with openness. The Creative is duplicated in the secondary influence position and underscores the idea of initiating where the Receptive as the Zong Gua shows that a period of reflection and retreat must give way to active expression. A new burst of inspiration has gestated and you can now bring it life. There is great potential waiting for you to tap it.

Lifted up by
what is pressed down,
the great untangles the night.

"The clouds pass and the rain does its work and all individual beings flow into their forms." Qián is made up of all Yang lines showing potential and beginnings where action is necessary to manifest this energy. Qián coaches you to take responsibility to become empowered in a current situation. Although circumstances might appear to be working at cross purposes to what you are trying to achieve, change is on the horizon that will allow you to express your greater capabilities.

The master says: *"you cannot plant a large tree within a small pot."* Plant yourself in an environment of expansion. Open yourself to wonder because what you experience is only limited by your beliefs. To be successful, you must ensure that any self doubt or insecurity is eliminated. Even if initial steps bring about a challenge open to how this hones your ability to succeed. Don't give up.

Be firm in standing up for what you feel you should to do in a situation where you may feel powerless. Without the freedom to keep growing, your authenticity is stunted.

You can no longer claim to be a victim. Everything that is unfolding is propelling you toward growth and actualization. If you feel stuck, look for the closed doors that are leading you toward an open door.

Meeting the world of events, you may believe that you have nothing to do with what is unfolding. There is an inconsistency of belief, each time you take responsibility for your success, but blame events for your failure. To discover Tao's fundamental harmony you must first uncover your connection to what unfolds.

The width and depth of your beliefs mirror the growth of your branches above. When you take inventory of what you are currently doing in thought and action, you will discover the seeds of what you are making of tomorrow. The Creative offers a message of inspired rebirth and a chance to harness your further capabilities. Creativity, inspiration or a new idea is secondary influence so loosen the borders of your paradigm and free yourself.

Take a chance and have faith that everything is coaching your real nature forward. You have an opportunity to be more empowered by confronting your fear of change. Once you remove the barriers of fear, you will experience life in more powerful and fulfilling ways. The Creative is a sign that you are ready for greater challenges and can open you to the ultimate reward it will bring.

Qián means force and as the great Creative Power is the inspiration behind all form and requires some sort of application to give it life. Open to the inspiration that is seeking to manifest through you.

Unchanging: Dragon stirring unexpressed = action is needed to give it form. The Creative unchanging shows powerful feelings or inspiration not acted upon. It can be a warning that insecurity may be inhibiting your ability to see opportunity when it presents itself. It can symbolize focusing on the hope that something will transpire rather than taking the active steps to make it manifest. Some sort of action is necessary to bring this opportunity into form. Like a fruitful seed that has landed on a rock, you need only move it into the soil of purposeful action so that it can grow. Otherwise it will remain as the dream of a flower that dried up and blew away in the wind because you failed to nurture it. You may have heard the call to do something but your fear is holding you back. A creative or transformative opportunity is in gestation and requires time before the birth of inspiration reveals itself.

Line 1 Hidden Dragon = do not act. Changes to (44) Coming to Meet. The timing is inappropriate for action. Have patience so your plan can develop further, avoiding negative repercussions. You are in the early stages of realizing your goal. Be patient. Those depending on you may require reassurance but check that guilt is not holding you back from making a change. Don't blame others as what you encounter may simply be your Shadow or the energy that you project on others so you don't have to acknowledge your real face. You are eager because the temptation to act is stirring the great power within you.

Line 2 Dragon in the Field = get helpers. Changes to (13) Fellowship. Develop your talent and explore networking ideas. Establish a plan of action and incorporate the feedback and/or skills of others. Don't be selective in choosing feedback because the more diverse the group, the better. Great potential is emerging but it is best realized when you are not going it alone. If you are diligent, your harvest will succeed.

Line 3 All day all night = powerful but does not threaten. Changes to (10) Treading. The power to succeed is rising although tread carefully, knowing that new ideas can bring about opposition. Gain consensus by showing that what you are attempting to do is of benefit to others. Ensure that you have the capacity to carry your plan forward. Don't rush. Monitor your

19

words and actions and behave moderately – the situation is delicate.

Line 4 Dragon leaping over pond = attempting to fly but safe. Changes to (9) Small Restraint .Your plan of action is ready for implementation and yet you may need to play it safe. Perhaps you must pay attention to the small details. While difficulty may have appeared at first, there is nothing to worry about so have confidence. Take it one step at a time. Big things are accomplished only by heaping up small things over time. Your power to succeed relies on gentle persuasion, not aggressiveness.

Line 5 Dragon flying in sky = realizing ambition. Changes to (14) Great Possessing. Due to connections and confidence, all lights are green and your success is assured. Be sure to reward those who assisted you in your success. This is a powerful line that is connected to a powerful hexagram. Timely action, confidence and virtue will pay off. You are in sync with your Tao and have the power to succeed. Whatever it is that you are creating for yourself can become the illumination for others. Stop thinking and fly. The energy is bigger than you and it is correct.

Line 6 Haughty Dragon = acts without support, cause to repent. Changes to (43) Determination. Success needs no aggression and pomp. Remove doubt and insecurity to ensure completion in your efforts. You may feel like you can go it alone or don't need support, but that will lead to misfortune. Victory may appear easy and within reach, but therein is the danger. The sixth line indicates the end of the opportunity so this might be your last chance to check your attitude to ensure you are sincere and not acting defensively.

Hexagram #2
K'un The Receptive

Action: Reflect
Hu Gua (secondary influence) 2 Receptive: Yield
Zong Gua (underlying cause) 1 Creative: Initiate
Received as 2nd Hexagram: A need to open is at the core of your question.

Reaction is how you defend the past against the future.

Take rest; a field that has rested gives a bountiful crop. –
Ovid

Reading at a Glance: K'un calls for a period of patience and reflection. Where you may have been reactive in the past, it is time to learn how to be responsive. Reaction is a defensive position to uphold the known while responsiveness is open to the unknown. K'un encourages you to yield to the way each day is a creative awakening. A sense of openness and the release of clinging to structure and form will be necessary to give birth to this energy. The difference between reaction and response is your ability to use your senses and not the memory mind while observing. Stand in the moment with a sense of openness to what is unfolding without defending the past. Connect with each sense: Are you listening? Are you seeing how life speaks to you? Remove preconceptions and judgment. All things change in time and a period of action, reflected by the Zong Gua of the Creative must give way to its opposite: Reflection. Like winter it is time to turn within and reinvigorate your inner world in preparation for a spring time to come. Embodying an open field in any activity – you are called to put your needs aside to serve, open and reflect before acting. K'un's power of success comes from within. Move into the world from the inside ~ out. The Receptive is the womb holding the energy of attraction by way of intention that requires the development of sincerity and patience.

And in the night,
the moon like a bow,
plays the song of the sun.

"The Receptive is in harmony with the boundless; it embraces everything and illuminates everything in its greatness."
K'un is composed of all Yin lines and coaches you to become more still, observant and *less reactive.* By 'not

doing anything' you become a spectator to see how circumstances unfold to guide you.

The master said: *"when closely related things do not harmonize, misfortune is the result."* Misfortune is simply how you fight against necessary change. Sometimes K'un can be a message about letting the past go and opening to something new. You may be too attached to what you believe you want, when Tao is bringing you what you need. Look around to see what life is saying to you *right now*. Pay more attention to your dreams to uncover the profound guidance that comes from within. When you cultivate a *natural response* to what unfolds, you react less and observe more. It is often in the things that you cannot change that you discover Tao's power to guide you the most.
Circumstances urge you forward, although reaction is how you defend the past against the future. A natural response means that you respond to life *without defending anything*.

We may find it odd that mystics deny the reality of the outer world, yet more people deny the immense power and reality of their *inner* world. Like the time of autumn when all things turn back to be renewed, you are coached to turn inward to reinvigorate your inner garden.

When you compose your inner world and control its gusts and storms, you will discover wellness and harmony in the outer world. Tao prods you forward, but misfortune is how *"those who go against the Way are called unlucky."*

If you are searching for direction, you will find it through your dreams, intuition and inspiration. When these inner clues are measured against events, synchronicity will validate your pathway. Be still and have patience so that you may begin to cultivate your personal connection to what unfolds.

There are times to push forward and times to remain still, as you *"move inward and outward according to fixed rhythms."* Stand in the moment and observe your reaction to what unfolds around you. When you stop reacting, you will find yourself *simply doing,* and you can move forward with a new sense of ease and power.

Unchanging: The quiet perseverance of the mare = do not lead, but follow. Without changing lines it is important to be open and acquiesce to others. There is not a lot you can do to change the situation, but your patience and receptivity is all that is required. If you are open and truly interested in serving and not taking, you can make something out of the fertile valley. Like the Creative unchanging, there is potential but it may be blocked for now. The confusion is real and serves the purpose of unleashing a more realistic perspective. Like a deep ravine, emotion is stirring but there may be no way to actualize it. This can happen when a relationship hits an impasse. The feeling is there but it can't be acted upon for some reason, at least not now. The energy that flows through the openings can suggest that what you think is happening is happening and you want to grasp your desire, but time is just passing by. Trust this time of flowing with something you have no control over. Without a true understanding of your motives, the question can be thrown back at you: "Have you considered where this action would lead? What purpose does your desire serve? Does what you want serve the other person's interests too? Can you make a commitment and follow through?" Therefore, examine your motives to ensure that you can be receptive enough to proceed. You may be meeting the moment with a lot of plans that won't have any effect on the outcome, so let them go. Your perseverance is recognized however, and another may be opening to you because of your undying loyalty.

Line 1 Treading on hoarfrost, surely turns to ice = each step solidifies your decision. Changes to (24) Return. It is important to follow your inner drummer but realize that some decisions cannot be undone. Once you take this step, there may be no going back. You may have to go against another's wishes to take the path you feel is right for you. However, you may Return to face the consequences of your impulsiveness. Observe cycles in nature because if it looks like winter is coming, it probably is. You may have to contend with another's coldness in response to your actions.

Line 2 Straight through the unfamiliar = speak your heart, it is not a disadvantage. Changes to (7) The Army. Everything unfolds naturally because it feels right and others recognize the value in following your initiative. Your open and honest invitation comes from the heart and is straight to the point. Any illusions or misconceptions are clarified. The situation has elements that you haven't dealt with before but being truthful can help gain allegiance to your cause. Move forward like a soldier of the heart, unafraid of what you encounter.

Line 3 Keeping the story to yourself = relying on another's completion of matters. Changes to (15) Authenticity. Acting humbly and working hard allows you to complete the job. You may need to work quietly for the benefit of another without seeking credit. Or, you may need to allow another to complete something prior to moving forward. Eventually success is ensured because you put quality work and integrity above your need for recognition. Authenticity can only develop through interdependency not dependency.

Line 4 Enclosing in a sack = no improvement because one remains closed. Changes to (16) Enthusiasm. Awareness may be too narrow or being fearful, you miss out on the joy of discovery. You may be hesitant about entering a situation where you will gain benefit. There is no reason not to trust events and invitations. Your own attitude and outlook are diminishing the opportunity for joy and fulfillment. Open to the mystery of life without the need to classify the outcome.

Line 5 A yellow lower garment = modest and ordinary so all goes well. Changes to (8) Uniting. Dreams and meditation allow you to tap into a higher sense of awareness. It may seem that ego is here to discover spirit, but witnessing life as spirit is just a shift in perception, an awakening that will connect you to the here and now. Ego understands time as limitation but spirit has a timeless and unbiased outlook. Union suggests two manifestations of one thing, like matter and energy, although nothing is separate. When in doubt about your nature, remember who you were as a child. What is unchanging about you? Be that. Find a way to give it expression to your field of dreams.

Line 6 Dragons fight in the field, their blood is old = fighting for a long time in an incapacitating situation. Changes to (23) Split Apart. The difference between having a response and having a reaction is the ability to listen and not defend your beliefs. Sometimes people defend each other's differences rather than identify their similarities. The opportunity for renewal in the situation requires a blending of opposite qualities into a higher order. The symbol of 3 in dreams is how an either/or outlook blends to allow for all possibilities. If you want to discover the other person's value, learn to listen to them. However, there is a limit to what can be done in this situation because the negativity has festered for some time.

Hexagram #3
Chun (Difficult Beginnings)

Action: Persevere
Hu Gua (secondary influence) 23 Split Apart: Regenerate
Zong Gua: (underlying cause) 50 Cauldron: Refine
Received as 2nd Hexagram: A need for patience is at play in your question.

**Dragging the adversary about when there is no adversary
will cost you your inner treasure.**

*Do the thing you fear, and the death of fear is certain. –
Emerson*

Reading at a Glance: Just as a seedling must crack open and push through soil and rocks to reach its source of solar nourishment, all new endeavors encounter obstacles in the beginning stages. The time calls for persevering into regeneration. Obstacles refine our sincerity about what we are doing, and hone our inner vision. The arrangement of the I Ching generally unfolds where each hexagram is viewed to be the cause or response of the preceding one. Yet Chun is the result of two hexagrams: The Creative and the Receptive interacting. Therefore Chun embodies how opposite yet powerful energies give birth to something new. This hexagram has a unique message where an unavoidable but difficult encounter must come together such as in marriage. Because the situation has never gone before, it lacks the clarity that comes from experience, yet how refreshing! It embodies the sense that the situation is meant to be and its opposing qualities are what brought it to life in the first place. Chun can appear when a commitment is being considered and the act of considering it is what changed an Easy attraction into something Difficult. Like nature which would remain stagnant without necessary friction, Chun embodies perfectly how to embrace conflict as the driving force of evolution. Often we want to cast blame when we fail, but we always take responsibility for our success. To succeed, you must recognize how Tao improves deficiencies by sharpening them into skills. Life has always been committed to your success but going it alone is not an option here because the dynamic of interdependency is central to Chun. Learn to see the 'teacher' in those who challenge you. Eliminate defenses and preconceptions so you can be lifted to a higher level. The secondary influence describes the Splitting Apart of a past way of thinking, while the Cauldron refines and boils down your capabilities. Connect with your passion and purpose and persevere until you find a way to manifest your dream. In that regard, Chun embodies the dream coming into existence. The path ahead is new and promises wonderful transformational learning regardless of the outcome.

> *Each day begins*
> *a silvery spray,*
> *a washing away*
> *a strengthening.*

"Clouds and Thunder: the image of difficulty at the beginning." Chun is the image of a seedling that must immediately push beyond dirt and rocks to survive. At times we face what appears to be an obstacle, yet circumstances are merely breaking away our protective covering.

The master said: *"Danger and opportunity grow on one stalk."* They are inseparable from the perspective of growth. Do not be frightened of how Tao cultivates your strength of purpose.

Like a blade of grass, we follow an inborn pattern of direction. Events peel away the seed's protective husk when it is time to blossom. The rock may appear as an obstacle, but it holds soil and moisture where it is most needed. Difficulty nurtures and stabilizes you when you can see all obstacles as opportunities and not barriers.

Adversity allows you to see how Tao carves away your unnecessary layers. To be skilled in the Way, be fearless in approaching change; to be one with it however, you must trust the special nuances of your pathway.

The master said: *"when you examine your heart and find no taint, what cause is there for self pity or fear?"* A heart tainted by fear projects the very barriers that reinforce a sense of self-pity. To rule the empire, you cannot have dragons lurking about.

Knowing that there are no adversaries allows you to move forward with a sense of power. *"Dragging the adversary about when there is no adversary will cost you your inner treasure."* When you unmask the adversary, you will see how having an enemy allows you to blame someone or something else for your condition.

The more you deny your power to be real, the more conflicted life becomes. Yet, Tao would set you free and is always seeking to prod you into being the best of what you can be.

All new endeavors embody a level of uncertainty but this is no reason to give up. Operating without obvious reinforcement is the only way that you can find your *inner* direction. The most amazing discoveries come from one individual following only their inner drummer. Something within you is struggling for definition and it is being shaped by unfolding events. Holding to a vision of being the best that you can be, nothing ever comes to block your way. It only makes you stronger. Difficult beginnings is how nature takes note of what is emerging and works to test and strengthen it. After a period of Difficult Beginnings your sincerity about what you are doing becomes clear.

Unchanging: Difficult beginnings as a gift = the path knows you are coming. If you receive this hexagram unchanging, you may not even be aware of a looming change on the horizon. It can be a message to start small and stay focused on the work, regardless of how inexperienced or unsure you may feel. The fact that Difficult Beginnings shows up static prompts you to look around to see what new beginning is not occurring because you are rooted to the past. A difficult decision may be required that you are avoiding. If you are rooted in the old, nothing should be continued. Chun unchanging is like a cosmic gift you may not deserve but the universe supports it in some way. Whatever the beginning, once you recognize it as the proper path, perseverance leads to success. You may not even realize how lucky you are to have the path cleared before you.

Line 1 Insurmountable obstacle, conserve and build strength = seek advice. Changes to (8) Uniting. An obstacle appears that seems insurmountable like stone, but there is someone who is able to help you. Your path is correct and you are offered support by a reliable person who won't let you down. In this line we learn the value of relationships.

Line 2 The wagon and horses are separated. It is not a robbery, but a wooing = commitment makes anything possible. Changes to (60) Limitation. Limitations are the breeding ground for nature's strengths. A period of waiting has to occur to test your resolve and allow you to discover a sense of commitment. Rather than change course, stay with what you have built. The power of commitment is like gravity and is unaffected by obstacles or time. If you know you want it then make a commitment to 'woo' it. In this line we see how the excited energy of opposing forces feels like a robbery, but has 'joining together' as its purpose.

Line 3 Hunting deer without knowing the way = resist acting without foresight or experience. Changes to (63) After Completion. Although a special opportunity has appeared, it is not wise to pursue it blindly because of the danger it presents. You do not have the experience or knowledge to make it work in your favor. Going forward leads to endings and humiliation. Complete a course of study or seek advice prior to moving forward.

Line 4 The wagon and horses are separated, you are cut off from something essential = striving for union. Changes to (17) Following. While following another, you may have become trapped. They may have followed you and feel trapped. The attraction is strong, but gaining union requires that you demonstrate your sincerity. Look at the situation more closely to understand what you are offering another and their intentions in accepting. Pursue the path that leads to fulfillment. Don't accept less than complete satisfaction. What you think you 'need' externally is actually found within.

Line 5 Difficulties that fertilize = move forward delicately. Changes to (24) Return. While you may have left the situation, returning is acceptable and is well received. The realization that comes from making a mistake actually improves the situation. The obstacle allowed you to connect with sincerity. It is still important to tread delicately.

Line 6 The wagon and horses are separated, an impasse is reached = brings great sadness and frustration. Changes to (42) Increase. While a door appears to close or an impasse emerges, know that opportunity for greater fulfillment is still possible. Perhaps the first approach to the situation was just too hard or unworkable. Don't allow failure to keep you from pursuing new opportunities or new approaches. Sometimes you need to discover what you don't want or can't have in order to discover the gift life offers you in what is. Until Difficulties are observed to be life's gestating force you cannot overcome them. Live the questions willingly until you realize that they are the answer.

Hexagram #4
Meng (Youthful Folly)

Action: Try Again
Hu Gua (secondary influence) 24 Return: Go Back
Zong Gua (underlying cause) 49 Molting/Revolution:
Transform
Received as 2nd Hexagram: An inability to process
what you are learning is at play.

To know success,
you must make peace with the idea of failing.

No man is free who is not a master of himself. – *Epictetus*

Reading at a Glance: The greatest thing Meng teaches is
how knowing something with inner certainty means
nothing needs to be defended. When we are ignorant
we use many words to defend our insecurity or vague
ideas. When we are enlightened, we need no words or
confirmation of our truth. Teachers come into our lives
in many forms. Be open to how this may be happening.
The time calls for going back and trying again. Criticism
can hurt our feelings, but if we desire to be the best we

can be then we need to be open to input. A teacher may say: "no, this isn't the right way – try again." However, when life does this to you by blocking your way, it is often viewed as a message to give up. Failing is no reason not to try again. Meng cultivates a state of mind that not only allows you to stand at the threshold of awareness without judgment, it also brings the joy of discovery that ensures your success. Life keeps us in a state of not knowing precisely to keep us growing. Much of the suffering we face has the purpose of leading us back to wonder. One who sees failure as a stepping stone for success always succeeds. The turning point during failure leads you to retreat, regroup and try again. The Zong Gua for Meng is that a period of Molting or Revolution has led to a state of Innocence where you can be led. It is time to become a student again.

Words,
like the shavings of a sculpture,
the substance revealed by silence.

"Youthful Folly means confusion and subsequent enlightenment." Meng asks you to recognize how failure is a prerequisite for your success. Do not hide your weakness. It can only be transformed into strength by exercising it. The journey is a process of discovery; the idea of a destination can be a trap, and the fear of failure can keep you from being the best you can be. Sometimes Youthful Folly can be a message that you already know or have the answer.

Like a student approaching a new course of study, know that trial and error will hone your expertise. This enlightenment brings forward a sense of stillness and power. Take everything in stride, but admit your mistakes so you can learn from them.

The master said: "*In search of stillness, you travel a journey of a thousand miles.*" The actual journey has the sublime effect of Returning you to your center and strengthening your trust in the way.

The Abysmal Water wells up at the foot of the Mountain, and portrays the inexperience of a youth who seeks a wider awareness. Folly describes the false starts that come from a lack of experience, but this trial and error is necessary to season you. If you want to know success, then you must make peace with the idea of failing.

In Tao's pursuit of excellence *"carving and polishing means removing the layers. Cutting and grinding is the cultivation of the self."* Meng is the symbol of something growing beneath a cover. It portrays the illusion of how you believe that you must conquer others to develop power. You will find that *"you must only conquer yourself."*

"Without looking out the window, you will discover the natural Way." Without looking out the window or following others, you discover a power within that grows beneath cover. You need not look to anything else to find your way.

The master said: *"One of little words has inner value."* In the process of learning, you will find that words are a measure of your inner certainty. To stand in silent knowing is real power.

When you feel the need to defend yourself, you are merely reassuring your own misgivings. At peace with who you are, energy can mount without the use of words. *"This is the inner strength that emerges from stillness."*

Meng can be a message that you are searching for something 'out there' to satisfy what can only be found 'in here.' You have attached yourself to an outcome that is blocking your inability to hear the message. Let go. Time is perfectly spaced to hear the echo of sincerity.

Unchanging: Foolish success = the fool receives answers but cannot hear. Don't continually ask the same question without understanding the message. It is as if you are being told to chew on the last answer before asking it again. You may need to give something time in order for the answer to become clear. Maybe you are operating on assumptions and are not open to hearing the answer. Perhaps the question needs to be tweaked a little before an answer is given. Like a student being given an answer in a koan, you may want an answer and instead, get only a riddle. But the riddle will disassemble your paradigm in a way that opens you to see beyond your question. One is only called a fool because of their beliefs and beliefs can change. With no changing lines perseverance in a changed approach to your questioning is in order.

Line 1 A fool needs discipline not fetters = inspire, don't humiliate. Changes to (41) Decrease. The idea of removing excess comes into play in this line. Whether you are learning or leading, subordinating your will to the cause is necessary. If you are facing an obstacle to your desire, how can the obstacle be transformed into opportunity through subordination? If you are leading others, follow behind and inspire their forward movement. Decrease force and open to possibilities.

Line 2 Bear fools in kindness = perspective comes from the unexpected. Changes to (23) Split Apart. In Taoism it is said that to overcome others we use power, but to overcome ourselves we are strong. While it may seem that you are powerless in this situation, you might benefit by the saying: "you get more bees with honey." A non threatening and lighthearted attitude works wonders. Just look how children achieve their desires through an innocent and playful attitude that adults simply cannot refuse. There is a way to succeed that a child already knows. You may need to spend time with the idea of not knowing or not having an answer in order to take off the glasses of preconceptions to truly recognize that anything is possible in this situation.

Line 3 Hold to strength = one becomes weak only by mimicking the strong. Changes to (18) Decay. In this situation you may be relying on dogma or other's ideas and opinions without exercising your unique perspective. As a leader, it may be time to reinvigorate the root of your teaching. As a student, you cannot just mimic the teacher but own the teaching by your actions. Integrity is called for rather than mimicry or copying. In a relationship you might be seeing the partner as your ideal and not necessarily as they really are. Avoid validating your weakness by giving your power to another.

Line 4 Confined by ignorance = entangled folly. Changes to (64) Before Completion. While you are close to your goal, you may be feeling rejection, failure or abandonment as Tao throws you back upon yourself to discover your folly. There is a final step to be taken. Silence your misgivings and return to the struggle. Don't entangle yourself in fantasy and arrogance, but open your mind to the possibility that you are not getting the message, or that your conclusions are not accurate.

Line 5 Youthful inexperience good fortune = brings opportunity. Changes to (59) Dispersion. Nature devises clever ways of sustaining life via the dispersing activities of different species. Bees pollinate flowers and seeds are carried about by animal fur. A childlike innocence and openness to innovation allows you to be led to new opportunity. You succeed because you are open to how life teaches and guides you.

Line 6 Attacking ignorance = insults build enemies. Changes to (7) Army. This line suggest how to apply discipline similar to how boot camp breaks down weakness to develop strength. The insult is superficial and serves to make you stronger. However, too much discipline or criticism can break the spirit. To develop ignorance into wisdom, one inspires greatness in others. Discipline works because the 'disciple' and teacher relationship means you can only lead if others respectfully follow. In this situation you are warned to keep respect for others above discipline and rehabilitation over punishment.

Hexagram #5
Hsu (Nourished While Waiting)

Action: Patience
Hu Gua (secondary influence) 38 Opposition: Yield
Zong Gua: (underlying cause) 35 Progress: Enlighten
Received as 2nd Hexagram: You are worrying about something that will solve itself with time.

Failure and success
come to test the depth and nature of your sincerity.

Too often man handles life as he does the bad weather;
he whiles away the time as he waits for it to stop. – Alfred
Polgar

Reading at a Glance The time calls for remaining patient while in a holding pattern. Waiting can be done with patience or worry, it really doesn't affect the outcome. All things take time to develop and the eventual outcome is never altered by your attitude while waiting. The journey however, is more enjoyable when you are patient. A lack of patience can lead to false starts, defeat and humiliation. Why not take a break and allow the situation to unfold? The nuclear trigram suggests a secondary influence of Opposition that causes a necessary delay. Yet, all of life is built upon the bringing together of opposites: high/low pressure systems, hot/cold weather fronts or positive and negative atoms clash and bring about something new. In order to fulfill the Progress required, a time of waiting is a way of allowing the elements of what you are seeking to move naturally to a conclusion. Perhaps you are waiting for something and need the time to explore sincerity about whether it is right for you. Use the time of waiting to re-evaluate your plan or to build up your reserves against any real future difficulty. A boiling pot won't boil any faster by watching it and a farmer cannot harvest corn when the seeds are barely sprouting. All is progressing nonetheless. Balance your desire for an outcome with the natural cycle that nourishes it. Trust that when the time is ripe, the situation will embody the answer.

Time
is perfectly spaced
to hear the echo
of
your sincerity.

"Waiting: If you are sincere, you have light and success."
Hsu reveals the force of attraction that resonates from
your beliefs. You are either nourishing a picture of
success or failure. This time of waiting will give form
and help you recognize which vision you choose to
hold.

The master said: *"it furthers one to Cross the Great Water."*
When you are fearless in testing the waters of the
unknown, *"failure and success come to test the depth and
nature of your sincerity."*

It may feel like you are in a holding pattern, although
sincerity or realizing what is important to you is
necessary before continuing. *"Nature does not give up the
winter because people dislike the cold."* If you are on the
right course, this will be a period of trial rather than
defeat because if the circumstances are right for
you, success is assured. The nourishment rests in
learning to gauge the time just like a farmer.

The Creative stirs below the Abysmal Water in the
image of planting a field, while waiting for rain. The
blossoming will come in its own time and impatience
brings about nothing, although the time of waiting can
be a time of cultivating. When the world offers no

43

response, you can hear the voice of your heart. This is your sincerity. You are being given the opportunity to reconnect with it.

Just as you test a rope by pulling on it, your sincerity is being tested against the tension of waiting to allow you to understand the nature and the correctness of your vision. Life always asks the same questions: *are you growing?...is this really what you want?* Hsu's message is that in the field of action, you generally find all that you are seeking.

You cannot interfere before the time is ripe, but if *"what you have planted is tended with sincerity, it will bear fruit. During the time of waiting, only the heart can reveal the answer."* Being forced to wait is the only way that you can validate the voice of the heart. Being forced to wait allows you to recognize whether you cultivate a positive or negative sense of attraction.

Sincerity is the root that keeps you connected to the germinating power of Tao. *"When things are still small, you should not leave them without nourishment."* While you remain in a holding pattern, you imagine all sorts of scenarios. After a time of waiting only sincerity remains; if it is real, it will endure. Cherish this opportunity to re-explore whether you are on the right course and how you think. Nothing is wasted during a time of waiting.

Unchanging: Waiting in sincerity = time reveals the answer. We generally seek answers that have to do with

44

the future or to ask about an outcome. This hexagram unchanging is a message that you may need to go without an answer or sense of direction specifically because this time of waiting is very important in allowing you to see whether your desire will really fulfill you. Rather than rush toward a future that hasn't arrived, or focus on the outcome of the matter, how is this time of waiting changing you? How are events nourishing you? Sometimes this answer is as simple as 'everything is still up in the air so just wait it out.'

Line 1 Waiting in the meadow = abide in what endures. Changes to (48) Well. The situation is new and there is a sense that not enough attention has been paid to it yet, so put your head down and just do the work as the results will appear in time. The meadow or countryside shows a sense of distance from the end result so do not be threatened by a need to wait, which may take quite some time. Waiting allows you to connect with the sincerity of what you are doing to see if what you desire is actually nourishing.

Line 2 Waiting on the sandy shore = the wasted energy of talk. Changes to (63) After Completion. You may feel a sense of being misunderstood or criticized, but the sandy shore is a message about watching the flow of water as a promise that things are still moving forward. There is also the idea of how actions speak louder than words. Instead of expending energy talking about what you will do, After Completion reminds you to just do it. This line is a message about finishing, but with the added warning to respect cycles. Just as waves come and go, chaos follows organization and opposition follows a solid structure, so be prepared to ward against it.

Line 3 Waiting in mud = being stuck leads to vulnerability. Changes to (60) Limitations. You may feel stuck by the limitations others have imposed, or you have failed to abide by their limitations, which has brought matters to a stalemate. In either case, it is difficult to proceed because leaving seems impossible. Explore the idea of limitations to see if a win/win solution is possible. Patience, receptivity and a change in speed may be required.

Line 4 Waiting in blood near danger = get out of pit. Changes to (43) Determination. This is a very difficult situation that might be unhealthy or dangerous. Determination can be a message to break free. Your words are falling on deaf ears because you are merely surrendering without giving up the argument. This can lead to the 'bloodiness' associated with battle. Either strive to see the validity of what you are arguing against, or leave the situation. Otherwise you are just waiting in a pit with no way to win.

Line 5 Waiting with wine and food = enjoyment without forgetting the goal. Changes to (11) Peace. This line shows the most useful way of dealing with a period of waiting. You have a sense of peace and can relax and enjoy the time of waiting. As long as you hold fast to the goal, all goes well. Life is about more than just accomplishment so enjoy its simplicity and nourishing qualities.

Line 6 Waiting in the pit = three uninvited guests arrive, respect them. Changes to (9) Small Restraint. You have a reached a critical point and have run out of the necessary resources to continue. The situation is not hopeless however. There is a need to either accept the help of others or bridge disagreements. Three, symbolically is tied to the transcendental merging of opposites, moving away from an 'either or' approach. Perhaps the solution requires that you look for the middle way between extremes in your thinking. You are hoping for a certain thing and not seeing that you already have what you need.

Hexagram #6
Sung (Conflict)

Action: Let Go
Hu Gua (secondary influence) 37 Family: Support
Zong Gua: (underlying cause) 36 Brightness Hiding: Reignite

Received as 2nd Hexagram: Hard feelings or resentments may require a sacrifice on your part.

When you open, all obstacles will disappear.

Truth fears nothing but concealment. – Chinese Proverb

Reading at a Glance: You are being sincere but may feel obstructed. A cautious halt halfway brings success in the sense of meeting another in the middle to regain trust. You are asked to let go of defenses in order to find proper support. The secondary influence of Family suggests that discussing expectations and agreeing upon roles can aid the situation. The Zong Gua of Brightness Hiding shows there are times where we must avoid contention and hide our inner light but a purely selfish approach may have brought this situation about. It is important to confront and discuss any disagreements rather than remain silent. Conflict is the driving force of evolution and life. Opposites are what turn the wheel of Tao. Do not be put off by a sense of opposition or conflict. Expect it and plan for it but understand its creative nature rather than respond to the friction defensively. Allow Conflict to lift you to a higher level in your thinking. This open and accepting attitude ensures that any difficulty can be treated with respect and transformed into an opportunity. When meeting contention in another, it is wise to let go of your point of view and look within.

Where the river flows,
the wounded let go.

Holding loosens a circular turning.

"Heaven and water go their separate ways: The image of conflict." The profound and Abysmal Water moves downward, while the Creative pushes upward and away in a situation of conflict and separation. Yet, in the Water, you can see your reflection in life's 'mysterious mirror.' Conflict offers an opportunity to see the truth of what you keep hidden. It may appear that something is taking place *out there*, when it is actually energy rising *in here.*

Although you may feel you are being sincere, opposition can still emerge. To hold to a hard line ensures failure so it is important to approach conflict with an open mind. How might looking at the situation with a fresh perspective alleviate conflict?

The master said: "propitious means that you attract the things you need." Like a trapped log in a river that encounters a spinning leaf, if two things are stuck and doing similar things, it is only a matter of time before they meet in the river of life. Believing in the idea of conflict is simply how you remain oblivious to how you may have become 'stuck.'

Life's creative and natural tension is always active, whether two highly charged individuals come together, or two unbalanced pressure systems collide. There will be change and there will be creative growth; it is simply nature's way. Allow the conflict to lead you to a higher order in your thinking.

Meeting contention in another offers an opportunity that will teach you about your condition. *"When meeting another of contrary character, one would do well to examine themselves."* Difficulty *out there* seems to come out of nowhere, but nature reveals how the energy released was always *inherent* in the things that crash together. From a psychological standpoint, we are drawn to explore the Shadow in another. Whatever you try to repress 'in here' finds expression in the situations we are unwittingly caught up in 'out there.'

Without defensiveness, try opening to a situation that you would rather not face. Like nuclear fission, there is enormous energy released in the 'bonds' that tie things together and bind things up. Obstacles may block your progress, but they also present a tangible vehicle that allows you to understand how you become stuck. Conflict comes to release you.

"When you open, all obstacles immediately disappear. When you learn not to contend with others, you no longer contend with the Way." Any barrier to your forward progress will always fill you with inner strength and clarity. As the image of pleading your case before an official, you can sometimes only understand what is important to you, when you are forced to defend it. Through conflict, your true potential finds definition.

Unchanging: Conflict, sincere, but obstructed = what is not 'out there' is 'in here.' Sung unchanging can have a variety of meanings. On one hand, conflict can emerge that serves no real purpose other than allowing for someone to vent their frustration. At other times, we may be timid about speaking up or rocking the boat in a situation in which we feel frustrated. Indecision and sweeping frustration under the rug leads us out to meet the world with a sour attitude. Conflict festering in a stagnant condition is unhealthy and needs to be addressed. You may feel wronged by another when you must realize that they made their choice based on their needs and there is nothing to be done except to seek closure. While conflict always offers a fertile atmosphere for constructive change, there may be no other solution other than to chalk the event up to a learning experience. The good news is that all things change in time so whatever the conflict, it too will pass. Trust has stopped and the only way to regain it is through sincerity.

Line 1 Conflict over a small matter = talk it out and in the end good fortune. Changes to (10) Treading. The matter is small and ultimately isn't worth fighting about. Treading is a way of dealing with difficult situations with care and respect, so as not to arouse anger. Whatever the conflict, try talking it out to improve the situation. The situation improves by dropping the issue.

Line 2 Don't engage conflict, give way = three hundred households without guilt. Changes to (12) Standstill. Everywhere you go, there you are. If you are having trouble with one person, fine. If you are having trouble with everyone, perhaps the issue resides in you. Standstill is a stagnant mindset that needs to be released. There is no disgrace in backing down. It is better to let the matter go and move with the consensus. You can't win them all.

Line 3 Basing expectations on past conduct = complete the task without recognition. Changes to (44) Coming to Meet. Not all situations should be judged on what happened in the past. This can lead to an unnecessary defensiveness that has nothing to do with reality. Coming to Meet is associated with Shadow projection where the present is overlaid with judgments from the past. What may feel like punishment may be a trial showing you that whatever strength you hold within your nature, cannot be lost. Do what needs to be done and let righteousness go. You are made stronger in the process.

Line 4 One cannot win = go on peacefully. Changes to (59) Dispersion. When situations dissolve, room is made for something new. This line suggests that there is no winning in this situation and a return to your center is necessary. To go on peacefully, forget the 'why' and replace it with the word 'acceptance.' There will be greater opportunities by letting this one go.

Line 5 Conflict and arguing = a satisfactory result. Changes to (64) Before Completion. Because the conflict has encouraged discourse, a satisfactory result is achieved. This last step was required to move all parties forward in agreement. There is a need to state your argument clearly without emotion to achieve success. The energy of two people arguing lifts both to a higher level.

Line 6 A leather belt won = stripped three times by the end of morning. Changes to (47) Oppression/Exhaustion. This line suggests you may be bullying and not thinking in terms of a win/win solution. Just like a prize fighter, winning the belt only guarantees that further battles will ensue with others having the intention of taking it back from you. Carrying a battle to the bitter end may wear others down, but given time, they will rise again in revolt. Conflict is solved through solutions that serve all parties, not through Oppression that only exhausts energy.

Hexagram #7
Shih (Army)

Action: Correct Discipline
Hu Gua (secondary influence) 24 Return: Go Back
Zong Gua: (underlying cause) 13 Fellowship: Socialize
Received as 2nd Hexagram: The situation may be founded on power plays or personal righteousness.

**To know fulfillment,
nourish what is for the belly and not the eye.**

If you do not stand for something, you will fall for anything.
—Chinese Proverb

Reading at a Glance: Shih is a hexagram that focuses on correct discipline and organization. It calls for delegation and structured behavior where everyone is acting according to routine. In personal readings, it can remove the emotional component where one takes a defensive or aggressive posture. The Army can relate to your inner strategy for pursuing work and even romance, but more from the standpoint of how to conquer and succeed without giving much thought to anything else. This is like a soldier disciplined enough to allow reason and forethought to override any emotional considerations. Even while it focuses on conformity to the group, the lines explore varying degrees of how to Return to one's integrity in different levels of success and failure. There is an element of the development of willpower as opposed to spiritual or emotional concerns at play. The Zong Gua shows a movement away from Fellowship or easy social interchanges to organize one's own foundational beliefs within the group to learn more about the Self. Ultimately, you must find a balance between the need to conform to others expectations against the need to express your authentic identity. When you receive Shih the message can be about a struggle that has become disjointed and requires some sort of organizational

54

thought to turn it around in your favor. You may have met your match in some situation where control is the dominating energy.

The wind excites
a thousand
different instruments -
each song is played
in its own way.

"When there is conflict, individuals rise up in revolt." The Abysmal Water stirs below the Receptive Earth, portraying how custom and duty can erode your sense of loyalty. Shih is a message about discovering value in what you do. As the image of many people gathering around a center, peer pressure and the expectations of others can sometimes lead you away from your center. At the same time, when you are cultivating 'original sincerity' circumstances also bring you together with those of like mind.

Army symbolizes the Collective Force, whether in love, business or professional goals you may need to establish a plan of action or strategy. Explore whether you are approaching your object of enquiry with a sense of battle or domination. Participating in the Collective Force requires balancing individual needs with the respect of others.

Shih can also symbolize conformity. Beyond the flowery show that bears no fruit, *"it is the fruit and not the flower that sustains life."* The flower is attractive, but if you cut it for display, you will find no nourishment or fruit to sustain you later. This is the image of trading your real nature for acceptance. The master said: *"nourish what is for the belly and not the eye."* You are reminded to do what nourishes and does not deplete you.

Whatever has left you feeling empty will lead you in the pursuit of instant gratification, as an endless cycle of fulfilling what is missing. When you find yourself drawn to this gratification process, you can be certain that something more fundamental remains unfulfilled within.

The nuclear hexagram of Return can bring you back to your center to ask: *"Which is worth more, the person or the title?"* You can find pleasure in what you do only when it taps and authenticates your full capabilities. In the great field of action, you can become an instrumental part of the collective force only when you are fulfilled and true to your own nature.

Shih is also a message about working with others in a group. Perhaps you have been isolated and it is time to return to more social interaction. The obstacles you may be encountering might be solved if you were to allow your vision to be added to and augmented by others. Stay true to yourself, but no person is an island.

Unchanging: In between conflict and union = is it a time of either peace or battles. Shih unchanging can show a stagnant situation stuck between the principle of (6) Conflict and (8) Union. Before the situation can move forward it might require more definition in terms of what it is really about and can show a self protective stance. Shih is also a message about not becoming obsessive about discipline. For example someone on a diet may place so much stress around not eating that the diet backfires from anxious overeating. It can be a message asking you to get organized or learn to delegate before you burn out. As an image of an Army, it can show a mindset of battle about your object of enquiry. Even in relationships, you can pursue for the thrill of the chase, rather than explore whether or not the person is right for you. The difference between discipline and control is the focus on the self vs. others. Discipline is an agreement about mutual growth where control can just lead to battles.

Line 1 Army marching in order = the discipline of team. Changes to (19) Approach. When overwhelmed with the needs of a group, be sensitive to others' skills so that each functions independently and at their best to fortify the strength of a team. In personal matters, you may need to start by organizing and planning a strategy. In emotional issues, you may need to follow the head and not the heart, or at least reign in your emotions.

Line 2 In the midst of an army = the king bestows a triple decoration. Changes to (2) Receptive. A triple decoration is like the 3 treasures in Taoism: compassion, moderation and not needing to be recognized, but to follow and remain humble. All of these treasures accord to serving others. While working fully in a team, each individual retains their own integrity. This shows the importance of core foundational beliefs functioning at all levels to achieve success. Ensure your individual principles resonate to what you are seeking.

Line 3 Carrying corpses = holding on to non essentials and wasting resources. Changes to (46) Pushing Upward. The imagery of this line shows an Army led by improper leadership, advancing and winning, but what is won has no value. They are carrying corpses in the sense of advancing without a goal into an empty town. This can also be a message that an old way is changing into one of greater discipline. Growth comes after a deteriorating situation is given a new sense of direction. If you are too much in the head – look to the heart and follow instinct. Balance emotion and logic but move forward with vitality, not routine. Discipline requires that you moderate thought, action and emotion with your purpose. The situation provides an optimum environment for spiritual discipline and transcendent growth.

Line 4 The Army retreats = no success but no blame. Changes to (40) Deliverance. Too much discipline can block your ability to move spontaneously to avoid danger when retreat is necessary. Therefore, in being disciplined it is important to know when to throw in the towel. This also leads to success. Deliverance can be a message about taking time out to relax and regroup so you can march refreshed another day.

Line 5 Birds in the field = stop speaking. Changes to (29) Abyss. You can use an army of discipline to succeed, but some things can only be learned through mistakes. Hidden soldiers must refrain from speaking when seeing birds in the field which will fly up and alert the enemy. In this case, discipline must be melded with expertise to ensure success. Seasoning and experience differentiate the great from the mediocre. Make certain you are up to the task or find someone to help you. There is more to the situation than what worked in the past. In this situation you would do well to listen and not force your agenda.

Line 6 Develop cities and support the families = don't give responsibilities lightly. Changes to (4) Youthful Folly. The word 'infantry' originates from the French word "enfant" or child. The proper approach for any leader is to develop the skills of the individual like a parent. After a period of difficulty, it may be necessary to reorganize or rebuild. Good relations with people require support and generosity. The battle is over so there is no reason to march against anyone. Youthful Folly is also a warning about making sure you are finding the right people to meet your needs.

Hexagram #8
Pi (Uniting)

Action: Unite
Hu Gua (secondary influence) 23 Split Apart:
Regenerate
Zong Gua: (underlying cause) 14 Great Possessing:
Shine
Received as 2nd Hexagram: The possibility for union
exists no matter the trial.

Merge the world *in here* with the world *out there*
and your destiny is revealed.

We sleep, but the loom of life never stops and the pattern
which was weaving when the sun went down
is weaving when it comes up tomorrow. – *H Ward Beecher*

Reading at a Glance: Holding together or Uniting is
something that plays out in the way we pursue and are
pursued by others, but also how we find a sense of
Union within. Where the previous hexagram Shih
(Army) had to do with organizing the will around the
collective, Pi places the focus more on uniting the

diverse aspects of the individual, or unifying all aspects of the individual with others. When receiving this hexagram one is asked to seek the oracle again to explore whether one is truly ready to transcend egoistic aims. The underlying cause or opposite condition of Possession in Great Measure led you to a pinnacle but the hidden influence of Splitting Apart now focuses on Regeneration. This may call for a transcendental perspective in the spirit of serving others. The second reading should provide more detail about the nature of a partnership or union and where you stand in your growth. You cannot know the love of another until you discover self love. You are called to be unified with others, with life and most importantly with all aspects of who you are.

Inner and outer
in seamless unity -
reflections
upon
the mysterious mirror.

"Holding together means uniting." When you are in a hurry, life moves quickly to slow you down; when you are angry, circumstances test your patience. *"The way does not speak; it reveals by deeds and events."* Take a moment to observe how current events are mirroring the condition of your inner world. Tao brings people together propitiously in order to strengthen deficiencies or to soften excesses.

The master said: *"Everything is destiny; all things are already complete in oneself,"* we turn inward in order to bring our vision forward. Uniting brings together what appears to be separate so that you can discover your seamless unity with what unfolds around you.

Dreams can offer a profound source of inner guidance. They reveal the impact of experience upon your development through symbols that portray a picture of your inner world. How are these two ways of learning separate? You are changed by both experiences. Just as you evolve through actual experience and not by denying the world, you cannot deny or ignore inspiration rising within. *"Even in sleep, you continue your practice."*

When you are trapped in a transformative process, inspiration rises, whether through dreams, intuition or events to reveal the 'way through.' Synchronicity is a word that describes this uniting process, where the inner and outer are drawn together in a way that reveals there is no separation between the two. The path of Tao leads you to tap your unique individuality (Te) while removing any sense of separateness from what transpires around you.

Therapists explore dreams to uncover symbols that can re-empower a client in crisis. Pi is the image of someone walking, who suddenly stops to become more observant. Bringing the inner and outer together, *'ming'* is a word that describes your destiny in the sense of the path, but also how the pathway is leading you to self-actualize your destiny. Without accessing the inner guidance of dreams you may float aimlessly in the river of life.

Ming is the unified awareness achieved when *me in here* and *that out there* have no separation. To cultivate fulfillment in life, you must live it from the inside - out. Life doesn't happen to you; it happens because of you. Cherish how the pathway leads you to understand your inner world. At the same time, recognize the importance of how your beliefs shape your experiences. Uniting is a message about looking for this connection.

Pi also offers a message about uniting with others as a type of leader. So great is the possibility of leading others by example that you are asked to consult the oracle once more to examine your character. In relationship readings, Pi shows a natural pairing or the way two individuals fulfill their needs in the mirror of each other.

Unchanging: The mysterious mirror is without blemish = inquire again if your will is correct. Pi unchanging can be a message that you have the power to achieve what it is you want but warns: 'be careful what you wish for.'' If you are asking a question about achieving union with another, the message throws the question back in terms of finding and standing firm in where you belong without forcing others into unnatural associations. Union flows because of timing and correct action. If you are in limbo, others will respond with the same lack of commitment. How can union be achieved if you are a moving target? As a static hexagram it is important to consult the oracle once more to understand your motivation and the current condition of your will. You might discover aspects at play that you hadn't considered.

Line 1 Trusting relationships = express your truth like a full earthen bowl. Changes to (3) Difficult Beginnings. In order to love another, it is important to love yourself. All relationships require sincerity and an offering of the Self which is like a full earthen bowl and not a begging bowl. Seeking Union can be Difficult in the Beginning, because we are often attracted to aspects in others we find deficient in ourselves, which can lead to fascination and disagreements. You don't need to go out searching for love. You need only open to love to find it was always there. Attraction is built upon opposite energy so there is no need to change anything in others. Hold to this truth and you will gain loyalty. If you are seeking union with others, celebrate their differences.

Line 2 Hold union within = persevere in intimacy. Changes to (29) Abyss. The danger of union is that one can lose themselves when associating with another. There is no need to impress or behave in a way to gain acceptance. Merely be yourself and others will be attracted to your steadfast and sincere nature. Retain your individuality and dignity when interacting with others to avoid the loss of authenticity. Don't be afraid to jump into the unknown.

Line 3 Union with the wrong people = leads to humiliation. Changes to (39) Obstruction. Avoid habitual needs that bring you together with the wrong people. This type of Union can only lead to Obstruction when you discover a lack of fulfillment. You are probably seeking a connection with those that are not of like mind. This can only lead to humiliation or injury.

Line 4 Hold union outwardly = determination is auspicious. Changes to (45) Gathering Together. There are times when it is appropriate to seek union with others beyond your circle of intimate associates. You may need to step out of your network or social sphere to seek union with people who can teach you or guide you to a higher level. Maybe you are spending time with someone you wouldn't normally associate with but are gaining wisdom through the association. By gathering diverse people in your sphere you are able to explore all aspects of who you are. By looking without, you learn more about what is hidden within.

Line 5 Manifesting Union = one way out, the other ways lead to trouble. Changes to (2) Receptive. When you are comfortable and secure in who you are, you have no need to hunt and capture followers. Your purity and strength is a magnet that pulls others to you. Impressing others or pretending to be who you are not can only lead to trouble. The Receptive force in life is magnetic and therefore, has no need to hunt or capture. Others come of their own accord because you are sincere and the freedom to come and go is key.

Line 6 Associating out of confusion = finding no head for Union. Changes to (20) Contemplation. One must examine the beginning of measures that are made for Union to discover if it will lead to the right ending. Commitment and devotion are things we possess, yet give to another. However, a fear of intimacy will ensure that we attract relationships that feel like abandonment. If Union is elusive, explore your mindset. You are seeking an association out of confusion.

Hexagram #9
Hsiao Ch'u (Small Restraint)

Action: Surrender
Hu Gua (secondary influence) 38 Opposition: Yield
Zong Gua: (underlying cause) 16 Enthusiasm: Align
Received as 2nd Hexagram: You get more bees with honey.

There is no real blockage that can withstand submission.

The universe is full of magical things patiently waiting for our wits to grow sharper. – Eden Phillpotts

Reading at a Glance: Because of the one weak Yin line holding the fourth place among strong Yang lines, we see the idea how something small or weak can tame the powerful. Yin is the gentle influence operating in Tao that magnetizes the powerful Yang. The feminine side of courtship shows how a strong element can be held in check through gentle submissiveness. In Small Restraint power is accumulated by gently withholding its expression. We see this in the 'coming soon' advertising that creates anticipation, and also in the mating dance of courtship. At the same time, weakness and insecurity within the psyche can become powerful because it is repressed. Anything locked in a vacuum can grow out of proportion to what it is. Ideas of failure can stunt even the most obvious talents. Opposition is the secondary influence or mirror of how we meet our Shadow, or repressed qualities of ourselves in another. We think someone is the enemy when they have come to set us free from self imposed restrictions. After waking from period of Enthusiasm or possible illusion, we discover how nightmares are a positive sign that power has begun to stir in the psyche. In Taoism, the idea of 'Te' is the inherent authenticity that you are born with. You need only peel away the layers of fear that keep you from expressing it. In either case, you will need to approach the object of your enquiry with gentle submissiveness to exercise, discover or release your power. Defensiveness ensures that the negative outcome is relentless. Submissiveness always opens new doors for success so simply surrender to the Way.

When obstacles are
insurmountable -
open to
the teaching.

"Holding together, restraint is certain to come about." The
Gentle Wind stirs above the Creative portraying how
constant action, regardless of how small, makes creation
possible. Hsiao Ch'u reveals how your power to
create always comes as a double-edged sword. On the
one hand, the smallest effort will eventually bear fruit
as the image of the fertile soil gathering in a river valley.
It also suggests how the tiniest seed becomes reality in
the ideas that you cultivate.

The master said: *"The Gentle has its own power, like water
dripping onto stone."* Hsiao Ch'u suggests the ways in
which your thoughts might either hold you back or
allow you to succeed. The power of intention is being
examined.

Hsiao Ch'u is a picture of how small things are
domesticated and suggests how habitual responses are
trained and can lead to self-imposed restraint. If you
chain a wild horse to a fence long enough, its spirit will
not only be broken, it may also forget that it ever
roamed free.
The nuclear trigrams suggest *"dense clouds, no rain."*
Condensation gathers energy above the Water, but the
Winds cannot disperse it, and the atmosphere is left
with an unproductive heaviness. Self-limiting ideas can

take hold like a dam that appears to block your forward progress. Let go and believe in yourself to find success.

You may be moving in circles, while obstacles appear to be everywhere. The smallest restraint can make you feel paralyzed, although when obstacles appear insurmountable, you must only release the dam within. Either take the time to understand what is created by fear, or you may encounter it later as an obstacle. The obstacle is merely a tangible vehicle that allows you to see how you become stuck.

To engage the energy of life productively, combine your power to create with the openness that makes anything possible. The greatest power we can express is through silence. When there is nothing to defend, we are strong.

Unchanging: Clouds gather = the rain has not yet arrived. If things are unfolding slowly and you get Hsiao Ch'u unchanging, the message relates to the way clouds are gathering but have not developed enough to bring forth rain. In this case, the idea of surrender or abiding means to just keep doing the work until the way becomes clear again. Nature moves season to season very slowly. We, on the other hand, want something and we want it now. Small Restraint is a message calling for patience so that some type of blockage within you or another might clear. The object of your enquiry is still developing. However, the time spent waiting is productive in opening you to greater realizations.

Line 1 Return to your path = how is this wrong? Changes to (57) Penetration. There is a sense of advancing and then retreating. Penetration or introspection allows you to examine the obstruction to recognize how it has emerged because you are on the wrong path. There is nothing wrong with retreating or going back to who you were before you started. It is more important that you return to your nature, rather than use force to obtain that which isn't right for you.

Line 2 Drawn to the home for return = good fortune. Changes to (37) Family. Observing what is up ahead, you are obstructed. Perhaps you have noticed a blockage where others are retreating too. Circumstances may be bringing you back, but this can be a time of sharing or providing care rather than achieving goals. Enjoy more and strive less. Personal relationships take precedence over ambition.

Line 3 Spokes of wagon wheel burst = husband and wife turn away. Changes to (61) Inner Truth. When the wagon spokes burst, it is important to recognize how to be in sync with partners. Pushing forcefully ahead is incorrect because power lies in your submissiveness and willingness to hear each other. It does no good to cast blame because nothing is inherently wrong. All is unfolding as it should and the situation will align you with your Inner Truth. Step back and allow the space for others to work through their own issues.

Line 4 With sincerity no need to be cautious = enriched by neighbors. Changes to (1) Creative. Being held back by fear, you may have become stuck in ideas of self doubt. There is no need to be cautious or fearful if you are sincere about what you are doing. In fact, the blockage is revealing your sincerity so you might commit and your inner reserves are awakened to discover solutions. There can be a lot of anxiety around the situation but confidence is the key to breaking through to a good outcome. The Creative shows you possess the power of creative flexibility. You may feel powerless in achieving the response you desire, but the ability to resonate your sincerity will be recognized.

Line 5 Confidence and sincerity = truthfulness in companionship. Changes to (26) Controlled Power. This line incorporates small taming outwardly with great taming within. Small Restraint draws on Controlled Power, relating to others out of a sense of confidence and sincerity where partners are truthful with each other. The difference between scarcity and abundance shows that what you possess within is mirrored without. No need to show your cards, but be confident and you will succeed.

Line 6 You have what you need = don't press for more. Changes to (5) Nourished While Waiting. By acting with submissiveness, you have achieved what you need. Don't get pompous and demanding because of your accomplishment. You may need to be patient and give the object of your enquiry further time to develop before proceeding as in "you have all you need to know at this time." The danger comes from being pushy and impatient.

Hexagram #10
Lu (Treading)

Action: Cautious Advance
Hu Gua (secondary influence) 37 Family: Support
Zong Gua: (underlying cause) 15 Authenticity: Balance
Received as 2nd Hexagram: There can be a sense of
everyone walking on eggshells.

Participate with life; do not mystify it.

Use what talent you possess; the woods would be silent
if no birds sang except those that sang best. – H Van Dyke

Reading at a Glance: At some point in our journey, we
begin to wonder about our life path. We look for
meaning and notice the signs around us, paying
attention to our dreams and flashes of insight. We begin
to have a sense of being led and we find meaning.
Spirituality isn't a way to avoid punishment or to do
right. It is how we begin to open to the way life guides
us and therefore, our footsteps become more cautious
and self reflective. Each individual has an entirely
different purpose, so looking to the path of others might

get you lost. The idea of Family is also at play, suggesting that even among family members nature endows each with unique variations to ensure that competition for short supply is minimized in close proximity. We see cycles that come and go, and we begin to identify a pattern. Lu is a hexagram that brings up issues related to what you are doing and why. It asks you to look at where you are going and to focus on your footsteps and motivations. It suggests a Cautious Advance because where you are going you have never gone before. Humility allowed for Authenticity and it is time to apply openness and all that you have learned from introspection. In times of difficulty, you may need to sit with emotion to discover how this 'tail of the tiger' can lead you inward to tap your Authenticity. Feel the emotion without acting on it. Allow feelings to have life within you without needing to give them a label. This energy will ignite deeper levels of awareness for you in the sense of what might be called Spiritual direction. Energy does not die and by allowing for its expression you can actually allow it to transform you. Each day is a piece of a puzzle, a gift that will unmask your character and reveal your destiny. The Tiger of emotion or fear only bites when you run from it or try to cage it.

*Discover the
pleasure
of treading
in life's
mystery.*

"Treading shows the basis of character; one who treads does not stay." Life always meets you half way, but as long as you feel that life is working against you, the world will appear as a glass half-full. Filling the other portion of the glass allows you to discover your full capabilities. Sometimes the way isn't easy - but it will make you stronger. Sometimes the path isn't clear, so we need only look down to see where we are currently treading. How is life speaking to you in the nuances of your journey? The tiger we come upon in the woods can be the passion within or the passion we believe is in others. How can they be separate? Dreams show us how others are a reflection of us. The Spiritual path is our own and you are being called into initiation. The small choices you make today will give shape to tomorrow. So tread carefully and observe the signs. If you are walking around with your head up in the clouds, you may step on the tiger's tail. Don't mystify life. Live it.

The master said: "*The truth is not a sign that points to something beyond itself; it just is.*" When you tread on the tail of a tiger, you have to be prepared for the nasty bite of truth that brings you back to earth. Treading means being present and participating with how life is shaping you.

The Joyous Lake is the daughter, reaching toward the Creative in the image of the weak treading on the power of the strong father. The exuberance of the child worries the father who looks upon his daughter with humor. Perhaps he finds humor in the innocent pursuit of something that cannot be grasped. Of the energy of life, the master said: *"whoever lays hold of it will lose it."* In the image of someone impersonating the deceased at a funeral - another's truth may not be your truth. The words of deceased masters must be made personal because one person's truth is not another's.

Sometimes the mind leads you away from passion and sometimes passion leads you into a pit. The message of Lu is to find the balance between learning from experience and being open to the unknown. Passion is not dependent on what you have. The passion of Spirit is an infinite fire that burns unattached to what transpires around you.

Let it burn freely behind eyes open to wonder.

"The scriptures are the dim footprints of ancient kings. They tell us nothing of the force that guided their steps. Footprints are made by shoes, but they are far from being shoes." Lu asks you to focus on your footsteps because life reveals itself differently in the unique pathway that you walk upon.

When dogma takes the place of actual experience, it shackles you to *"lectures that are no better than footprints in the dust."* Yet, of the evolutionary power of life, *"go up to it and you will not see its head; follow behind and you will not see its rear. Treading on the tail of the tiger, it does not bite."* It does not bite because you follow behind. You must be present to see how life is guiding you.

If your path is leading you to be continually bitten, examine whether you are moving too quickly and not appreciating the sensitive environment in which you find yourself. At times you are the tiger. At times you bring out the angry tiger in another. Treading carefully is not a message to stop; it is a message to be more conscious of your steps.

When you have lost interest in the mystery of life, Lu becomes a shining light upon your footsteps. It coaxes you to reconnect with your journey. The truth is revealed in every moment that unfolds before you. In life, we rarely make choices. We know what we don't want and life shows us what we can't have...all that is left is the answer.

Unchanging: Treading on the tiger tail = become fearlessly yourself, no need to rush. Lu unchanging is often a clear message to slow down. Perhaps you need to gain greater clarity about your object of enquiry rather than asking so many questions. It can present the idea of walking on eggshells or feeling that you are in an environment of heavy judgment and criticism. It can also suggest that you are failing to see any deeper reason for why events are unfolding as they are, perhaps feeling like a victim. The deeper aspects of your journey are lost to you. Character development can also be at play. It helps to identify the silver lining in difficulty or the part you play in hitting walls. You are not a victim and a frenetic pace is sometimes the reason you lack comfort. Slow down. Look for meaning. Chances are life is protecting you from making the wrong choices.

Line 1 Simply going one's way = progress without blame. Changes to (6) Conflict. Many enlightenment seekers begin their journey when the ego is wounded. Interacting with others and not fitting in will throw you back upon yourself. This is necessary when you are searching for your own path. Don't be angry at others to vindicate yourself. Remember that conflict has one purpose ~ to transform you. Just go your way. If it is real, it will come back to you.

Line 2 Taking the easy path = perseverance of the dark man brings good fortune. Changes to (25) Innocence. Any breakthrough in enlightenment is usually followed by an encounter with the Shadow, whether in dreams or daily life. This is the powerful side of you that once allowed expression and given a home, can guide you. Without judgment means to use the Innocence of a child, accept your trials with wonder. The path is always easy when you don't fight, but follow. How is the path teaching you about your hidden potential?

Line 3 Stepping on the tiger tail and getting bit = the lame man walks and the blind man sees but this leads to misfortune. Changes to (1) Creative. Success is a journey of self completion and the seed is always within you. The ego is only a part of who you are, like the lame or blind 'man.' Your dream life gives definition to a more complete picture of who you are. The tiger is initiation and something is still unknown in the situation so you might look deeper. Study your dreams for guidance or explore the perils before proceeding. To proceed without wisdom leads to folly but even folly can be a teacher.

Line 4 Stepping on the tiger's tail = cautious and circumspect, all goes well. Changes to (61) Inner Truth. You have what it takes to proceed although the environment appears dangerous. All obstacles that you face become opportunities for further insight into your purpose in life. It is your integrity and commitment to the truth, mixed with cautiousness that allows you to succeed. Synchronicity reveals the dissolving of barriers between 'in here' and 'out there.' Overcome fear and you will succeed.

Line 5 Making a decisive step = preparing for danger eliminates risk. Changes to (38) Opposition. The most appropriate way to meet the conditions you face is with a deep respect and the wisdom that everything and everyone on your path is your teacher. Expecting difficulty makes things stressful. Expecting to transform the opportunity that an obstacle presents brings peace. Risk is the window that allows you to escape from your prison.

Line 6 Watching the steps = examining omens. Changes to (58) Joy. At the precipice of enlightenment we measure insight and inspiration against the path to find a correlation. Finding meaning in this way brings Joy and success. You can play victim or look back upon your conduct and consequences to see how you brought about the result. There may be conditioning or early beliefs that you need to release in order to overcome fear and participate more intimately with others. How delightful to discover meaning in life!

Hexagram #11
T'ai (Peace)

Action: Relax
Hu Gua (secondary influence) 54 Propriety: Subordinate
Zong Gua: (underlying cause) 12 Standstill: Release
Received as 2nd Hexagram: There is a strong need to lighten up and not take things seriously.

**Being free of desires, you will discover
that the empire is at peace of its own accord.**

*If I keep a green bough in my heart,
the singing bird will come. – Chinese Proverb*

Reading at a Glance: Heaven is below Earth and all things move upward in harmony   and transform. Peace is a message about going with the flow. What you are worrying about today won't be as important tomorrow.

Anything that had previously been out of place or difficult is now receding. Chances are you will feel relieved by seeing this hexagram. However, in order to know Peace, one must experience discord. Hot is only relevant to cold and similarly up is meaningless without the idea of down. More importantly, Peace is an outlook you can carry with you at all times by remembering cycles. Yet Peace can be lulled into tranquility and lead to stagnation as suggested by the Zong Gua of Standstill. The message might be to calm down and relax...take it easy, but there is still an element of change happening. This change however is permeating the situation and might be difficult to grasp because you are being coached to discover rather than overlay experience with past assumptions. It can be a message about seeing the profound reason that heaven's answer can sometimes be "no." But with it comes the words of the mother to a child: "shhhh...everything is going to be okay..it all has a good purpose and will work out fine." If you are feeling stressed, the secondary influence of Subordinate asks you to align your will to the way. Rather than rush ahead to organize tomorrow – enjoy and learn from today. A period of Stagnation is transforming into growth and openness. If you have had any disagreements, things should improve considerably. This is an excellent answer for relationship questions because it shows that the will of heaven is flowing so go with it.

The moon goes, the sun comes.
The body circulates -small world.

80

"Good conduct, then contentment; thus calm prevails in the image of peace." T'ai is the image of moving harmoniously with the flow of events. *"All weak elements are forced to take their departure as the two great forces of Yin and Yang come together."* The master said: *"Make your home the inevitable, then grief and the pursuit of joy cannot intrude."*

In life's relentless pursuit of a better way, anything that would block its forward progress must *'take its departure.'* Perhaps that is why the Tao te Ching states: *"Tao treats the creatures like straw dogs."* What is held tightly in your arms will leave you unable to embrace new opportunity. Sometimes what we cling to is taken away even when we don't understand why. All that you hold is only borrowed; you might as well let it pass freely from your grasp.

Being free of desire and clinging to nothing, you discover a pathway of Peace. This is how you can keep a *"green bough in your heart"* so that the singing bird will come. Cultivate this garden daily where the joy of spirit can roost.

When you look backward, you can trust that tomorrow will take care of itself because yesterday was meaningful. This allows you to be present and observant *now.* The master said: *"be in awe of timelessness. This is how you can dwell in timelessness."*

"If I cease from desire and remain still, the empire will be at peace of its own accord." Nothing of value can be

threatened because if it is meaningful, it will remain. What is relegated to the past, were those things that were unnecessary. Representing your evolutionary journey, T'ai is the image of a person flowing in the great river of life.

Trusting in the Way joyfully, events unfold with no need to shake you from your self-imposed obstructions. Each day, the mysterious carriage appears. *"The clouds are the carriage and the sun and the moon are the steeds."* Embarking upon each new day with a sense of discovery, you can move joyfully to receive the gifts that each unfolding moment brings to you.

In relationships, T'ai can show the need to develop self love or to open to the idea of love, rather than treating it like something to be pursued. It bodes well for partnerships of any kind as it shows a movement toward harmonious relations. Don't overwork or force anything but allow it to unfold naturally.

Unchanging: Peace like lullaby in the darkness = the small departs and the great approaches. Peace unchanging can show the development of a proper mindset of accepting what you can't change. Often it is a message to forget focusing on the small details or negativity because the bigger picture is more important. One of its clearest messages is to stop worrying. Everything will work out fine. As the Creative pushes upward to transform your situation, you discover that something beyond you and what you believe you need is at play. Stop worrying and go with the flow because the flow knows exactly where to go. It can also show that the current situation has become stable or unchanging which can be good if you are in a relationship or satisfied with events but frustrating if you are seeking reunion or progress. Its positive message of providence however, still holds true because everything works out for the best.

Line 1 Pulling out grass, entangled roots = each according to its kind. Changes to (46) Pushing Upward. In order to succeed, you may need the help of people of like mind. Any changes may reveal that under the surface things are more entangled than had first appeared. Proceed anyway. Honor differences in another and don't try to change them. Actions that you take will be beneficial for all. This is also the idea of 'grass root' gatherings or uprooting something as a way of weeding out the confusion so new growth can emerge.

Line 2 Meet the uncultured with gentleness, resolute in crossing the river = the middle way abandons nothing. Changes to (36) Brightness Hiding. To walk the middle path, you must neither abandon your principles or others. There are times however, when you must respond with gentleness and only your inner vision even while the way is dark or harmony is threatened. Tolerate other's weaknesses with grace but follow your own drummer. There can be a gentle action of kindness needed to ward off disunion. Make the most of all opportunities in serving the larger goal. Be at peace with whatever unfolds. In this way you fjord the great river so as not to neglect what is distant or what is close by.

Line 3 The easy and difficult change in cycles = don't complain but enjoy what you do have. Changes to (19) Approach. If you know that light follows dark and the way goes up and down, you can balance difficult times with the knowledge that there will be light at the end of the tunnel. When times are good, you can draw on this memory during difficult times. Relationships too, move in cycles so be patient and ensure that you offset difficulty with sincerity. Communication should be honest and not just a means of avoiding difficulty. Enjoy the simplicity of what you do have.

Line 4 The wealthy exchange with the lowly = neighbors being sincere. Changes to (34) Power of Great. Don't measure others with a common denominator and avoid cliques or distinctions of class. When disaster strikes in a neighborhood, everyone is equal. The simplicity of each member of a household fulfilling their roles will return when judgment and anger are allowed to evaporate. Harmony begins with those closest to you and a spontaneous coming together reveals that the heart of all are in agreement. This leads to mutual benefit for all. A spiritual rebirth happens when heaven (Spirit) eclipses the Earth (Ego). All pretension and masks fall away as heaven's will manifests.

Line 5 Imperial princess given in marriage = a sacrifice for peace and goodwill. Changes to (5) Nourished

While Waiting. The princess was often of higher rank than her husband but still obeyed him. To achieve peace, put aside right and wrong or high and low and make a peace offering. The highest form of expressing harmony is through sacrifice. In the middle of a stalemate, bring nourishment to yourself and another by forgiving. Those issues we fight against are often to our benefit. Go with the flow. Make a gesture of peace.

Line 6 The wall falls back into the mote = being vulnerable and accepting this. Changes to (26) Controlled Power. While things are not as great as you would have liked, you are in a vulnerable position and may need to concede to that. During change, everything appears confusing. With Controlled Power you don't need to fight the flow of events. Strengthen your ties with those you can rely on and take time out to reflect on the lesson. This time too will pass. In time, you will come to a crossroad that helps you understand why this period has come to an end. Further action might lead to humiliation but also allows the transformation to complete itself.

Hexagram #12
P'i (Standstill)

Action: Release
Hu Gua (secondary influence) 53 Development:
Permeate
Zong Gua: (underlying cause) 11 Peace: Relax
Received as 2nd Hexagram: What you are asking can
only be solved through a changed perspective.

**Contentment cannot be held in the hand,
but lives perpetually in the heart.**

Fresh activity is the only means of overcoming adversity.
Goethe

Reading at a Glance: Our desire for the familiar and to
know peace can often lead us away from further
growth. Therefore, after a time of Peace as the Zong
Gua, a situation can lead to stagnation or Standstill. You
are asked to release something so that Development can
proceed. The purpose of receiving this hexagram is to
remind you that all of life changes and moves toward
growth. Humans cannot remain on the sidelines. It can

be frustrating to throw your enthusiasm against the course of events that seem to have placed you in a holding pattern. Patience is how you release your sense of urgency and allow the outcome to unfold. The secondary influence allows for the Development of a new awareness, skills or ways of interacting with the world. In order to learn how to be steadfast one must relinquish expectation, assumptions and impatience. Just as winter appears as a time when the world appears lifeless, there is much going on in your underground world. Ten thousand seeds are becoming the landscape of your spring. If you feel frustrated, take a walk in the woods. You'll be amazed at the realizations you will have when you are away from your phone and computer. In fact if you were to have a conversation with trees and bushes they might ask 'why do you walk in circles when life plants you exactly where you need to be?' Nature is the greatest teacher of how to be steadfast and move in time with the changing cycles. Discover the contentment of following life on its terms. Follow the great circle and allow Standstill to unleash an innovative approach within you.

In a time of standstill
open the gates of the mind.

"Things do not stay forever united and can lead to standstill." The danger of Peace is that it can lead to progressive stagnation. This is because of the lack of *necessary tension* that life generates to drive change. In other words, too much of a good thing can unwittingly lull you to sleep in the arms of stagnation.

87

The master said: *"Everything flows on and on like the river. We can appreciate the changes taking place in nature, while wholly unaware of our own mutability."*

Finding a balance in contentment that still allows for growth becomes an important lesson in following the energy of life. P'i suggests that you are holding on to something that is keeping you from moving forward.

Observing nature, you will see that nothing comes to a standstill. A pool of water that has separated from the rivers and sea will eventually stagnate or dry up. The nuclear trigram of the Mountain is immovable, while the Gentle Wind encourages movement. Together, they ask you to release your expectations, so that you can discover the joy of following life on its terms.

Do not root yourself in the momentary thing that made you happy because contentment is simply the proper response in following. If you do not expect anything, you can discover the magic that life has in store for you.

Exploring what it means to follow, the master said: *"contentment cannot be held in the hand, although it can live perpetually in the heart."* You can plant something in a pot and fill it with water, but if it is not provided proper drainage, it will die. As a lesson about letting go, P'i suggests how desiring not to remain full will allow you to be fulfilled anew.

The empire will be at peace of its own accord, whether you choose to worry about it or not. If you find that you are not moving forward, you will discover that it is your will and not the Way.

As an image of the mouth and the symbol for 'not,' it suggests how *"standstill is giving way."* You can let go, or find that something more profound will come to make you give way. To follow the easier path, try releasing your attachment to something that no longer serves you. Ultimately, you will discover how *you* were blocking life's greater movement that left you unable to receive something new. Its message is simple: *if things are at a standstill, let go.*

The Yang lines of Heaven are moving upward and the Yin lines of Earth are moving downward, and the energy cannot connect. Harmony is gone and it is easy to get discouraged. Use this time to retreat and explore new ways of approaching experience. If you are feeling disconnected from others, take a class or attend social gatherings. This can be a time of testing which will ultimately lead you toward greater fulfillment.

Unchanging: Everything at a standstill except you = the great usurped by the small. Standstill unchanging can be a message to stop wasting energy attempting to change a situation that has reached an impasse. Sometimes the message is that the answer is 'no' and you must come to terms with that. Sometimes the message is that you need to wait out a period of Standstill in this situation and give it more time to develop. This is not a very encouraging answer because we would rather bang our heads against a wall rather than accept defeat and move on. You can be certain however, that its clearest message is to stop. Focus on other areas in your life and allow the period of Standstill to pass. Whatever the blockage, it is external so there is no need to take it personal. You are facing strong opposition and can only wait it out or move on.

Line 1 Weeding out grass, sod comes with it = each according to its kind. Changes to (25) Innocence. During a period of stagnation it is important to make changes. This is a period of rebuilding and a need to let go of old preconceptions and judgments to approach the atmosphere with a fresh perspective. An outward event may be guiding you toward big inner changes. To pull grass with sod attached can mean that the changes need not be dramatic. The soil allows you to make changes without upsetting what you have built. Honoring differences among others brings success.

Line 2 Bear and endure = no need to seek favors. Changes to (6) Conflict. Others may feel insecure during periods of stagnation and overly needy or seek instant gratification. The enlightened ones use this period to uncover the reason for stagnation and care for the welfare of all. Discover your higher purpose beyond fear responses and self gratification.

Line 3 Surroundings entice = shameful action. Changes to (33) Retreat. Someone wasn't entirely honest yet still succeeded in some way. Now they are paying the price. Behavior can lead to retreat out of a fear of rejection, attack or because of anger and may require time before moving forward. Admitting fault will lead to better developments. Don't let the surroundings incite you to action that isn't authentic. Respect others and don't try to change them.

Line 4 Working from a higher purpose = those of like mind participate. Changes to (20) Contemplation. Your integrity has brought the admiration of another who understands your message to break through the Standstill. The hexagram of Contemplation shows a monument where one can get a better view of the path. While you are holding to a higher purpose out of respect for yourself or another, an enlightened message brings a sense of union.

Line 5 Standstill is giving way = what if it should fail? Tie it to a mulberry tree. Changes to (35) Progress. It is normal to feel trepidation on the precipice of change. Whatever blocked you is being released and progress can continue. If you can learn from your mistakes you will successfully create lasting change that leads to good fortune. Don't expect it to be easy though because without a serious change in attitude the blockage can recur. This is a line that encourages you to transform doubt or fear based attitudes into acceptance and a strong inner core committed to Progress.

Line 6 The Standstill has ended = at first frustrated then glad. Changes to (45) Gathering Together. The impasse has ended. Much inner strength is achieved when a situation reaches Standstill so the time was not wasted. Like a sailboat without wind, now the wind returns and things begin to flow again. To avoid this type of crisis in the future make sure that you incorporate sustainability in all you do. All good things require the freedom to change and evolve. Go out and meet experience with your new found insight.

Hexagram #13
T'ung Jen (Fellowship)

Action: Socialize
Hu Gua (secondary influence) 44 Coming to Meet: Encounter
Zong Gua: (underlying cause) 7 Army: Correct Discipline
Received as 2nd Hexagram: Friendship and associating with others is at the root of your question.

**If you understand nature's symmetries,
you will use no counting rods.**

*Humankind has not woven the web of life.
We are but one thread within it.
Whatever we do to the web, we do to ourselves. – Chief
Seattle*

Reading at a Glance: T'ung Jen is a hexagram that explores your principles, character, integrity, and how you interact with others. In joining with another, the relationship will allow you to share a special connection, but is not always a romantic or harmonious interaction . This is because there is more of an emphasis on gaining Clarity about how you behave in relationship to others. Yet, there is a lot to learn from these partnerships. We are often attracted to groups because of our shared interests. Once in the group however, we discover the ways in which we are different. The secondary influence of Coming to Meet allows for the exploration of the Shadow in your relationships. It is an opportunity to own the dynamics you bring to your relationships rather than blame others for your condition. If you can discover even the smallest insight about yourself through a relationship, regardless of its duration, it has been successful. Moving away from the Zong Gua of Army, we had the opportunity to put individual expression aside to work as a Team. Now partnerships have to be viewed in terms of how you can best serve them while discovering more about yourself. Fellowship places emphasis on socializing so if you have been introspective, it is time to return to the group. There is a sense of caring and emotional well being at play as you interact with others. If you are isolated from others, Fellowship is a call to realize that no person is an island. We are part of a tapestry of interaction, yet each individual fulfills their own destiny. Fellowship presents a relationship with an emphasis on what it can teach you about yourself.

Nature nurtures
unity,
while honoring diversity;
it is a crossing
holding hands.

"Heaven together with fire: the image of fellowship." The
Clinging Flame reflects the Creative fire and sparkles
like stars that mark cosmic time and order. T'ung Jen is
a message that asks you to overcome feeling separate
from everything around you. Discover your connection
to others and transcend the boundaries that separate
you from life.

The master said: *"Everything in the universe is interacting
and exchanging energy in some way."* Although you
cannot see nature's symmetries and connectivity, they
are there. *"One who understands the activities of Nature,
uses no counting rods."* The meaning of one thing can
only be understood in relation to what stands next to,
and influences it.

Fellowship provides the opportunity to merge with the
whole to understand the importance of the part you
play within it. Let go of the limitations that hold you
back from seeing your unity with all that unfolds
around you. If you are experiencing rejection, check to
see that you are not stalking the relationship with a fear
of abandonment.

The planets moving through constellations in a fixed
rhythm above demonstrated a predictable method of

marking time for the ancients. Observing these cycles provided the knowledge of when to plant and harvest, allowing civilization to thrive. While these patterns reveal our dependency on what is taking place above, it also shows the outline or behavior of a *larger* organism connected to what is below.

All people are complex networks of cells, but we only recognize them in one form. Your perception makes distinctions in the natural world that are not necessarily there. In the same way, you can project qualities on others from past experiences or repressed fears that make a person appear different than what they really are. Interacting in social circles allows you to learn about yourself through your differences to identify your unique gifts. You sometimes discover your deficiencies too, or uncover unhealthy dynamics that you carry forward into relationships. Fellowship can be a learning journey through interaction.

In the image of quietly knowing, without being able to describe it, when you give and receive through others, you are able to move beyond your self-limiting structures and orientation to life. Through giving you learn more about yourself. Through self love or opening to love, you find it was there all along.

"Life becomes brilliant when purpose is a light that shines upon it." You are not made meaningless and irrelevant. On the contrary, by becoming a part of the group or joining in an attitude of caring and service to others,

you are awakened to greater meaning and purpose in life.

Unchanging: What you seek of others is really your gift to give = offer it freely. Fellowship unchanging can mean that you are not being social enough or social situations are causing you frustration. However, something deeper is going on with you which has nothing to do with others. You may be approaching a new type of social interaction and are not sure how to act or what will be expected of you. Examine your attitude about associating with others. If you receive this in relation to a romantic enquiry, the message can be that there is a connection, but it is not a passionate one, and probably will remain platonic. Ensure that you are associating with people who are right for you.

Line 1 People meet at the gate = a superficial connection but nothing wrong. Changes to (33) Retreat. Fellowship has success at the beginning only because the connection is superficial or based on serving mutual interests. This partial involvement does not offer much in the way of personal needs. The gate combined with Retreat can show a lack of deeper connection. The interaction could lead to deeper personal growth but barriers prevent this from occurring.

Line 2 People meet in a clique = shutting others out is not good. Changes to (1) Creative. In any group or partnership remaining exclusive or shutting others out will prevent the dynamic input of diversity. The Creative can only manifest by allowing for the innovative and even the conflicted energy of different opinions working like friction to create the fire of creativity. When the opportunity to grow through interaction is presented, one chooses to stay within familiar circles.

Line 3 Weapons hidden in thicket = mistrusting others is not good. Changes to (25) Innocence. This can show the influence of defensiveness or fear in interacting with others. A change in attitude is called for that releases judgment and preconceptions. While this barrier exists, Fellowship is blocked. An innocent outlook is the only way to Fellowship.

Line 4 Climbing a wall but not attacking = reconciliation emerging. Changes to (37) Family. Erecting walls creates a barrier for protection, but one does not retaliate and reconciliation is considered. The wall can symbolize the need for healthy boundaries which needs to be respected. Family suggests that discussion and clarifying expectations and roles will bring about union.

Line 5 People cry, then laugh = after a struggle a meeting occurs. Changes to (30) Clarity. While you may feel outwardly separated from someone, in your hearts you remain connected. Regardless of the obstacles keeping you apart, Fellowship emerges again. Clarity shows the synergistic connection among people connected in Spirit. Because of the vicissitudes of emotional interaction, the connection grows deeper.

Line 6 People outside the city = distance prevents Fellowship. Changes to (49) Molting/Revolution. Warmth and connection is missing from Fellowship as people are interacting with a sense of distance. The connection may be bringing about transformation but there is an aloof quality to the interaction. Dislike isn't the issue as the connection isn't very strong. Deeper intimacy can only occur via personal transformation.

Hexagram #14
Ta Yu (Great Possessing)

Action: Shine

Hu Gua (secondary influence) 43 Determination: Breakthrough

Zong Gua: (underlying cause) 8 Union: Discover

Received as 2nd Hexagram: Whatever you are seeking, you already possess it.

**If you are not playing the host,
you will discover that you are the guest.**

*In the depth of winter, I finally learned
that there was in me, an invincible summer.* – *Albert Camus*

Reading at a Glance: Ta Yu is formed when Fire moves over Heaven. The idea of mental clarity or the sun in the sky shows its auspiciousness in describing your current condition. The sun sustains life and if we rise like the sun, we need only activate our hidden powers of expansion. Like the sun, by simply being, we set off a chain reaction of abundance. Obstacles disappear because of the secondary influence of Breakthrough. We cultivate the seeds planted in the dark of winter that break through the soil of difficulty and emerge stronger and wiser. This is Great Possessing. Perhaps we learned to play the guest of life and not strive so much to fight against what can never be. Where the Zong Gua of Union was a time of joining and partnerships, Great Possessing is a time when our star shines or our sun is rising as an individual. Life has offered you its greatest gift – the power to shine with an inner certainty that need not be defended. Strength and clarity unite and you can move forward in the knowledge that Grace is your teacher and power is merely aligning your will with the way. The message can be about wealth, success or just a sense of knowing you have arrived.

When the hand opens
to reveal
its unbroken line -
the host
rumbles in the belly.

"The character is firm, strong, ordered and clear: the image of possession in great measure." Ta Yu is the image of an

inexhaustible source of energy that is available when you open yourself to nature's drive toward excellence.

The master said: *"Do not play the host, but become the guest."* If you can transcend your need for control, you can become the recipient of the subtle treasures that life has in store for you.

In the natural world we are the only creatures who attempt to play the host. We have become so disconnected from knowing what it is like to hunt for our nourishment that we behave less like animals and more like trees. You might argue that unlike trees, you can move freely about. Yet, you come and go to the same places each day, drawing sustenance from a refrigerator. Even while you barely look over your dashboard, desktop or television, life still finds productive ways of coaching your authentic nature forward. Opening to life's power to lead you aligns you with a power and energy that cannot be depleted.

As a message about the illusion of control, a tree provides shelter to the tiny nests hidden within its branches, but it does not play the host because it opens itself to the wind, rain and the tiny insects that nourish and steward its pollination and rebirth. The wind and the rain are not the host because they are generated by the changing pressure systems in the atmosphere. The earth is not the host because it responds to these atmospheric changes, and the moon makes its great bodies of water rise and fall. If the oldest things in the universe are not in control, then why do you attempt to play the host?

Playing the host without understanding the host is how you unwittingly create your own misfortune. When you learn to become the guest of a greater unfolding, you can flow into life's purposeful movement toward the best of what it might become. Knowing your place within the larger flow of life allows you to discover power in great measure.

Trusting that something more profound might understand your needs in ways that you cannot, *"all things in the universe have a purpose; is it right that you should be different?"* The future must remain a mystery because life has a special predisposition for exploring possibilities. Through its dance of randomness, it generates innovation and novelty. When you are not busy organizing your life, you will discover that you are the guest of something that demonstrates a greater purpose in leading you.

The greatest teacher learns by the process of teaching and the most celebrated artists allow their work to lead them. Similarly, if you open to the energy of life to lead you forward, you can access power or inspiration in greater measure.

The more you open, the more this great energy of discovery will fill you. The Flame burns away any barriers that keep you from experiencing yourself *just so*. As the image of a hand opening to present an offering, when you open in this way, you will receive.

Unchanging: Nothing has been lost = shine your light without searching. Ta Yu unchanging can be a message that you already have all that you need. In relation to the object of your enquiry, it can be a cryptic answer like Hexagram 4 when you keep pushing for additional clarity and the answer is "it is what it is" for now. Unlike Hexagram 4 which is an admonishment to stop asking, Ta Yu adds the additional message that your life is full of abundance if you can stop focusing on what is missing. Sometimes we can operate like a magnet rather than being magnetic. One gathers a lot of possessions, relationships, and whatever satisfies their desires, but they have not incorporated the work that is required to make Great Possessing fulfilling. It can be instant gratification or just a desire to win or have the most toys. What is missing from the flow is that abundance fulfills and renews daily because it is shared. Your life is given more definition when you experience it through others. Examine your desire to see if growth rather than need is operative. Ta Yu is a positive message showing how clarity of mind and strength of character have made your abundance recognized and is something valued by others.

Line 1 Releasing what causes harm = eliminating arrogance. Changes to (50) Cauldron. Since this is the beginning of Great Possessing success can go to your head. The only thing standing in between you and your object of desire is the need for humility. Things are not

102

as easy as they appear, so there is a need for caution. Because you refuse the easier path and seek a higher aim, you are respected. Not holding a grudge and rising above the superficial works wonders.

Line 2 A wagon arrives = you have the means to succeed. Changes to (30) Clarity. Remaining true to yourself is important in achieving your aim. The wagon refers to gaining the consensus and support of others. You have shown you are worthy of greater responsibility. The situation shows a connection to passion and the synergy of Clarity. Your aims are in agreement with others.

Line 3 You are in a unique position to help another = no one else can do this. Changes to (38) Opposition. This is a line that suggests an attitude of abundance ensures that you don't fall into conflict with others. Don't measure what you give, it will only undermine your success in achieving your aim. The empty vessel of being open is always filled when in the service of others. A sacrifice may be required and another may rely on your support. However, know that sacrificing to others can also lead to their resentment which is not something you can control. There is a fine balance required, so if you open your hand make sure the gesture is with the attitude of abundance and not what you will receive in return.

Line 4 Making a difference between oneself and neighbors = envy is a counting rod. Changes to (26) Taming Power Great. It is normal to look around and measure your success against what others have. Perhaps you haven't quite arrived where you thought you should be. You are filled with inspiration even if you haven't yet found a way to express it. Looking over the hedges to see what the neighbors possess just distracts you from seeing the gifts you are being given. Accumulating this great energy of self direction is progress so tame it.

Line 5 Truth accessible and dignified = it is the character that attracts good fortune. Changes to (1) Creative. There are many blessings at your disposal that only require that you keep your relationships balanced with sincerity. You are received like plants greeting the sun. You offer unconditional sincerity that transcends the material world because your radiance is inspired by truth. Other's respect you for your actions but your dignity is at the core of who you are. You are seen for who you are and trust is not misplaced.

Line 6 You are blessed by heaven to receive what you **need** = great good fortune. Changes to (34) Great Power. Great Power means being vigorous but Great Possessing is one who becomes a vessel of abundance that overflows. Because you have no need to cling to anything, all things come to you. Great Power focuses on movement and strength. Great Possessing at its pinnacle shows that you have done the work required to prepare yourself to be a vessel of abundance for others. A period of testing has proven that your dignity is unquestionable.

Hexagram #15
Qiān (Authenticity)

Action: Balance
Hu Gua (secondary influence) 40 Liberation: Untangle
Zong Gua: (underlying cause) 10 Treading: Cautious
Advance
Received as 2nd Hexagram: Achieving balance is
central to your question.

**If you know no boundaries,
you will meet with no limitations.**

*One who rides a tiger is afraid to dismount. – Chinese
Proverb*

Reading at a Glance: After a period of feeling fulfilled,
perhaps full of yourself, it is normal to return to reality
and not take yourself so seriously. The secondary
influence of Liberation or freedom needs to be balanced
with the cautious conduct of Treading. Watching the
steps and checking unfolding events against inspiration
led to a greater sense of having purpose in life. Now
humility and moderation return you to a place where

you need to ensure that all parts of your life are moving in harmony. The Receptive is above the Mountain where Keeping Still returns you to your nature. It is normal to succeed at a point in life and want to keep doing the same thing. Suddenly what worked before isn't working anymore. This is because life moves in cycles, and the future will never be anything like the past. Moderation and modesty return you to the center of your Authenticity. Your unique path hones you for the next level of growth. It is Tao's way to fill what is deficient and to reduce what is in excess. No matter where you look in nature, you will find it balancing out its extremes to ensure the well being of the entire tapestry. Yin is receptive while Yang is active. They push and pull until all of life is in equal balance.

Authenticity can be a message to step back and slow down to connect with sincerity. Trust that everything is unfolding in its own time and exactly as it should. Moderation is a way of taking stock of your life to ensure that one area has not become so important that other areas are deficient. Pride generates enthusiasm and inspirational freedom, but humility keeps you focused on how you tread on the path so you don't become disconnected from what is right for you. It is said that *those who go against the way end up being called unlucky."* Authenticity is every step you take and all the steps together that reveal your path. The journey of 1,000 miles begins under your feet.

This long
upward climb -
with periods of falling.
Balance ensures
a stable footing.

"One who possesses something great should not make it too full." The Mountain bows down to the Receptive Earth in an unusual display of modesty and temperance. Even the summit of Mount Everest contains proof of its humble beginnings, in rocks that were once formed in a shallow sea.

The master said: *"The vessel in the temple of Chou stands upright when empty, but overturns when full. Rather than fill it to the brim, it is better to stop in time,"* so nothing gets overturned. Qiān offers a message about turning back and ceasing action to ensure that nothing needs to be undone.

Humility is a necessary virtue that reveals the fine line between taking and giving. In our effort to grow abundant produce, we apply chemicals that ward off disease, although they destroy the bees and ladybugs that keep the plants healthy.

Tourists are attracted to colorful reefs where they can snorkel with abundant fish populations. As hotels appear along the coastline, they tear out the mangroves that trap and process excess nutrients and pollutants in the water. As the water quality in the coral reef environment diminishes, the reefs soon die, and all that the tourists came to see is destroyed.

As nature finds ways of purifying itself, we discover that what we throw away does not necessarily go away. Because you cannot trace the line of excess, *"it is better to stop in time."* In all you eat and do, strike a balance between productive and fiery Yang and replenishing or earthy Yin.

"The way that leads forward seems to lead backward." Nature achieves forward movement sometimes by turning back, and you too, can be moving forward when it appears as if you are going backward. After every rise, you may fall, but you only appear to be rising and falling in relation to your expectations. In the larger scheme of things, you are always moving forward toward Authenticity.

The master said: *"what is vast resembles nothing because if it resembled anything, it would become small."* Turning back to replenish, while still moving forward is the constant motion of life. This is the essence of moderation.

Turning back, you can find contentment in modesty; through authenticity, you will re-connect with the way. Do not become so distant from your actions that you forget that you are a part of both the smallness and largeness of life. *"There are times when you climb and times when you fall. The climb is difficult, but the fall is quick and inexorable."* As you rise, offset your times of falling with your knowledge of this turning.

Authenticity ensures that you do not close your mind with structures and ideas that can become obstructions to your sincerity. In your search for absolutes, you must succumb to the gravity of the unknowable.

"When there is nothing that you cannot overcome, no one knows the limit." When there is *something* you must overcome, you discover your limits. A path of Authenticity suggests that if you are content to know no boundaries, you will discover no limitations. As the image of establishing limits on the outer world through words and ideas, it asks you to turn back and be content not to know.

"The Way goes round and round. Being great, it is described as receding. Receding, it is described as far away. Being far away, it is described as turning back." In the Great Circle, turning back is how all things continue in their forward movement.

Unchanging: Words, ideas and structures = let them fall down. Authenticity unchanging can be a message about having expectations that are too high or unrealistic. This answer can be the sound of a mother quieting a child : "Now you know why I told you not to eat so much cake." You may be overly enthusiastic or stuck. Instead of the balance that is brought about by combining modesty and enthusiasm, one or the other is running amok. Both K'un and Ken are images of stopping in meditation. The absence of lines suggests stopping to take a breath. Whatever you are seeking – it is either not the time or you need to gain more clarity. Be patient, the way will unfold and you will be glad you didn't act so impetuously.

Line 1 Authentic about modesty = good for crossing the river. Changes to (36) Brightness Hiding. Being humble doesn't mean being timid or false. Being modest doesn't mean being a 'yes' person. There is a difficult task ahead. What you are attempting may not be easy, but you will succeed. Respect the energy of the time that is guiding your forward movement. Keep your story to yourself while pushing through to achieve your goal.

Line 2 Making humble gestures = persisting in this yields success. Changes to (46) Pushing Upward. At this time you may need to make a sacrifice in order to succeed. Gaining the support of others because you are authentic and not threatening ensures the success of Pushing Upward.

Line 3 Modesty is demanded to get the job done = don't underestimate and under deliver. Changes to (2) Receptive. Your dedication to do the work required is more important than accolades or compensation. There can be some sort of boundary where you can only do what you can and then must let go without expecting anything in return. Authenticity leading to the opening suggested by the Receptive can describe being humble enough to know what is beyond your power to do.

Line 4 Modesty gains merit = but gaining prestige is not the goal. Changes to (62) Overwhelming of Small. It is your work or actions that define your character. Keep to a modest approach and express humbleness to the other. Overwhelming of the Small shows that small things done over time lead to great rewards.

Line 5 Not getting what you need = to balance modesty with success force is required. Changes to (39) Obstruction. There is no need to show you have the upper hand. However, to achieve success, you may have to be more assertive. Take what you need which doesn't harm the other. All benefit because you are being authentic. This is the only way to work through the Obstruction.

Line 6 Modesty comes to expression = don't blame others. Changes to (52) Keeping Still. Even though you have not achieved your aims, you have learned a valuable lesson about authenticity. Blaming others is useless. Real strength is first and foremost the ability to conquer yourself. A friendly attitude prevails. Perhaps you set your sights too high. As the highest point of Modesty, being authentic is the surest way to your goal.

Hexagram #16
Yu (Enthusiasm)

Action: Excite

Hu Gua (secondary influence) 39 Obstruction: Innovate

Zong Gua: (underlying cause) 9 Small Restraint: Surrender

Received as 2nd Hexagram: Enthusiasm is at play and can be either too much or too little.

**If you make your home in the inevitable,
you will arrive exactly where you need to be.**

*Chance is always powerful. Let your hook always be cast;
In the pool where you least expect it, there will be a fish. —
Ovid*

Reading at a Glance: Yu shows Thunder over Earth which can bring new energy and inspiration to your situation. In ancient times, people gathered around the fire at the end of winter, sharing stories meant to jar the clan from stagnation. In ancient China, Chen or Thunder was believed to ignite the seeds into rebirth. Yu was believed to be the energy that connects people to the Gods. It is associated with art and music and any inspirational work that ignites our imagination and lifts us out of this world for awhile. The trick is to work with this Enthusiastic and inspired energy in a way that you don't become lost in it. Yu can be a warning to take off your rose colored glasses if you are still waiting for that answer when all signs have already told you all you need to know. Enthusiasm should not to be confused with the law of attraction. If you place preconceptions against the ability to see *what is,* you may suffer disappointment. Yu is a child riding an elephant joyously. The child is the Taming of the Small or Small Restraint, like the weak force in the universe that holds much of life together. It was your joy or willingness to meet life face to face with innocent excitement that generated this opportunity. The child doesn't know, so operates without preconceptions. This is the innovation suggested by the secondary influence of Obstruction.

Trusting the wild and powerful elephant can be both good and bad. Enthusiasm needs to be grounded in moderation otherwise it can lead to escapism and pipe dreams. The elephant embodies the creative power of emotion, which when harnessed, tramples any barriers to forward progress. You are asked to connect with this innocent enthusiasm for inspiration and to inspire others. This is a hexagram which combines how walking the path, allowing life to guide you and meeting experience innocently will create the joy and enthusiasm that makes all things possible. Like a child, *"those who don't know what can't be done accomplish great things."* Align your will with the way and believe that anything is possible. Something magical is on the horizon so stay grounded while you look for that magical elephant to ride upon.

The earth's power
to thrive
and succeed
resides
in your core.

"One who possesses something great and is modest is sure to have enthusiasm." Yu is the image of a child riding an elephant where spontaneous enthusiasm, combined with nature's enormous transformative power will allow you to trample any barriers that would impede your forward progress.

Like the athlete who enters 'the zone,' by overcoming resistance, movement is effortless, and you feel as if you can accomplish anything. Yet, nothing in the environment has really changed, although somewhere within, the illusion of resistance dissipates. Enthusiasm is your devotion to moving forward when you tap life's positive and free flowing energy.

The master said: *"The power of becoming resides in a positively charged core."* The only similarity between Lu and the power of attraction is positive intention. Lu coaches modesty or a willingness to stay practical and grounded. You can fill intention with a concrete desire or preconceived outcome and wonder why it doesn't arrive. Perhaps you are gaining something fulfilling by playing in fantasy. The texts warn that you need not wait a whole day...you've been given the answer. You've already seen the signs. Enthusiasm embraces what is. We must sometimes close the door to fantasy so that reality can show us it is even better than we dreamed.

You can approach life with a positive attitude of acceptance, or you can resist and fight against it with your will. The way is much easier when you follow the path of least resistance.

Banging endlessly against a closed door, you might discover that another door remains open. This is the sublimity you will discover when following the energy of life. The nuclear trigram of the Abysmal suggests a wellspring coming up against the Mountain of a closed door.

Water cannot flow up the hill of a hardened perspective, but a profound inner shifting can open the doors of inertia where your devotion to movement magnetizes opportunity. The door was always open; it is a shift in awareness that will allow you to find it. Let your will be the enthusiastic expression of celebrating what comes to pass. In other words, go with the flow because the flow knows where to go. And your boat ride is waiting.

Unchanging: Knock on the door of enthusiasm = the joy inside will open and let you in. You are going to have a date with enthusiasm. It is a hard thing to kick start and takes momentum to keep it going, but look for that first burst of inspiration that ignites a new idea. You can be receiving a message to bring more enthusiasm and passion into your life and an opportunity is coming. You can also be at a plateau of inspiration and riding a wave that will eventually recede, so prepare for the change. The other message can be enthusiasm running rampant while you close your ears to any realistic input. Whether you need a burst of inspiration, spiritual guidance, or an unexpected date with reality – change is coming. The good news is that whatever it is – it will lead to greater fulfillment. Enthusiasm must be grounded to be meaningful.

Line 1 Boasting enthusiasm = not uniting does not further. Changes to (51) Shocking. A false sense of well being has led to pride and a surprise encounter with failure. Something important to you may be brushed off by someone else who thinks you are too overly excited. Your behavior may appear Shocking to another. Better to use enthusiasm with humility without bragging. Emotions are interfering with the ability to see clearly. There may be a loss of purpose or blocked aspirations. Excess is at play in some way which a return to humility will cure. Bring it down a notch and trust the flow.

Line 2 Separated by rock but aware of the signs = persistence brings good fortune. Changes to (40) Deliverance. There is much that can deceive one who cannot read the signs and cycles of change. Perhaps you know the answer and just don't want to face it?

Enthusiasm leads to liberation or Deliverance if you are not swayed by passing fads and remain persistent. It is your vision that carries the day so examine your outlook. Firm as a rock, one does not allow enthusiasm to run away with them. If you are in a holding pattern, the Way should open soon.

Line 3 Relying on others to support enthusiasm = waiting wastes opportunity. Changes to (62) Small Exceeding. Instead of proceeding, one hesitates out of fear and misses an opportunity. Perhaps you feel that the call to align appears needy or reveals weakness. Others are offering support although timing is important in order to seize the opportunity. Remove the barriers that are causing unnecessary discomfort and delay. You do not need the support of others to keep your enthusiasm alive.

Line 4 Enthusiasm without doubt = gathering friends. Changes to (2) Receptive. Shining with enthusiasm without any sense of doubt attracts others to your cause. Confidence and trust in others leads to their willing support. What you need and how you express yourself resonates with others. This is an excellent line showing a strong team based on devotion to each other or a greater good.

Line 5 Persistence = chronically ill but does not die. Changes to (45) Gathering Together. Enthusiasm is obstructed and creates pressure, slowing down a sense of joining others. However, the blockage is a source of enlightenment for all. This is an uncomfortable situation which has the potential to lead to a breakthrough. You may need to accept that this is as good as it gets but growth and potential are still possible.

Line 6 False enthusiasm = if after completion one changes, no blame. Changes to (35) Progress. You may be staring longingly at the past and are not seeing the present or are living an illusion. If you can let go of being deluded by enthusiasm, there is still time to move toward a more practical and grounded opportunity for growth. The sober awakening is actually a good thing. Perhaps your enthusiasm has run away with you and you need to bring it back down to earth for others to grasp it. Continuing in fantasy won't lead anywhere. Look realistically at the situation and Progress indicates that you can succeed.

Hexagram #17
Sui (Following)

Action: Show by Example
Hu Gua (secondary influence) 53 Development: Flower
Zong Gua: (underlying cause) 18 Decay: Remedy
Received as 2nd Hexagram: Others may be following your lead.

If you return from the darkness with gold, others will naturally follow.

We can easily forgive a child who is afraid of the dark; the real tragedy of life is when men are afraid of the light. –
Plato

Reading at a Glance: You may need to take the initiative and show the way in order to get others to follow your lead. When doing anything remember that actions speak louder than words, so recognize that you are setting an example. Joy above Thunder can be a message about stepping back to delegate. Inspire forward movement in those you lead, don't make demands. You may receive a promotion to lead others because you have integrity and are not a threat to superiors. At the same time, don't threaten your subordinates. This hexagram calls for Joy in leading. Ignite the passion of others to tap their seeds of genius. Don't burst onto the scene with an agenda that may be threatening. Working on what has spoiled in Decay as the Zong Gua shows that your transformation has been successful and you are recognized for what you have accomplished. Gradual Development as the secondary influence indicates patience and care when approaching the object of your enquiry. With the proper approach this is an auspicious time to connect with others who will follow your lead.

Follow
behind,
tranquil
in your
visionary cave.

"Where there is enthusiasm, there is sure to be a following."
Observing nature as your role model, you can begin to
lead others by emulating its ways. The sage who had
become master of the self and the pathway was
encouraged to develop *"harmony in one's larger*
relationship to life." Transcending your personal
journey, you are called to lead others as a pathway to
growth.
The master said: *"if you are a model to the empire, then the*
constant virtue will not be wanting. To benefit others without
extracting gratitude, and to steward without exercising
authority is virtue."
Your object of enquiry may require that you take the
initiative so that others believe in what you are doing
enough to follow your lead.

The Arousing Thunder rests within the middle of the
Joyous Lake, representing a calm withdrawal and the
image of delegation. When winter gave way to spring,
the electricity of the lightning was believed to withdraw
into the earth to regenerate the unseen seeds below. In
the image of withdrawal and retreat, it is time to
cultivate the unseen talents of those that follow.
Empowering those you lead, you can nurture each
individual to build the strength of the group. Sui is the
image of how footsteps naturally follow each other.

120

Sensing the appropriate time when things are in their proper place, you may leave what you have built in the hands of those that follow. *"Desiring to lead the people, one must, in one's person, follow behind them. One takes the place ahead of the people, yet causes no obstruction. That is why the empire supports the leader joyfully and never tires of doing so."* Firm like a Mountain, you can inspire and not impede. Gentle like the Wind, you can bring projects to completion by trusting others to carry forward your vision.

As a leader, you may operate from insecurity, threatened by the strengths of others; or, you can cultivate the talents of those that follow in a way that *you* are lifted to a higher level. Only by delegating, can you be made stronger.

The empire or enterprise will only support the leader who nurtures others in this way. You can take your place ahead without causing any obstruction behind. To lead in a way that others follow joyfully, is the sign of true leadership. *"When the task is finished and the work done, the people all say, 'it happened to us naturally.'"* A leader, guided by the laws of nature will not be worn down by failing to rely on the strengths of others.

Thus, when you master something, you naturally develop a following. The message of Sui can also lead you to explore commitment. If you are having difficulty getting support for what you are doing explore your level of commitment. The universe is always manifesting your desires. The question is: is this really what you want?

Unchanging: There is nothing to follow = if you don't open the door. Because of the lack of movement in the lines, following has a message more related to non action in its unchanging form. You are being asked to learn how to gain deeper insight into others. This means listening and being there to support one another. You may find yourself in a situation where you have to make a choice to follow of stay. Following your heart will leave you without blame. However, following the mind can get you into trouble. The heart is motivated by the passion that the trigrams Joy and Thunder inspire. The head can be susceptible to fear which only makes you go in circles. Take a chance and open to intimacy. At the same time the message can be: don't be a bully but be magnetic, you will get more bees with honey. Or, don't push – give someone time. If you are unhappy with another's response, do nothing because this waiting period throws them back upon themselves and often brings the other to a change of heart. Finally, the question this hexagram presents is: what are you following and why? Pause and reflect. You may need to look long and hard at your motivation. The idea of others following, or you following them is at play so examine their motivation and yours. Is it real intimacy or simply an opportunity to meet each other's basic needs for survival? Are both situations acceptable to you?

Line 1 The situation has changed and minds have changed = impulse rising, going out of the gate. Changes to (45) Gathering Together. Adapting to a change requires new approaches that can only be explored by leaving the familiar. Allow the time to reveal itself in the changed minds of others. Be open to input. There are consequences that affect all involved. A discussion or meeting brings people together to make amends. Influence is an outer prompting while impulse is an inner sense. Allow someone the space to discover the impulse rather than attempting to influence or push.

Line 2 Attached to the child = ignoring mature aspects. Changes to (58) Joy. In making a decision, an element of self indulgence is at play. Perhaps you are attempting to re-ignite the passion and carefree attitude of youth. Clinging to an outmoded path stems from immaturity or a lack of wisdom. You may need to connect with the child in some way to ignite passion in maturity. However, there is a danger of being influenced by inferior people. A lack of growth can occur if you follow another, but it can certainly be fun. Examine that which you follow to see if it aligns to the person you want to become.

Line 3 Attaching to maturity = ignoring the child and following what one seeks. Changes to (49) Molting/Revolution. In making a decision, you are exploring whether or not to follow another. It seems that they can teach you something that will allow you to evolve. The logical pursuit of goals is fine as long as you can recognize the need for passion. You make a more mature decision following logic rather than fantasy. Following in this way will lead to transformation.

Line 4 Persevering but trapped = following leads to success. Changes to (3) Difficult Beginnings. A flattering situation has trapped you. While it seemed perfectly okay to follow, you need to examine your motivation in following or another's motivation in seeking your company. Sincere actions are fruitful. Gratification brings illusion. Be true to yourself and look at the real foundation of this situation.

Line 5 Confidence and appreciation = all goes well. Changes to (51) Shocking. A decision needs to be made whether to follow what other's want or to follow your intuition. A bolt out the blue type of insight or a Shocking event may have changed your attitude. Only you know what is right for you. If underappreciated, confidence grows anyway as a sudden feeling that awakens you to your real path.

Line 6 Rewarded for wisdom = other's cling to you. Changes to (25) Innocence. Your wisdom and conscientiousness have been recognized. After retreating from a situation you have the opportunity to return with a fresh perspective. Your willingness to help those in need is appreciated. Others seek you out because of your steadfast character and willingness to provide guidance.

Hexagram #18
Ku (Decay)

Action: Remedy
Hu Gua (secondary influence) 54 Propriety:
Subordinate
Zong Gua: (underlying cause) 17 Following: Show by
Example
Received as 2nd Hexagram: An overhaul is required in
this situation.

All things are supple when alive,
but become hard when dead.

The real voyage of discovery consists not in seeking new
landscapes,
but in having new eyes. – *Marcel Proust*

Reading at a Glance: Success in business is often
measured in an "S" like curve. Initially costs are plotted
against time, revealing a flat beginning. In the middle
when costs are no longer an issue, the line rises as
profits grow. Later, competition flattens the line as
market saturation offsets profits and the line recedes. If

the business recognizes that innovation and responsiveness has to occur at every turn, perhaps the line would progress upward unimpeded. That is not usually the case. People wait until sales fall or something is broken before they take action. We do this in our personal lives too and that is the message of Decay. Mountain over Wind suggests how the Wind must change course as a remedy for forward advance because the Mountain of ideas has blocked progress and Decay grows unchecked in this situation. The secondary influence of Subordinate suggests recognizing how you are interdependent on others. All relationships thrive on win/win solutions. A business explores demand prior to manufacturing the product.

You may need to put your personal goals aside and make a sacrifice based on the needs of another. Where Following as Zong Gua suggests how one thing follows another naturally, in this situation, the old way needs to be overhauled if you are to be successful. Ego games and self serving approaches to others will not work. Following old routines can lead to shoddy work and design. Whatever the situation, it is time to clear out the old and prepare for the new. Ku has a lot to teach you however. If you know that Decay can set in, you can prepare in advance to avoid it. The necessary ingredients are the ability to offset deterioration by ensuring innovation and that constant change is sustained.

Wind over the Mountain.
One chisels away,
the other
inspires
leaders.

"Work on what has spoiled; afterwards there is order."
Routine can take on a life of its own and over time, all
things require renewal. You must work on what has
been spoiled by decay to foster a rebirth. Bringing
vitality to what is old and outworn, Ku portrays how
being placed in a yielding position to nourish others can
sometimes turn the Wind into the image of drifting.

The master said: *"you are supple when alive and hard when
dead."* Even a business environment, being comprised of
individuals, must be established on a foundation of
individual growth to keep the enterprise alive.
Observing what has led the situation to become hard
and dead, prune away what has stymied forward
progress.

Failing to recognize the necessary cycles of completion
and renewal, a situation has been allowed to move
steadily toward a state of stagnation.

Perhaps you have defined your worth by solving the
problems of others, and those that follow look to you as
a problem solver. You may have lost your vision of the
larger picture by tending to its many parts. Regardless
of the reason, the situation has lost its suppleness.

127

"The Mountain is the beginning and end;" it is associated with autumn when the height of creation ends and begins anew. In the image of seeds falling to the ground, harvest the seeds of the future by removing the outer husk or protective covering of the past. To work on what has been spoiled, separate what is dead from what will bring new life.

"You observe life's power in what you can see and hear. Its potential remains in the unknown and mysterious." Crossing the Great Water to observe the situation with a fresh perspective, success is assured through systematic renewal. There is a need to overcome complacency so you can lift something to a higher and more functioning level. Stagnation only exists while you avoid the inevitable death of the old way. To tap the future potential of something, you must come to terms with what must pass.

"Before the starting point, three days. After the starting point, three days." Three months of spring follow three months of winter to bring about growth, but only because three months of summer was followed by autumn to usher in decline. If you are inspired by the laws of nature, you will be undaunted by the changing climate, and merely set upon the task of reinvigorating renewal.

Unchanging: During autumn = leaves fall to nourish spring. You may not immediately see Decay or its cause, although you can observe the lack of vitality or hardness surrounding your situation. The new beginning cannot manifest until you are willing to allow the ending to come. A situation may be beyond repair because of your refusal to acknowledge that there was anything wrong in the first place. Something requires transformation and care if it is to succeed. Sweeping a problem under the rug won't work – address the issue. Since propriety or Subordination is the secondary influence you may need to be more of a subordinate and stop pushing or fighting. Step back and let others approach you in their own season.

Line 1 Neglect of the father brings investigation = consequences and blame released. Changes to (26) Taming Power of Great. This line can describe karma or past actions rooted in tradition and their consequences. Investigate whether actions have been too impulsive spoiling an otherwise good situation. Perhaps a more modern approach to the matter will correct what is wrong. An investigation of inherent weakness is in order where a new idea can invigorate it. To allow for the Taming of the Great, respect of another is in order.

Line 2 Neglect of mother = sensitivity needed. Changes to (52) Keeping Still. Emotional responses have gotten out of control and sensitivity is needed. A relationship is delicate and applying remedy drastically might wound. Through weakness an imbalance has occurred. Someone is choosing not to act for the time being. Give the situation gentle consideration by Keeping Still and allow for the space needed for reflection.

Line 3 Minor neglect of father = hasty correction of humiliation. Changes to (4) Youthful Folly. A mistake is easily rectified, although you may have been a bit hasty and judged as inconsiderate. No real blame because it is better do something rather than nothing. In fact, you may have to bend over backwards a little to make amends. State your case and then back off to allow another to assimilate your change in attitude. Approaching correction too hastily can lead to regret or you might be viewed as acting Foolish. Since intentions are toward correction there is no blame.

Line 4 Setting right what was spoiled by father = seeing what is wrong leads to praise. Changes to (50) Cauldron. Ignoring decay leads to problems because you'd rather not rock the boat. Perhaps your respect for another has left you unable to speak up. The Cauldron can show co-dependency or giving your power away. Eventually this will lead to humiliation. Better to rectify the situation and speak up. The weakness is obvious but to discuss what is wrong without remedying it is futile. You will be respected for speaking your mind.

Line 5 Setting right the father's corruption = one meets with praise. Changes to (57) Penetration. It will take some time and probing to remedy the situation but it is necessary and will lead to respect. A long needed reform is in order and you are in a position to make it happen.

Line 6 Transcending the entire situation = turning away to attend to higher goals. Changes to (46) Pushing

Upward. Something important to one isn't important to another, so one minds their own business. While the decision to go one's own way may not bring popularity, it is the right thing for the time. An ability to rise above right and wrong allows you to see the 'just so' flow of events where not embroiling leads to acceptance. After letting go one is able to achieve loftier goals.

Hexagram #19
Lin (Approach)

Action: Advance
Hu Gua (secondary influence) 24 Return: Go Back
Zong Gua: (underlying cause) 33 Retreat: Disengage
Received as 2nd Hexagram: The opportunity to meet and discuss is available.

When you place yourself in a position to help another, you will discover your greater capabilities.

In creating, the only hard thing is to begin:
a grass blade's no easier to make than an oak. – James Lowell

Reading at a Glance: Earth above Joy offers an opportunity where one is favored by circumstances and superiors to advance or receive a promotion. Joy rises to permeate the earth. The secondary influence of Return allows you to connect to your center where you can express your talents while at the same time demonstrating your integrity. Now is the time to show others that you have a sincere desire to Advance. Approach is a message about making or seeking contact. The Zong Gua for this hexagram is that a period of Retreat should now lead to Advance. But be warned that after favorable times, downturns and a need to Retreat may occur again as life moves in cycles. In this way, we go 'inward and outward in fixed rhythms.' The moment is ripe and won't last forever so seize the opportunity to make your Approach. Now is the time to reach out to others or expect that they will enjoy hearing your ideas. Your confidence is appreciated and your demeanor is non-threatening. Even in small ways, you will discover that if you open yourself to helping others you will discover untapped potential. Go for it and enjoy this time of Approach.

Earth's reflection
on a lake;
its hidden depths
coaxed upwards -
where clouds rise.

"When there are things to be done, one becomes great."
Approach describes new work before you that will enable you to tap your latent talent. You receive a new

job or promotion because you have delegated in a way that leaves you open to greater opportunity. Advance cannot happen however, if you don't take the initiative to seize the opportunity.

The master said: *"If you place yourself in a position to help others, you discover your greater capabilities."* Lin show how leaders must remain approachable. A steadfast character and willingness to serve is noticed and you are approached with an opportunity for advancement.

As a leader, you may know the destination, but those that follow must discover their own way. When achievement rests upon the shoulder of the individual, through systems that both ensure and reward growth, you set a course for success that has the momentum of a wheel in motion. It is put in continual motion by the enthusiasm that comes from an unfettered structure focused on growth.

"The firm penetrates and grows; Great success through correctness." Being firm in helping others grow, you must sometimes approach the difficult task of breaking through their walls. With nature as your teacher, this is no different from how you are led; life is always breaking down your walls to unleash the best of what you can be. Serving others with honesty and without fear makes the difficult always easy.

"The Earth above the Lake, the image of approach." Lin is the image of making contact and is associated with a

willingness to serve. You can only serve others if you are steadfast in helping them grow. *"The sage is inexhaustible in the will to teach without limits."* When you 'make contact,' you create a truth environment where growth occurs exponentially. Anytime you find yourself working in an environment where truth and growth are non-existent, the lack of integrity undermines productivity in a way that makes the work a chore.

Inspired by the laws of nature, you become a leader who allows others to bring forward their own vision. Holding to a vision of where you are going, you must also foster 'ownership' in those that follow. When subordinates can create their own vision, and identify a sense of 'owning the outcome,' the enterprise achieves a sense of fullness, of which *"use will not drain."*

Harvesting good fortune reminds us to also save for a rainy day. When times are tough, it will be periods like this we can draw upon as inspiration that all things change in time. This is a good time to increase your skills or learn from others. Whatever abundance you hold should be shared with others.

Unchanging: When you rise each day like spring = everyday is a flowering. This is a fortunate hexagram to receive with no lines changing. The message is that Approach is more than a momentary event for you. Your abilities and compassion have already led you into the service of others. There is an eternal flow of abundance at your disposal. Your positive attitude makes every day feel like spring. The only warning Approach offers is when you are not being approachable. Perhaps you have cut yourself off from communication in some way? A high level of focus is placed on reaching out to someone. If that is not an option or contact isn't reciprocated then the message of quickening suggests allowing events to unfold naturally, like seeds beneath the earth at Springtime. Perhaps a period of waiting for Approach has allowed you to cultivate talent or a type of 'inexhaustible teaching' that puts you at service to others. Your day will come. Just keep being patient, present and willing to do what you can to nurture others.

Line 1 Joint approach = persevere and succeed. Changes to (7) Army. Moving into influential circles, others join or contribute to your upward trend. Being sensitive to another's feelings helps to bring good fortune. A need to clarify expectations with another might be necessary. A joint approach combined with discipline allows everyone to be served in a way that all talents are harnessed.

Line 2 Joint approach with sincerity = everything furthers. Changes to (24) Return. Being sensitive and showing integrity wins sympathy from others. A need to stay strong in who you are while respecting another is necessary. A discussion leads to a return. If you are sincere in seeking advancement you will succeed.

Line 3 Comfortable approach does not further = to see the mistake no blame. Changes to (11) Peace. Being sweet or expecting a response in approaching another isn't right for this situation. While maintaining the peace, you may have become too intimate or careful with someone. Be yourself and if you share something do it in the spirit of expressing your truth not manipulating. Recognizing this gives you a chance to change your approach. This is the time of year that requires work although the situation may be so comfortable that nothing profitable is accomplished. You also may need to face your mistaken idea that things will flow easy. It may seem that harvest is near but it will take additional work and effort. Much enjoyment from simple activities is promised while it is important to remember this is a situation that is fostering growth. Ensure that your goals are accomplished and don't just sit back expect an easy ride.

Line 4 Complete approach = no blame. Changes to (54) Propriety. A truthful discussion is required in order to draw others into agreement. Propriety shows respect for the steps necessary in achieving a proper connection to the success you seek. This is a favorable exchange where nothing is left unsaid. It is important to work within the context of Propriety and not assume that there is a deeper connection than what exist. You may find yourself in a subordinate position that cannot be changed. In a relationship the other party may currently be involved with someone else.

Line 5 Wise approach = this is right for a leader. Changes to (60) Limitation. Approaching with knowledge beforehand is good for a leader. A need to be selective when choosing associates is recommended. Knowing and respecting other's boundaries, while pushing them beyond their self imposed limitations makes a leader exceptional. Sensing the seeds of genius in those you lead and helping them tap that genius without interference allows subordinates to truly own their work and creates sustainable success.

Line 6 Great hearted approach = good fortune. No blame. Changes to (41) Decrease. A compensating sacrifice takes place in an exchange, like a Sage returning from retirement to teach others. Put the needs of another before your own needs to harness this great hearted approach. The exchange will lead to good fortune for you as well because you decrease expectation and selfishness in the service of union.

Hexagram #20
Kuan (Contemplation)

Action: View

Hu Gua (secondary influence) 23 Split Apart:
Regenerate

Zong Gua: (underlying cause) 34 Great Power:
Invigorate

Received as 2nd Hexagram: Examine the patterns in
your thinking that create the same outcome.

**You can only lead others toward growth
if you are willing to grow yourself.**

*Life can only be understood backwards,
but it must be lived forwards.* – Kierkegaard

Reading at a Glance: A period of Contemplation can
come about for a variety of reasons. Perhaps your ego
has been wounded and you are stepping back to
understand the part you played in getting hurt. You
may have completed a job and are now stepping back to
examine future direction. After a time of Great Power
and invigoration, the Zong Gua suggests that an anti

climactic period follows. The secondary influence calls for Splitting Apart the past from the future. It is a time for regeneration. This hexagram has the appearance of a tower and there is a need to gain a wider view – and take time out to consider your future direction. Others are drawn to those who exhibit an evolved understanding of life that can only come from showing their objectivity and willingness to listen and grow. This means even as a leader, you are called to keep growing. Nothing in nature is stagnant and careful Contemplation is necessary prior to making changes.

Remove
the red dust.
Arouse the child
to the
endless field.

"The wind blows over the earth: the image of contemplation." You have the opportunity to climb the heights of what you have built to obtain a wider view. In the image of a tower that allows for a bird's eye view, find the white space that will allow you to remain objective in finding your way forward. You establish a course for the future by reinvigorating your roots.

Wind suggests purity and the washing of the hands. The master said: *"the ablution has been made, but not yet, the offering."* The 'ablution' or washing of the hands is how you *"remove the residue of red dust,"* or the hardened perspective that can accumulate on your journey and open with reverence. The 'offering' is your willingness to remain malleable in all you do. Whenever the Wind blows over the Earth, it ushers in a changing climate.

The most common celebrations of ancient times revolved around the harvest festivals of autumn. Perhaps it was out of fear and reverence as the days grew darker, and the natural world began to die away. It was an important time however, because what was done in earnest during this time, laid the seeds for a springtime to come. This is the meaning of contemplation: take inventory of the past to reinvigorate the seeds of the future.

"The sage understands the way forward by observing the cycles that endure. If you don't believe, just look at September, look at October!" When you look backward, you will see the cycles that remain constant, although you barely remember the vague situations that become meaningless over time. By recognizing all that is transient, you can observe the 'carved block,' but only hold fast to that which cultivates growth. In each situation, *"retain the lesson but not the carved block."* Other than its transitory manifestations, *"the great image has no shape."* It is time to let go and become the uncarved block in the hands of the 'woodcarver.'

The *"thread running through the Way"* becomes your footsteps through the path of change. Your destiny is revealed by that part of you that remains constant against the wheel of changing events. *"Returning to one's roots is known as stillness. This is what is meant by returning to one's destiny."* You can move through the changes without being pulled from the center of your unfolding. Although you walk less, you discover more. The core of who you are only sharpens against the vicissitudes of experience. Allow yourself to open to whatever life is shaping you to be.

The master said: *"When one is at ease with themselves, one is near Nature. This is to let Nature take its own course."* When you are 'just so,' you are not defending anything. *"When 'this' and 'that' have no opposites, you discover life's very axis."*

Contemplation allows you to see that all things are equal: the good and bad, the difficult and easy are merely the ebbing and flowing of energy. *"When a leader is right with themselves, things will get done without giving orders. When they are not right with themselves, they may give orders, but they will not be obeyed."* You can only lead others toward growth if you are willing to grow yourself.

To others, your humility makes you the representation of *"how great fullness seems empty. Full of trust, they look up to view the divine Way where the four seasons do not deviate."* In contemplating, *"you partly give and partly take."* You take time for yourself, but also become *"something for the world to view. The more one gives, the more one comes to possess."*

A student asked: *"Sir, how is it that you are old, but have the appearance of a child?"* The master replied: *"It is because I have not been worn down by going against the Way."*

Unchanging: Life moves in cycles = find the thread in the eternity at the end. Receiving Contemplation unchanging asks you to take a bit more time to contemplate the object of your enquiry because your approach may be too vague or there are elements that you haven't recognized. Contemplation can mean reviewing solutions that worked in the past, however you may need to adopt a new approach more appropriate for the future. Something has changed and perhaps you are not seeing this. You have to Split Apart the situation and look at it objectively rather than viewing it subjectivity. Clarity is missing so wander back through the situation from a perspective other than the one you already know. You might ask or the oracle again: what am I not seeing in this situation?

Line 1 Childish contemplation = acceptable for a child but not an adult. Changes to (42) Increase. You may not be taking responsibility for how you are contributing to a difficult situation. There is something to be learned that will be beneficial to your success if you can approach it with maturity rather than childish fancy. However, until you stop acting childish or like a victim, nothing can be solved.

Line 2 Contemplation through the crack of the door = not seeing everything. Changes to (59) Dispersion. It is not helpful to place yourself in the center of a situation with a selfish or wishful attitude. You will only see what you want to see. There is much that can't be seen because your view is limited. Look at the situation from a broader view. Expand a self serving perspective into something that allows you to see more clearly.

Line 3 Contemplation of one's life = a decision to advance or retreat. Changes to (53) Development. An important decision must be made. Taking responsibility for the part you play in succeeding and failing allows you to make better choices. In a past situation one examines the truth of what transpired and comes to understand why things unfold the way they do.

Line 4 Contemplating what others experience = looking broadly at their benefit. Changes to (12) Obstruction. Beyond purely selfish motives, you observe how your actions influence others. You may need to make a sacrifice for the benefit of the team beyond selfish aims. Social awareness furthers your growth where you can make significant contributions. Until you climb out of a purely self centered perspective you may feel Obstructed.

Line 5 Contemplating my life = one is without blame. Changes to (23) Split Apart. Since you are open to removing any faults, you are able to make a decision that will have lasting consequences. It is not so important to scrutinize what you do, but what you've done. Determining between what yields tangible results and what wastes your time, you can set a productive plan for the future. Split Apart the ideal from the actual and make changes where necessary. Looking at what you do and its affects allows you to fix what is not working.

Line 6 Contemplating this life = one is without blame. Changes to (8) Union. Beyond taking responsibility for correcting actions that are not serving you, contemplation of the bigger picture allows you to see the effect you have on others. Unifying perspective as if there are no lines separating your thoughts from experience or the impact others have on you and the impact you have on them is a very broad view. Each moment and all you meet are a reflection of how you might grow. Remaining open to the teaching, you remain without blame because you see failure as a stepping stone to success.

Hexagram #21
Shi Ho (Biting Through)

Action: Discern
Hu Gua (secondary influence) 39 Obstruction: Innovate
Zong Gua: (underlying cause) 48 The Well: Inspire

Received as 2nd Hexagram: There is something you are not seeing in this situation.

To keep others down,
you would have to live your life on your knees.

Honest differences are often a sign of progress. – Mahatma Ghandi

Reading at a Glance: Oftentimes we feel that life is unfair. However, if we look at the natural world there is nothing resembling justice. Nature merely evens out its extremes or removes blockages to achieve balance and this truth will eventually come to light in the situations that you face. You are a part of nature. If you have attached yourself to illusions of right and wrong that block your forward progress, Biting Through will dispel the illusion. Unless growth is in the equation, life tends to re-organize by breaking things down. Ideas that foster separateness or boundaries blocking renewal or union need to be 'chewed over' or presented through experience until the illusion is transformed into clarity. The Well as the Zong Gua can suggest living too much in the inner world leading to a time for your debut, whether or not you are ready. You can create a false sense of reality and believe it is real. Obstruction as the secondary influence shows that any blockage will come down . Discernment is how the truth has to be given careful consideration even if you'd rather not face it. The focus on the mouth in this hexagram encourages clear communication. If there is something to be said to another then speak up. If it is real, it will endure and truth spoken is the only cure. If you are expecting clarity from another, it might not be forthcoming. This is because they may feel too severely judged by you.

The best way to communicate during a time of Biting Through is to put personal agendas aside to truly understand the needs of the other party. Clarifying roles and boundaries might be in order or you may need to simply be there for someone while they figure out their own confusion. Biting Through can lead to union but you must have a willingness to listen. This is not about sacrifice however. The other party's needs and sense of purpose must align with your needs and sense of purpose. Often when exploring another's intentions, the answer shows unavailability because of an immutable truth or law that blocks union. A prior commitment such as marriage or an incompatibility of age or lifestyle can obstruct progress. The truth is more important than wishes when receiving Biting Through. It is time for you to see the truth in this situation and until you do so, your progress may be blocked. Open to the possibilities that can emerge after the truth is clearly recognized.

The truth
cannot be silenced.
It is the child
ever asking:
"why?"

"There is something between the corners of the mouth: the image of biting through." The master said: *"when the firm and yielding are distinct from each other, when the high and low move separately; when anything reaches its extreme, it must turn back."* Lightning precedes Thunder and similarly, the Fire ignites the Arousing Thunder to illuminate how balance is corrected. What is missed by vision is reinforced by sound. Balance and truth is nature's only focus. By Biting Through difficulty ~ you can speak honestly about what has disturbed your sense of balance.

Anytime varying pressure systems collide, or when lightning crosses the expanse of sky to ground itself in the earth *"the high and low incline toward each other."* Whether something is hot, cold, high, low, empty or full, energy is exchanged as life pursues a state of balance. In this situation something is out of balance so emulate how nature finds harmony, even while it honors differences. Real success should be a win/win situation for all. Differences fine tune collective strengths and provide the roadmap for productive growth.

In the natural world, justice is how the high is brought low so that the low can be lifted up. Life does not demonstrate retribution; it merely seeks balance and improvement. Biting Through is a foundation of impartiality that allows balance to be restored. Harmony must sometimes come without justice. If justice is held to be higher an impasse will continue.

Speak up ~ you have nothing to lose. At the same time, you need to look honestly at what another is, or is not saying or doing. Perhaps you are not listening? Only you can know the truth of whether a situation can achieve union or dissolution by allowing clarity in perspective. Biting Through can be a message about realizing that hopes and wishes cannot withstand not being supported by the observable actions or words of another.

"When two sides raise arms against each other, it is the one that is sorrow-stricken that wins." The voice of the oppressed is woeful and has lost value in living. We see how their voices are heard through violent acts of frustration. Nature is a profound teacher in the way that all things remain equal, although they are not the same. When opposition emerges, change is already taking place. It is better to follow the course of where the changes might lead. By letting go, you find your proper path. Whatever you believe you can only get from another ~ you already possess.

Shih Ho is the image of teeth biting through what is blocking communication. *"Leveling out is going two ways at once."* Going two ways at once describes how you succeed through a win/win situation where all parties are served.

A free economy is one example of how the *natural way* is not always the obvious way. It works because it allows 'what is' to take its own course, unimpeded by unnatural restrictions. View the situation to see how

148

success does not have to come at the expense of loss. At the heart of the difficulty, the solution has already begun to manifest itself so open to it.

All things are equal in the eyes of nature; equality is a level playing field for life's diverse creatures. It is unnatural to think that one way is the only way. The master said: *"the owl can catch fleas at night but cannot see a mountain during the day. This is because different things have different natures."*

Do not measure others with a common denominator. When you observe nature, you will discover how Biting Through allows life to move beyond all obstacles. Whenever fireworks or arguments arise - understand that the storm is unearthing assumptions to unblock communication. Its sole purpose is to release the obstruction of illusions, regardless of where that might lead.

Unchanging: Nature is impartial = its only purpose is growth. This is a message that the need for clarity is not being recognized or acted upon. Perhaps you don't want to rock the boat or prefer to go on believing that you can live in illusion. When a demand for justice over-rides a need to simply move on, only you will suffer. You are not being punished. You may be over-idealizing the situation or taking an easy path that can only lead to the Obstruction of your own growth. The situation is not hopeless but the outcome must clearly serve all involved. The need for clear communication and a sense of establishing boundaries is paramount. In many cases Biting Through unchanging is a message to wait because more information is coming. If you make a decision in haste you will miss out.

Line 1 Feet bound and immoveable = learning something for the first time without fault. Changes to (35) Progress. While attempting to get at the core of a situation you have become stuck. An impasse may be occurring with another. Since this is the first time a grievance has occurred, the punishment or response is light. This restriction has the effect of slowing you down. Progress shows that in time you will move forward and chalk this up to a learning experience.

Line 2 Biting tender meat and submerging the nose = without fault. Changes to (38) Opposition. Another is holding the position of power and causing restraint. Perhaps you have been unfairly judged. You are only seeing the obvious in this situation and need to look deeper. While you may have done nothing wrong, your actions have aroused Opposition. Perhaps you stood your ground and regret it. There is more to this situation than meets the eye so blame can be a smokescreen that covers up a deeper issue. Noses can 'be out of joint' and time is required to heal the misunderstanding.

Line 3 Biting dried meat and encountering decay = humiliation, but without fault. Changes to (30) Clarity. The matter at issue is an old one and will keep resurfacing until Clarity is achieved. By attempting to change something it arouses a spoiled attitude. There may be a sense of humiliation playing out rather than seeing the lesson as a learning experience. Clarity as the Clinging can be a situation of co-dependency. Resolving this situation will take some effort and patience to change button pushing into mutual synergy.

Line 4 Biting through dried, gristly meat and encountering a metal arrow = laborious persistence brings success. Changes to (27) Nourishing Vision. A difficult situation feels like punishment because it is persistent and difficult to understand. This situation is an old one, but biting through it will provide rich nourishment. The punishment enables fault to be made clear, and by doing so, relations can improve. You are being taught by punishment to have more appreciation for what you have taken for granted. Success comes from understanding what you did wrong. The situation is not as gloomy as it appears and contains a silver lining if you can Nourish Vision through the trial presented.

Line 5 Biting Through dried, lean meat and getting a yellow arrow = don't push too hard. Changes to (25) Innocence. Although there are not many alternatives, a decision is still difficult to make. One is ready to make a lasting change that will have ramifications so a cautious attitude is required to face a complex issue. Innocence is a way of starting over so don't push too hard or expect past solutions to work. The yellow arrow can be how one learns to walk the middle path between extremes, learning to overcome judgments and not losing oneself while interacting with others. There is a great learning opportunity in this situation.

Line 6 Neck confined in a cangue with covered ears = nothing learned. Changes to (51) Shocking. You are not willing to learn from the situation and may be forced to learn the hard way, perhaps through an unexpected and rude awakening. You fail to take responsibility for why the situation has you stuck and your inability to listen or grow from the experience may lead to unwanted consequences.

Hexagram #22
Bi (Grace)

Action: Accept
Hu Gua (secondary influence) 40 Liberation: Untangle
Zong Gua: (underlying cause) 47
Oppression/Exhaustion: Adapt
Received as 2nd Hexagram: Divine providence is at play in this situation.

When you lose your way,
life always hands you a map that says: 'you are here.'

If a man carefully examines his thoughts, he will be surprised to find
how much he lives in the future. His well being is always ahead. —Emerson

Reading at a Glance: The master said: *"untangle the knots and soften the glare."* This means if you stalk life with a scowl expecting difficulty, you will find it. When meeting Oppression we had the opportunity to learn to Adapt or make changes to better fit in with the changes around us, but now it is time to connect with your inner source of light. Grace is an attitude of Acceptance that radiates outwardly as joy regardless of what is unfolding around you. Anxiety and constant worry can make you unattractive both inside and out. You can cover yourself with nice clothes and possessions but if the scowl remains you remain unattractive. The secondary influence of Liberation from worry is at the heart of Taoism because if you are following life on its terms with an Accepting attitude you will discover more and lose less. The greatest lesson Bi teaches you is that no amount of outward adorning will ever conceal what is going on inside of you. If you want to attract others to you, begin within. Loving the self makes one loving. Accepting the way makes one accepting. When you have no preconceived expectations you will open to the beauty of Grace. Brilliant inner beauty is like a magnet that others can't resist. If circumstances are less than favorable, turn within and release the expectations that are making your outlook hardened. Take a breath and return to the moment. You may have the opportunity for Grace to shine down upon you where your wish is granted.

> *Open what is closed.*
> *Light the darkness.*
> *Grace is the life*
> *of the lifeless.*

"Fire at the foot of the Mountain: the image of grace." Seasons can change gracefully or destructively; either way, nature's behavior cannot be classified in terms of good and bad. We build homes in what was once a desert, irrigate our gardens during times of drought, and wonder why the trees in the hillside catch on fire. The seeds of higher elevation plants actually require fire for regeneration.

In the image of how things are valued, the master said: *"the Way is benevolent and excels on bestowing."* Through wildfires, nature accomplishes new growth by removing old growth. Although you may put labels of value on experience, you sometimes cannot see how *"good fortune perches on apparent disaster."*

Mountains and islands are created by the violent shifting of tectonic plates; nature paves the way for renewal through fire, floods and landslides. Living within a sliver of time in geological terms, we erect our structures on an ever-changing landscape. Since the beginning of its existence, the earth has always been very much alive.

Obstruction 'in here' is often overcome through the breaking down of what we cling to 'out there.' Over time, you will recognize all experience as the graceful way that life leads you where you need to be. Pi is translated to mean 'because;' and suggests that life doesn't happen to you, it happens *because* of you.

"One, who is open to the Way, will gladly embrace it. One, who is not open to it and told about it, will laugh out loud at it." Similarly, one, who is crying might not realize how life nourishes the unseen garden within through tears. Something has yet to grow and in this case, awareness must evolve before value can be found in the experience.

Bi is a message about seeing the silver lining: *"who knows what is good and what is bad?"*

"Once a farmer's mare ran away and afterward, his neighbor came by to console him. The farmer said: "Who knows what is good and what is bad?" The next day the mare returned with a stallion and the neighbor congratulated him. The farmer responded: "Who knows what is good and what is bad?" The following day the farmer's son was thrown from the stallion and broke his leg and again the neighbor consoled him. "Who knows what is good and what is bad," said the farmer. Within the same week, the army came to conscript the farmer's son, who was dismissed because of his broken leg. The neighbor finally agreed: "Who knows what is good and what is bad?"

The Mountain has a Fire within it, like a volcano where pressure accumulates and demands release. You can

155

emulate grace and open joyfully, or you will find that
events will force this energy out of hiding. Whenever
you become lost, life hands you a map that says: 'you
are here.'

Grace works to soften the vicissitudes of your emotional
states. As you grow older, the sharp edges of extremes
are made softer by experience. All that remains is the
light of understanding, which grows within and
illuminates the eyes. Capturing your journey of a
thousand miles in this way, no matter the trial,
everything always works out.

The monuments you build to commemorate the past
can become prisons. In proportion to your
unwillingness to leave them, you will experience the
power of grace. If you measure the vicissitudes of life,
all things become equal over time. Grace is a message of
optimism without judgment or the silver lining you
have yet to see. On the pathway, you will discover: it is
all good.

Unchanging: Grace on the outside = the heart and mind
made manifest. In some cases Grace will come up
unchanging as a message about forgiveness. Sometimes
we are given a break even when we might not deserve
it as Grace shines upon us. Other times Grace
unchanging can be a message that the situation is
blocked by superficialities, as if appearance is held
higher than the truth of what is actually transpiring.
You may not realize that your own bitterness is causing
the world to appear as a glass half full. You may be

looking for answers as to why something isn't happening or someone isn't responding when the situation has resulted from your own actions and thoughts. Do not fall prey to believing that the projections you place on others are real. Open yourself to life's Grace and benevolence. Celebrate your inner Grace and allow it to rise to the surface. Unleash any expectations and flow in the dazzling river of life. The greatest makeover begins within. If you want to be attractive adorn yourself with the Grace that resonates from the sincerity of trusting the Way.

Line 1 Grace to the feet = abandoning the carriage, walking instead. Changes to (52) Keeping Still. While one has the opportunity to take a path of ease or that is flattering and comfortable, it is more important to remain simple, humble and true to oneself. Don't rely on others but stand on your own two feet. Keeping Still can show not taking an opportunity, but staying put.

Line 2 Grace to the beard = saying something and stroking the chin. Changes (26) Controlled Power. Give consideration to what it is said in terms of substance with careful reflection. Habitual responses will not do. Communication is measured so that it is not superficial. One is affected in a thoughtful way as if stroking the chin. A message is received that embodies Controlled Power in thoughtful and Graceful communication. Perhaps stroking the beard can suggest how one feels pleased with themselves.

Line 3 Graceful and moist = constant perseverance brings good fortune. Changes to (27) Nourishing Vision. You can find yourself in a position to help someone but that doesn't mean you should be manipulative. Providing or taking comfort is not a replacement for real fulfillment. You may need to strip away the 'glistening' façade and look clearly at the situation because it may not be what it seems. Don't cover feelings or the truth with denial or escapist behavior. This line can indicate that a deeper commitment is needed where being 'impregnated' by vision has lasting influences that will affect generations to come. Perpetual trials lead to stronger connections so persevere.

Line 4 Grace of simplicity, a white horse on wings = not a robber but he will woo at right time. Changes to (30) Clarity. While the situation seems threatening, positive forces are at work. Any misunderstanding is short lived and dies down. If you can return your thoughts to the purity and objectivity of Clarity you won't complicate things by reacting inappropriately. Another's feelings toward you are benevolent, not sinister. A winged horse embodies thoughts or a connection that transcends space and time. Through trust a commitment moves to a deeper level.

Line 5 Grace in the hills and gardens. Meager roll of silk = humiliation but good fortune in end. Changes to (37) Family. You may feel insecure about what you can offer the situation but if you are sincere you will be received well. Your inner worth shines so that your merit is acknowledged by another. Don't be confused by appearances and remember that less is more. Good fortune comes to you in the end.

Line 6 Simple grace = no blame. Changes to (36) Brightness Hiding. Being unpretentious, your inner light radiates in Grace. If you can rely on this inner Grace rather than what you possess or what shows in outer appearances, you will know joy. Defer to your inspiration rather than ego and its aims and all will be well. In fact re-imagine yourself in a pure white garment untouched by the past to prepare to receive the future. If it is meant for you – it will come in its own time.

Hexagram #23
Po (Split Apart)

Action: Regenerate
Hu Gua (secondary influence) 2: Receptive: Yield
Zong Gua: (underlying cause) 43: Determination: Breakthrough
Received as 2nd Hexagram: Nothing can change until you open to the idea that a change is needed.

All of life will not change you;
it unfolds as a way to unmask you.

*Life is a quarry, out of which we are to mold and
chisel and complete a character.* – Goethe

Reading at a Glance: There are times when
disintegration or letting go is the only pathway to
regeneration. Po is a message about how things become
stronger by removing outgrown elements. Pruning a
tree allows its branches to become more luxuriant. In
this situation there is a need to release what is outworn
or which no longer serves you so that you can return to
a path that is more fulfilling. Sometimes you have to
separate aspects in your life in order to achieve balance.
A relationship that is in this stage can reach an impasse
where either release or renew is at play. It can no longer
operate within the unhealthy dynamics of the past.
Similarly, a relationship reaching a commitment phase
can also become more stressed as each partner examines
the other more acutely. Like autumn leaves are stripped
away in preparation for the rebirth of spring. When
familiar landscapes die away it can be frightening,
however this is how nature moves upward into the next
cycle. The time requires patience while emptiness can
be returned to fullness. Some type of overhaul is taking
place. It requires great courage to wait the situation out
without acting until the way becomes clear. What a
delightful lesson in patience! Where Breakthrough
would have been a time to push through the difficulty
with action, now you must acknowledge that there is
little you can do to change events other than to let go

and open to the experience. The secondary influence of K'un shows a need to respond inwardly while waiting for the change to complete its cycle outwardly.

When the seed
falls,
adversity breaks away
the protective covering.

"The Mountain rests on the Earth: the image of splitting apart." Po reflects how feelings must break through the firm ideas that are rooted above. Nature does not remain stagnant and brings rain after a time of oppressive heat. Too much thought and life returns you to your feeling nature. Too much feeling and life brings you back to logic. Whether it is the emotional, logical or spiritual awareness, in actuality it is only one mind seeking balance.

Too much of anything and nature brings forward opposite energy. Like the high and low pressure systems that bring change in the weather, emotions rise to reinvigorate your internal atmosphere. Sometimes we must lose something before we understand its value to us. While we may not be able to hold onto what is being removed, we will proceed more cautiously in the future to avoid losing it again.

Relationships synergistically exploring love and adventure can take on a more somber tone when commitment is in the air. Splitting apart is how life separates the necessary from the unnecessary, whittling

161

away the husk until only the germinating seed remains. In the image of carving, pruning or being 'split apart,' your feelings are being brought to the surface. Like fruit that has fallen to the earth, the seed can only take root when its protective covering disintegrates.

You may understand that change must come, while clinging to the illusion of what you need. During the time of splitting apart, you will discover new life stirring beneath the mind's abstractions. Sincerity is the stirring of your authenticity. It is something, which is shaped by feelings, not mind. Feelings make life valuable and without them, you will be forced to 'turn back' and become open again. If feelings of fear have created a situation that moves toward Splitting Apart, we learn that fear can only lead to decay. It takes unconditional love and care to keep anything thriving.

Po reveals how sensitivity funds the urge for transformation; it is not an intellectual endeavor. Splitting apart is your willingness to remain compassionate in all you do.

The ancient text seems to suggest that our normal perspective has everything backwards. Conflict makes us defensive, although it comes to break our protective covering; the unnecessary blockages we create will merely evaporate when we become open. You may defend your concrete perspective when approaching others even while they have come to help you let it go. All of experience presents you with a mysterious mirror that reflects the well-being of your inner world.

Following the energy of life becomes a profound exercise in learning to overturn your mindset. Splitting apart is how the protective covering of the past is removed so you may grow to meet the future. The same hand that is forced open to give will now be open to receive. Whatever it is, let it go so that your inner garden can be cultivated. Allow the way to guide you toward the appropriate path.

Unchanging: During winter 10,000 seeds lay dreaming = become the landscape of spring. With no changing lines, Po can be a message that after holding on to the past you might explore a new way of moving forward. An intense transformation is at work and the situation allows for shedding of old patterns and beliefs. The secondary influence and lower trigram of K'un or submission can suggest that deterioration from pushing your way into the world is giving away to a natural rebirth where you blossom from the inside out. There is not much you can do in this situation other than become receptive to what the events can teach you while the change is upon you. Being benevolent or submissive to others might help. Trust that whatever is being removed is making room for something more fulfilling to grow in its place. Open yourself to this opportunity for renewal.

Line 1 The leg of the bed is split = those who persevere are destroyed. Changes to (27) Nourishing Vision.

Seeking nourishment through others rather than real sustenance can erode your self esteem as you place yourself in a disempowering situation. In dreams, the bed symbolizes ideas we rest upon and the leg refers to support so change comes to a foundational level of your thinking. The support offered may have led to disappointment as disempowerment or manipulation undermines the situation. A change is happening that will lead to balance in relationships. The good news is that the old situation can no longer erode your sense of self worth. Be patient while clarity emerges. Relying on the opinions of others can only confuse you.

Line 2 The bed is split at the edge = those who persevere are destroyed. Changes to (4) Youthful Folly. Something is being removed because of separation. Don't attempt to force the status quo because you are no match for the forces of change. To succeed, admit that your need for protection or boundaries may have sacrificed union. Take a non prejudiced outlook willing to see what must change within. Normal avenues of advice can be misleading however, a sensitive and innocent outlook allows for a rebirth in your thinking. Allow a child to be your teacher.

Line 3 Breaking ties = one splits with those who are leaving, no blame. Changes to (52) Keeping Still. You may need to create boundaries, leaving a difficult situation or relationship. Others may be going in a direction that isn't right for you but this may bring greater clarity in recognizing the one person or group that does support your vision and you may declare your loyalty. Do not be influenced by fear because this is a necessary step in finding greater fulfillment. Stillness allows for greater clarity in making a decision.

Line 4 The bed is split up to the skin = no choice but to embrace change. Changes to (35) Progress. The good news is that the situation cannot get any worse. The bad news is that you must make changes and cannot ignore the deterioration of this situation. Don't pretend that nothing is wrong. Holding to the past can only trap you and erode clarity. This is a very difficult time so take the time to nourish the heart while you wait for the sun to rise again. However, Progress ensures that things are changing for the better.

Line 5 A string of fishes = favor comes as a gift. Changes to (20) Contemplation. A difficult situation is improving because you gain support. A favor once bestowed is now returned as others Contemplate your character and find no flaws. Since you are recognized for being blameless this helps your position however you may need to make a sacrifice. This is a line showing how your generosity in the past comes to serve you in the present.

Line 6 The highest fruit uneaten = the good are carried and the evil lose a home. Changes to (2) Receptive. The uneaten fruit of a tree has the opportunity to become a new tree. When we have no agenda life leads us where we need to be. Those who let go find reward, while those clinging to their attachments become lost. Difficulty is stripped away but the generous and open spirit is the remaining Yang at the top after all else is removed. At such times the spirit becomes visible allowing you to reach the fruit that hadn't been considered close enough to reach. Through sacrifice the spirit becomes manifest as fruit. Through generosity you obtain the love and respect of others.

Hexagram #24
Fu (Return)

Action: Go Back
Hu Gua (secondary influence) 2: Receptive: Yield
Zong Gua: (underlying cause) 44: Coming to Meet: Encounter
Received as 2nd Hexagram: Going back, looking back or returning can be at play in this situation.

Progress is often marked
by a slow return to original sincerity.

Sow a thought, reap an action; sow an action, reap a habit.
Sow a habit, reap a character; sow a character, reap a destiny.
— Proverb

Reading at a Glance: Sometimes we need to stop and go back. This can arise when we have taken an improper course or the wrong path and need to return to where we started. Other times we can get so far away from who we really are that Return is necessary to re-connect with the core part of us that has remained unchanged over time. The secondary influence of the Receptive shows a need for an inner opening while the cause or past condition was one of focusing on Encountering others. After a time of Splitting Apart, a Return to the Self to develop authenticity is necessary. You are at a turning point in this situation and *"progress is often marked by a slow return to original sincerity."* It may seem like you are not moving forward although progress is still occurring because through Return, you reconnect with your true path. This can be a time to examine your intentions. A disconnect may be occurring where you seek a specific outcome yet experience something different. Examine your commitment to the situation and whether or not it truly serves you. There is a need to align intention and commitment with the truth of what you are truly capable of achieving. Return can come after false starts with the sole purpose of showing you what is truly important to you. This is a time when you have a fresh start to proceed more carefully.

Sincerity opens
the shameless
to a life
without shells.

"*Thunder within the earth: the image of a turning point.*"
The Arousing Thunder stirs the Receptive Earth and
represents a turning point or a time for Return. There
may be a homecoming or a return to a past situation.
Sometimes Fu is about simply returning to the core of
who you are.

In virtually all cultures, solar rituals were performed
during the winter solstice when the sun was believed to
be reborn. As the days commenced to grow longer in
the west, the ancients burned Yule logs and decorated
world trees. Using celestial orbs, they celebrated the
birth of the sun's return.

The master said: "*The kings of antiquity closed the passes
during the winter solstice.*" The birth of the new sun
embodied Yang's return to the earth and because it was
new, it was weak and required nurturing. By closing
the passes, people stayed indoors and businesses came
to a halt, while the empire focused on nurturing the
power of the newborn Yang.

Return is a recurring cycle in nature that returns all
things to their beginnings. As the image of moving in
the opposite direction or retracing a path, events lead
you back to your authenticity.

The master said: "*When one does nothing at all, nothing is
undone.*" Although you may not appear to be moving
forward, "*progress is often marked by a slow return to
original sincerity.*"

"Return shows the stem of character." After your flowering, you turn inward to regenerate. The stem of character is made stronger by recognizing your connection to what unfolds. When you *own your condition,* constant rejection reflects your inability to commit. Obstruction 'out there' always reveals the closed door 'in here.' If you are contemplating leaving, everything seems to validate why you should go. To break the chain of cause and effect requires that you explore the beliefs that you live by. This is the essence of Return.

Adversity has a way of shaving away illusions that no longer serve you. Let go and return to sincerity to prepare for your flowering. You may need to re-visit a past situation to see it in a new light.

"Composure straightens out one's inner life; righteousness will square one's external life." Circumstances reflect what emanates from your center. Like the birth of the new sun, return is an opportunity to begin anew. After a period of struggle or darkness, Return ensures that things can only get brighter.

Unchanging: Without looking out the window = one sees the whole world. There are patterns or cycles in your life that become apparent during a time of Return. You may be focusing on external conditions without realizing the part you play in always returning to the same place. Before seeking further information about the situation it is important to examine this pattern and how it may be at play. In a relationship, rejection can be the result of your own fear of intimacy. Failure can be the result of your lack of commitment. There is a sense that nothing is happening but the cycle is moving from the darkest point to a transition of increasing light or clarity. Unchanging, Fu can throw you back upon your own motives. If you are examining a new direction, explore how it relates to the cycles you have always known. Look for that part of you that has remained unchanged over time and explore your original sincerity. You may need to transform it if it is no longer serving you, or hold to it if you can validate its importance in leading you toward fulfillment. If your question is about the return of something or someone, this is often affirmative.

Line 1 Return from a short distance, no remorse = great good fortune. Changes to (2) Receptive. You realize that a path was not correct and return. Your decision has consequences for others who might be expecting you to continue in a different direction. You need to follow your own insight and not just blindly follow others which will lead to good fortune.

Line 2 Quiet return = good fortune. Changes to (19) Approach. You realize that returning is the proper course and have no need to seek advice from others although you remain sensitive to their views. By remaining humble during a quiet comeback after a time of adversity, your virtue and tenacity are recognized. It won't be an easy path of Return but you will succeed. The return to success after a period of heavy defeat is the only way to self mastery. Others will seek your counsel because of your experience.

Line 3 Repeated return, danger = no blame. Changes to (36) Brightness Hiding. You return because of a crisis and while it may take a few attempts to finally settle, your decision is correct. Following your own insight is not always the popular way but keeps you deeply connected to your Tao. How can this be wrong? Keeping your intentions to yourself minimizes any danger or opposition.

Line 4 Walking in the midst of others = one returns alone. Changes to (51) Shocking. It is a difficult decision to go your own way, even when it means abandoning friends. Even if you choose to ignore the need to return to a path of real fulfillment events may lead you there anyway. Shocking can describe unexpected events that alter your course for the better.

Line 5 Noble hearted return = no remorse. Changes to (3) Difficult Beginnings. There is nothing keeping you from seeing that the proper course is to acknowledge a turning point and to return. There are no mistakes in life even in Difficult times. Sometimes we need to see what we don't want or can't have in order to find ourselves where we need to be. You return holding your head up knowing it is the correct path.

Line 6 Missing the return, misfortune = misfortune from within and without. Changes to (27) Nourishing Vision. Defiantly seeking an objective only gets one lost. This is a lesson of knowing when to act and when to Return to the truth. Being in denial and believing an opportunity exists when it doesn't leads to humiliation so examine your motives. The opportunity for Return was missed and there is nothing to do but learn from your mistake.

Hexagram #25
Wu Wang (Innocence)

Action: Open
Hu Gua (secondary influence) 53: Development: Flower
Zong Gua: (underlying cause) 46: Pushing Upward: Ascend
Received as 2nd Hexagram: Preconceived judgments can cloud your perception of the present.

**If you don't know what cannot be done,
you will accomplish great things.**

*Like a kite cut from the string,
lightly the soul of my youth has taken flight.* – *Ishikawa Takuboku*

Reading at a Glance: A Taoist perspective honors Three Treasures: *San pao* is the ability to know compassion

172

when relating to others, where you treat all experience as if it is a part of you. This is called owning your condition. *Jian* is your appreciation for the 'uncarved block,' or the ever changing aspect of life, by remaining malleable in your observations and simple in your desires. *Bugan wei tianxia xian* is how you do not play the host but remain the guest of a greater unfolding. You rise from sleep where your mind was open and then climb back into a type of sensory awareness that classifies everything. Just as you do in dreams, it is important to hover at the doorway of perception, without judgment or attachment to an outcome. Innocence asks you to keep an open mind so that the Creative can lead you toward environment that is beneficial to you, suggested by the secondary influence of Development. Where Pushing Upward required action, Innocence is best developed through non action. Step back and allow events to show you what and why a situation is unfolding. Without this purity of perception calamity can ensue. Yet even in calamity you can discover the Sage's greatest lesson: tranquility in disturbance. Synchronize your inner thoughts to events. Know that you are free of blame if you follow the course of events rather than attempt to coerce a solution for the sake of speed or gratification. Be like the child who has not yet learned to smile but simply remains observant to unfolding events.

Hover at
the doorway
of
perception.

"When you turn back, you are returned to a state of innocence." Approaching the gateway of perception, you can cherish the opportunity *not to know* to move beyond all sense of boundaries. Baby birds do not develop their colorful beaks and feathers until adolescence, when the territorial urge begins. Until then, their coloring allows them to remain hidden and protected. This is the protection offered to a state of innocence.

Like a hatchling protected from early danger, you can approach the threshold of perception with a sense of discovery. The master said: *"Those who do not know what cannot be done can accomplish great things."*

Wu Wang means 'not attached,' or not caught up in defending yourself against unfolding events. Exerting the will can sometimes create disharmony in the flow of life. Unattached, you can observe your fundamental harmony with what unfolds. The master said: *"those who know no limits meet with no obstruction."* This state of innocence ensures your success.

Innocence allows you to see how events cultivate your power of your Te. It requires three things: compassion when relating to others, an appreciation for the 'uncarved block,' or the ever changing aspect of life by remaining simple in your desires not playing the host but remaining the guest of a greater unfolding.

Even while you are the ruler of your empire, you do not dare take the lead, but follow. You can discover a new way of perceiving the world where a return to a state of Innocence will allow you to cultivate what is to come.

"One who possesses virtue in abundance is comparable to a new born babe. The baby goes without knowing where it is going, and merges with the surroundings, moving along with it." Wu Wang is the image of not wasting time lost on the by-paths where you wander away from where you need to be. Unattached to that place that would generate a response, you do not contend and therefore, nothing blocks your way.

Transcending unnatural distinctions, it is now, you have arrived, and you are just so. You make the choice of whether you use mind to establish boundaries or tear them down. Observing the emotions that trap you in your ability to discover, trace their illusions and let them go. At this threshold, observe how anxiety and fear attach you to expectations about the future, while guilt and anger tie you to actions of the past. Discarding these responses, all that is left is innocence.

"Like a baby that has not learned to smile," move to that place before the response to participate with how life is shaping you. Although *"desire brings you to observe life's manifestations,"* having no attachment to the passing scenery, is the key to your success.

Evolution brings about variations, but these random changes rarely improve what already works well. Creatures adapt in ways that are not always beneficial, and natural selection comes to purge mutations and reveals why the Way is described as turning back. As one of nature's self-organizing systems, you seek stasis, while life leads you to transform. Every plant and animal on the earth has outlasted a struggle for existence that is three and a half billion years old. This means that moving forward without worry will not be second nature.

Wu wang, 'not attached,' and wu wei, 'taking no unnatural action' allow you to move forward unattached to the past and not creating an unnecessary response. *"I alone, am inactive and reveal no signs; listless as though I have no home to go back to."* The home you would have gone back to houses your paradigm. Let go of what you believe cannot be done and you will accomplish great things.

Unchanging: If you push too hard to be in the world = the unexpected cannot find you. You may be blameless in a situation although you feel guilty. However there is not a lot you can do other than to wait for the situation to right itself. Prior to taking any action explore whether you can do it with sincerity. Do you possess enough facts or certainty to proceed? Whatever is going to happen will not be what you expected so it is better to step back. Something amazing can happen if you can practice not pushing and prodding. Innocence unchanging can be a message that you don't yet have all of the information needed to proceed because an element of the unexpected is still at play. Be receptive to whatever unfolds.

Line 1 Innocent behavior = brings good fortune. Changes to (12) Standstill. Even during difficulty it is important to be non judgmental and accepting. A situation may be more entangled than you realize but don't sacrifice your integrity for an easy solution. Acting without prejudice and with an open mind leads to success. When in doubt, follow your heart. Standstill met with openness and submission leads to success

Line 2 Plow without thought of harvest, clear the land without thought of the use = it is good to go on this way. Changes to (10) Treading. The moment has called you to do the work it requires in a calm and precise manner. Anxiety rises when you forget what you are doing and start worrying about the future. To develop Innocence while working in this way you can apply this awareness to all you do. Show up to do the work and forget everything else. Be here now and deliver all that you are in this moment. This is the art of being 'just so' and it aligns you with Tao.

Line 3 Undeserved misfortune = the wanderer's gain is the citizen's loss. Changes to (13) Fellowship. An unexpected event may not benefit the one who stays in one place as much as the one who might be called a wanderer, who gets a boon. Releasing what you thought you needed helps another in their time of need, but opens your arms to receive something better: a sense of trust that all is perfect in the world. If you can't change the direction of the wind, adjust your sails and let life guide you. Innocence is best developed by learning to follow the course of events. Fellowship is

177

achieved by responding to the needs of the group without selfish aims. While not a complete win for both sides – there is good companionship suggested by Fellowship.

Line 4 To be persevering = one is without blame. Changes to (42) Increase. You may need to pick yourself up, dust yourself off and keep pushing on. You are not a victim and nothing is wrong. If something is meant for you it will come to you. Operating from abundance allows you to let go of attachment with the certainty that you always have what you need. To be persevering is the type of consistency of character that allows you to proceed with an optimistic attitude.

Line 5 Let nature take its course = don't use medicine to cover uneasiness. Changes to (21) Biting Through. You need to explore what the situation truly offers you. Substances or illusions that hide the real problem won't cure anything. If something about the situation is bothering you then acknowledge it. Let nature takes its course by allowing the truth to reveal itself. You may need to address this situation gently to achieve the best result. Co-dependency means that another may have the dependency, but you show the symptoms. Your unconditional support may be innocent but is it really serving the other's higher needs?

Line 6 Innocent action brings misfortune = nothing that would further. Changes to (17) Following. If you are meeting resistance it is futile to demonstrate overly emotional behavior. Even the most innocent actions can create further difficulty. It is best to step back and sleep on it. Follow another's lead in this situation. Difficulties are challenges and the reward is the freedom of non attachment. Your open and accepting outlook attracts Followers.

Hexagram #26
Ta Ch'u (Controlled Power)

Action: Amplify
Hu Gua (secondary influence) 54: Propriety: Subordinate
Zong Gua: (underlying cause) 45: Gathering Together: Network
Received as 2nd Hexagram: Don't underestimate the power of silence and actions speak louder than words.

**Your vital force is not wanting,
only waiting for you to tap it.**

*We are told not to cross the bridge until we come to it,
but this world is owned by those who crossed bridges
in their imaginations far ahead of the crowd. — Anonymous*

Reading at a Glance: True power need not be demonstrated as Creative energy is restrained beneath the mountain of Keeping Still. Ta Ch'u focuses on the power of silence and stillness. While others are running around demonstrating their power, one who is strong has no need to prove anything. Controlled Power has Propriety as its secondary influence because a will under the sheer steadiness of a mountain allows it to become incredibly powerful. There is also a need for timing in appropriate expression. Another's insecurity is no match for the power of silence. Since Controlled Power follows Innocence, all that is learned from patience and non action is now ready to be harnessed creatively. When the will is in the service of acceptance and the good of all this deliberate intent is unstoppable. The message we deliver is amplified because our inner truth radiates as the embodiment of Tao. Combining holding firm, holding steady, holding to heaven's way and nurturing others, this is the hexagram of the true Sage. When water meets a dam, it continues to rise in power until it overwhelms whatever blocked its flow. If you renew your willingness to marry to your Tao daily, you become a reservoir for enormous creative expression that benefits all. You can draw on a power that need not be demonstrated but is 'just so.' Its simplicity makes everything easy.

Become
the master
of
your response.

"When innocence is present, it is possible to tame."
Innocence cultivates virtue, yet virtue, renewed daily,
ensures a state of innocence. The master said: "*The
perfected nature, sustaining itself and enduring is the
gateway of life.*" An innocent perspective allows you to
approach *the gateway* or threshold of perception to
become *"the master of your experiences."* By taming your
response, you are able to tame experience. Controlled
Power is the hexagram of the true Sage.

"*The firm is able to keep strength still; this is great
correctness.*" Much time is spent preparing for and
delivering your response. Only when you are not
defending, do you activate the Controlled Power of the
Great.

You can change what the *"world will look and feel like,"*
by approaching it differently. *"Acquaint yourself with the
teachings of antiquity"* and you will see how desire can
both, draw in experience or close you to it.
Approaching the gateway of perception, you make the
choice of what you will find.

The master said: "*Do not listen with your ears, but listen
with your mind. Do not listen with your mind, but listen
with your vital force. Ordinary hearing does not go beyond
the ears and the mind does not go beyond its symbols. Your
vital force is not wanting but waiting. Life brings together all
that is void to itself. Be empty ~ that is all. Thus you can
master things and not be injured by them.*"

When you tame your desires, *"not eating at home brings good fortune,"* because you move beyond your perceptual routines to be nourished by *discovery*. Gather the energy of desire's outward attachment, and tap it as the inner fuel that activates a powerful peacefulness. Stand at the threshold, connect with your Te or vital force and simply observe. *Find comfort in your strength.*

In China, the lion protected the forests, and its likeness was used to protect the gates and temples. Another gatekeeper, the Dragon Carp, had only one goal: crossing the Dragon Gate. Beyond this Gate, many believed paradise could be found. Like the salmon, the carp swims upstream and jumps the rapids, and came to symbolize human advancement and achievement in life. The Dragon Carp is a constant reminder of the pursuit of excellence, reflecting how following instinct makes obstacles non-existent. Where the lion symbolizes great passion and fearlessness, the carp is a symbol of *instinctual perseverance*. This is your Te, the instinctual awareness that knows exactly where you need to be: in the here and now and it is perfect.

Transforming the illusion of how you must conquer and take, you can develop the powerful peacefulness that comes when you no longer see the world as a place of obstacles. Just as the tree requires the storms for regeneration, and the stone carves away the seed's protective covering; like the creatures that feel the cold as a call for hibernation and migration, or the plant that instinctively knows the time to flower, you too, are fundamentally connected to the evolutionary force of life.

Te is your instinctual endowment and connection to life. When cultivated alongside of fearlessness, it is like water that finds its own course, without any sense of barriers. Water can dissolve mountains and evens out, regardless of where it flows. The power of Te connects you to the germinating power of life. Transcending the gate or 'the illusion of obstacles,' leads to a type of paradise in consciousness. This paradise is simply a place without boundaries.

Life's secret is that it has been committed to your success since the beginning. *"Mystery upon mystery: the gateway of its manifold secrets."* To take no action that is unnatural to your instinctive nature ensures that you will meet with no resistance. *"Overcoming others shows force; when you overcome yourself you are strong."*

"Generating movement even in the hardest things is how the great is tamed. Creating movement even in the greatest things is what makes Tao mysteriously powerful. The most submissive thing in the world can ride roughshod over the hardest in the world – that which is without substance enters that which has no crevices." Beyond the constant disillusionment that results from trying to be who you are not, there are no crevices or valleys. This is the essence of Controlled Power.

Unchanging: Domesticating the wild beast = soften the glare. A lack of movement, connection or release has stored an incredible amount of Creative Power beneath the meditative Mountain of Keeping Still. We can be drawn to another who is mysteriously powerful because of their silence. At some point however, we recognize that they might just be horrible communicators. Another may see our independence and power as a threat and seek to undermine it through actions meant to unseat us from our center. Determining who is in charge in this situation becomes a lesson about assumptions, fears and the need for control as a power game ensues between very potent individuals. You may need to wait for the right moment to proceed, or tread carefully because the release can be explosive. It can suggest a necessary respite or retreat in order to heal or recharge. It can also show a person afraid of their own anger so they retreat. The Creative desires expression, but rests beneath the immovable Mountain in unchanging form, so there can be a lot of energy building that will seek some type of release. On a positive note, when the great tame themselves, others submit to their will so growing in a sense of power while you do nothing can lead to success. You may feel held back, but trust that whatever is happening will lead to the expression of greater power in this situation. Not getting what you want, you get what you need. There may be a need to establish limits or boundaries that will allow for greater individual freedoms. To tame another you may need to tame yourself, but make no mistake, this situation is highly charged. The standoff can be quite spectacular and is witnessed in nature during mating rituals, territorial fights and even at the molecular level so it is not necessarily bad. There is no need to stop believing in the goodness of those you care about or serve. Nothing lasts forever and this situation will resolve itself. If you are asking about acting, don't be impulsive because there is something going on below the surface that needs to be investigated. Learn to tame your response and be a better listener.

Line 1 Danger is at hand = it furthers one to cease and desist. Changes to (18) Decay. Something is blocking your progress and without examining the misunderstanding or decay of the situation, further progress can only lead to danger. This is a time to explore what you can learn about the obstacle through inaction. Exerting your power will lead nowhere so step back until you have a clear understanding of everyone's motivations.

Line 2 The spokes are taken from the wagon = it is not possible to move. Changes to (22) Grace. You are held back from proceeding because of events beyond your control. This is a time to explore acceptance of what you are powerless to change. Grace offers the message: if you can't change the direction of the wind, adjust your sails and let life guide you.

Line 3 A good horse is trained to operate a wagon = beneficial to have somewhere to go. Changes to (41) Decrease. You are kept on your toes because another proves difficult to handle and self restraint is necessary. The way ahead is opening and you find a way to deal with a difficult situation or person. Powerful energy is now gathered by the strength of your will to proceed and by working in tandem with others. Identify goals and clarify limitations or boundaries and the way will open.

Line 4 A young bull is restrained = a source of good fortune. Changes to (14) Great Possessing. That which has held you back is observed to be the reason for your growth. By taming a wild impulse into focused power your success is assured. Since everything is under your control you can move forward. Interacting with another proves difficult but through the experience both harness great power and enlightenment.

Line 5 The tusks of a castrated boar = good fortune. Changes to (9) Small Restraint. Something that was potentially a threat is now harmless. Since you understand its nature you can make its power work for you. This leads to mutual trust and great success.

Line 6 One obtains the way of heaven = success. Changes to (11) Peace. After a time of success you may find yourself at a crossroad where a difficult decision must be made. The way of heaven or Tao ignites your Te or inner knowing so follow what feels natural. When in doubt follow the current that life presents to you. A great opportunity awaits because you have achieved the highest level of Controlled Power and have aligned with your Tao.

Hexagram #27
Yi (Nourishing Vision)

Action: Nurture
Hu Gua (secondary influence) 2: Receptive: Yield
Zong Gua: (underlying cause) 28: Critical Mass: Adjust
Received as 2nd Hexagram: Neediness needs to be
checked to ensure that what you want aligns with what
you truly need.

"Ignorance is the night of the mind,
but a night without moon and star."

Everyone sees the unseen in proportion to the clarity of the
heart,
and that depends upon how much one has polished it.
Whoever has polished it more, sees more – more unseen forms
become manifest. – Rumi

Reading at a Glance: Thunderous change now moves
within the Mountain of Keeping Still. The secondary
influence is the Receptive or a need to reflect on the
type of inner Vision we are Nourishing. This is a time to
consider what type of thoughts you nourish in order to

understand why events unfold as they do. Your
motivations can be understood by looking at what you
attract to yourself. The cause is Critical Mass, or the
idea that after a breaking point you must look for the
real essence of what might fulfill you. Perhaps
dissatisfaction or defeat is merely a way for you to
understand the hunger pain for change. Before
proceeding take time to understand how your thoughts
shape and nurture experience. We have two minds. One
that exists in the carbon based organic body that is
focused wholly on survival. It is trained to detect
anything that is *wrong* in the environment. The other is
energetic and guides our dreams with a boundless
optimism focused on growth. Both are natural in all of
us although their focus can be at odds. The omniscient,
dreaming mind has the purpose of unleashing the
patterns of thought that lead to stagnation or a lack of
fulfillment. In Nourishing Vision, we see what is
important to people because of where they focus their
energy. Are you cultivating a picture of success or
failure? How you nourish your body is no different
from how you are organizing your experiences. Are you
in a hurry or do you enjoy eating? Is your philosophy
manifesting the feeling that all is well in the world or
that life is working against you? If you have hit a wall,
is this wall just the fear of making necessary changes?
What we think about all day colors the environment we
meet. This is a time to examine your motivations,
thoughts and actions so that you can move in sync with
what you are creating for yourself. Smile and watch
how the world responds. Reboot your mind into an
open and non judgmental perspective and watch how

the world opens to you. There are no lines separating
what is happening 'in here' from what transpires 'out
there.' The highest expression of Yi is not just personal
sustenance but an ability to create nourishment that
fulfills those around you too. Critical Mass is also a
message that you cannot fill yourself up and hold on to
the great energy or it will overwhelm. If you seek
abundance in life you can only remain open by
allowing this abundance to flow out into the world.
Because you are open to life's benevolence it fills you
daily.

Defensiveness
ensures
that the outcome
is relentless.

"The Arousing Thunder moves within the Mountain."
It suggests how thought is excited into action. The
master said: *"what the people determine as great, they*
nourish." The energy of thought becomes manifestation
simply in how you interpret events. Many people can
witness the same event, but each will project a different
experience.

"To know what is important to the person, one must only
observe what they actively cultivate." Although you come
to give life labels, *"the Way passes through the mouth*
without flavor." If you are participating in your growth,
you will see the Way as being good; if you are not, you
will call it bad, and yet, it remains without distinction.

189

Observe the person by what they nourish. *"A person who understands the Way will conform to the Way. A person who lives by the rules of others will conform to the rules of others. A person who knows only loss will conform to loss."* In the image of a mouth, nourishment goes in and expression comes out. What you nourish in your heart and mind becomes the image reflected upon experience. If you want to experience life differently, begin to approach life differently.

"There was a student who watched a bee, spinning upside down in a shallow pond. When it began to drown, he pulled it out, and was stung. The master watched as another bee crawled into the pond. When it started to drown, the student pulled it out and was stung again.

The master asked: "Why do you keep doing the same thing, when each time the bee stings you in return?"

The student replied: "It is the bee's nature to sting, but it is my nature to save it."

This is an example of how what you repeatedly do comes to define your character. If you are not happy with the course of events then do things differently. Both nuclear trigrams emerge as the Receptive Earth, suggesting a time to reflect upon habitual behavior. You receive nourishment or reward in many ways, but this sustenance merely reflects how you sustain your way of living. If the outcome or response to what you do is always the same, then you must derive some benefit from it, or you would change your actions.

You have the power to shape your experience simply in the way you approach them. Your destiny unfolds from a seed within, although life will always meet you half way, with the events that will cultivate it. Sincere in your Te and remaining open in your response, nothing ever comes to block your way.

"The Way is easy, yet people prefer by-paths." You can know what your path will look like by what you nourish. As Thunder is aroused within, you have the opportunity to observe what motivates you, and what you nourish at the root of each experience. At the threshold of perception, *"pay heed to what you provide with nourishment, and to what you seek"* because you will find it. In knowing that a defensive attitude will always bring about events that will set you free from it, relax into the fulfillment that comes from witnessing life's power to nourish you.

Unchanging: Nourishing vision = unaware of its manifestation. Without changing lines this can be a message about the need to look at your desires. It can also suggest that you reap what you sow. You have your heart set on something but your insecurity may reveal itself in the mirror of what unfolds. Spending so much time thinking about negative outcomes has created a negative environment for you. If you want to experience life differently break out of your pattern of negativity and do a spring cleaning in your mind. Once all of the cobwebs have been cleared away, make a commitment to cultivate an open and non judgmental outlook daily. Slow down and relax. Spend a day just

191

smiling and see how the world reacts to you. Reboot your mind into openness and watch the world open to you. Perhaps you have noticed this negativity in the 'mirror' of interactions with others? How you meet the world determines how it will respond to you. Examine the object of your desire to see if it is truly what will nourish you.

Line 1 You let your magic tortoise go and look hungrily at me = misfortune. Changes to (23) Split Apart. Rather than follow your own intuition, you are looking for answers in the wrong places. Perhaps you have given another the unjustified power to validate your worthiness. This type of thinking will not lead to fulfillment and will be Split Apart. The magic tortoise is how we carry our world like a shell on the back. It houses our love, our dreams, our nourishment and even our home. All that you are seeking can be found within. Take this home with you as you go out into the world.

Line 2 Not a sage on a mountain but a beggar on a hill = misfortune. Changes to (41) Decrease. Someone is not feeling good about their inability to get their needs met. Even a pauper can find joy if intentions are simple while integrity is intact. In this case being provided for by others only diminishes self esteem. Being anti-social or retreating from interaction may be part of the problem.

Line 3 You turn away from nourishment in seek of gratification = misfortune. Changes to (22) Grace. If something is unfulfilling and you ignore it then you live a life of instant gratification. Find the root of your true desire and fulfill that. If you feel bad about yourself you can live a life of looking for acceptance from others which only validates your low self esteem. True nourishment comes from seeing how unfolding events are leading your toward fulfillment. Live your life from the inside ~ out rather than looking to outer events for nourishment.

Line 4 Nourishment from the mountain like a tiger = chasing desire, no blame. Changes to (21) Biting Through. Both images focus on acute awareness arising from investigation and the idea of providing nourishment and support. You have your sights set on something and you intend to give chase until you capture it. There is nothing wrong with this as long as you are hunting the right people or the right situations. Are you prepared to nurture what you capture? A time of retreat or Biting Through might allow for incredible personal insight. Finding value in what you seek, you work diligently to succeed.

Line 5 Turning away from the path, not striving = one seeks enlightenment. Changes to (42) Increase. If a situation has become challenging there is not much you can do but seek inner clarity. Don't attempt to change or force things. A time out would be beneficial and allow you to succeed later into an environment of Increase. Not striving means not forcing your way into the world, but remaining at the threshold of perception where you can witness events without judgment and simply be.

Line 6 One finds the real source of nourishment = a vision to cross the great water. Changes to (24) Return. If you can let your desire be without acting on it, you will discover a more real form of nourishment. Questions about resources and fulfillment might reveal that nourishing others with your spirit is all the nourishment that you need. Chasing something out of habit can lead you astray. One who shines the light of abundance without attachment attracts exactly what they need. To move forth in this way will lead to enduring fulfillment. Transcend purely personal goals to see how you are a light for others and in that, you find great reward.

Hexagram #28
Ta Kuo (Critical Mass)

Action: Adjust
Hu Gua (secondary influence) 1: Creative: Initiate
Zong Gua: (underlying cause) 27: Nourishing Vision: Nurture
Received as 2nd Hexagram: Something is too much in this situation - tone it down.

To follow the energy of life, you will discover that it is always seeking the best of what you might become.

The study of Nature is intercourse with the Highest Mind. You should never trifle with Nature. –Louis Agassiz

Reading at a Glance: The situation is in a condition of Critical Mass and an adjustment is needed. The roof is too heavy for the support of the ridgepoles which shows that exuberance of thought and energy surpasses the foundation that is being built to support it. Excess of some kind is at play. Ta Kuo can shows the secondary influence of the Creative at the root of the situation, where tension is the driving force of great creativity and accomplishment. Even while Critical Mass feels uncomfortable, it will lead to a readjustment. In this case, you may have to push beyond what you feel is limiting you by adapting and adjusting. The image is of a ridgepole sagging because the weight of accumulating tension is too much. You may need to stand alone with no support during this time of crisis and simply give form to your vision. Too much of a good thing is not always good so Ta Kuo can also suggest moderation. Nourishing Vision without putting it to proper use is shown as the Zong Gua so you may need to 'come out' and show the world what you have been working on. This can be a perfectionist who spends a lot of time practicing but is fearful of competition or feedback. Look to your work to stand on its own merit. Believe in what you are doing and don't worry about support and acceptance because that is the message of this hexagram: be undaunted. Keep going. However, this can be a situation where ideas have taken over what is actually witnessed as experience. This way of interacting with life is not sustainable and the paradigm will crumble. Critical Mass holds the essence of the Sage's greatest lesson: tranquility in disturbance. It is not expectation that you hold to; it is the certainty that everything is unfolding perfectly so you are free to grow. You succeed because you find that the tension actually leads to excitement and the joy of doing the work.

Like erosion, you are no match
for life's perpetual
gusts and storms
that come to soften
a hardened inner landscape.

"Nourishing something without putting it to proper use, will finally evoke movement in the image of the great becoming overwhelming." Like a heavy roof that rests upon a weak foundation, the structure sags in the middle and will come down. Ta Kuo is a message about putting accumulating energy to work.

Unbalanced energy always generates a chain reaction. A series of events ensue, in which each event is both the *result* of the one preceding, but also, the *cause* of what follows. Ta Kuo demonstrates how protecting a weak foundation or outworn idea is no match for the power of nature to bring it down.

The master said: *"if you must stand alone, be unconcerned. If you must renounce the world, be undaunted."* Natural action can only manifest when you eliminate your sense of right and wrong, or good and bad. Following how nature is unbiased will return you to a pathway of wellness and balance.

Nature, in its Creative form, explores diversity by bringing opposites together. At the same time, a constant movement of the Yielding takes form in life's pursuit of balance. When you defend yourself against Creative change, you are forced to become open or Yielding. Floating along Yielding to past beliefs, events will force you to embrace Creative change. When either is overly demonstrated, the other emerges to strike a balance.

Hunted to near extinction near Yellowstone National Park, wolves were reintroduced to control the exploding bison and elk populations, and a chain reaction ensued. Biologists recorded numerous scavengers, including animals, birds and insects that fed on the new carcasses. They discovered a food chain impact not previously appreciated. Once the park reverted to a more natural environment, the elk were again prey. They moved more, and grazed less on the willows, which also began to thrive. The flourishing willows allowed beavers to build dams and transform small meadows into lakes, where fish, waterfowl and other insects began to thrive. Protecting the elk and bison from being the top of the food chain is like *"nourishing something without putting it to proper use."*

This unnatural intervention caused a chain reaction of stagnation. It denied sustenance to a myriad of creatures. This is how beliefs can interfere with life's natural drive to explore the best of what it might become.

When the excessive overwhelms the weak, the weak will rise in a chain reaction, whether in politics, the natural world, or within the paradigm of the individual. The Wind, with the Creative at its center, is seeking a transition, but the Lake can be viewed as *joyous oblivion*. From within you, the Creative seeks expression and being naturally yourself is your only option.

While the ridgepole sags, *"it furthers one to have somewhere to go."* The transition will lead you somewhere. Ta Kuo suggests an unnatural condition that contains within it the power for renewal. Critical mass is like the explosion of the Big Bang, where new life emerged from a point of nothingness. In actuality life was already there. Authenticity and naturalness is life's main thrust. Meeting the challenge becomes your point of re-entry into a more stable way of interacting, even in difficulty.

Unchanging: Stalking crisis = good for heroes but not peacemakers. Critical Mass unchanging can mirror a situation where you are busy or overwhelmed at work. You may need a vacation to avoid burnout. It can be a warning that the object of your enquiry has stress attached to it in a way you aren't recognizing. Unchanging, Critical Mass portrays trying events that stay in suspension for a long period, such as the test of faith that comes from being a caregiver in a difficult situation. It can also show a person who complains constantly without changing anything. It can portray someone who stalks crisis to avoid commitment. It can show how others might be using the shock factor when interacting with you, either leaving you hanging or as a way to get a response out of you. Some people thrive on pushing the envelope, but others thrive on pushing our buttons. Some become the mover and shakers of the world, while the constant pursuit of a challenge can make them either loners or lonely. However, if you are feeling a sense of abandonment, you might want to look at the type of environment you are currently creating for yourself. Drama and keeping balls in the air can hide a fear of commitment. Perhaps you refuse to move on in some way or are failing to get the message that the current situation is just *too much*. In other words, it is not sustainable and the roof will come down. You may need to build a stronger foundation that can bring you a better sense of peace. Allow change to move you through a transition toward a more peaceful atmosphere. You may soon be making a tough decision you are avoiding.

Line 1 Spread white rushes underneath = no blame. Changes to (43) Determination. There is a need to take preparatory steps or be more cautious about building a careful foundation prior to proceeding. Don't put the cart before the horse. You may need to examine how resolute you are in actually going after your goal. The white rushes symbolize a mat of calmness beneath you as your Determination leads to a Breakthrough of clarity in a challenging situation.

Line 2 A dry poplar sprouts at the root, an older man takes a young wife = everything furthers. Changes to (31) Influence/Wooing. There is a fresh start to a situation that may have seemed to have withered or died. A renewal can take place because fresh ideas or new insights invigorate a decayed situation. You can encourage new growth by exciting or Influencing others by your ideas. Pushing forward willfully will get you nowhere.

Line 3 The ridgepole sags to the breaking point = misfortune. Changes to (47) Oppression/Exhaustion. During critical mass a change is needed and just pushing blindly ahead will not allow you to succeed. Obstinacy and Oppression will not reinvigorate an already deteriorating situation. Your main support is about to collapse, placing you in danger. The situation is too much and requires an innovative approach. You may feel closed in or trapped but it can be your own negativity. You have gone as far as you can and need to change direction or focus.

Line 4 The ridgepole is braced = good fortune. Changes to (48) The Well. The situation seems robust but you may still find that something is inadequate. Facing this truth may be humiliating but it is the key to making the situation better. Examine the source of your sustenance like a Well. Simply rebuilding the old city will only lead you back to Critical Mass if the Well has gone dry. The

Well can be a symbol of dysfunctional dynamics that can be corrected through honest discussion. It is also a symbol of a situation that is not easily changed.

Line 5 A withered poplar produces flowers, an older woman takes a younger husband = no blame no praise. Changes to 32 (Duration) This is a line often associated with an incompatible couple, unstable love or a relationship that remains friends to stand the test of time. Something you thought was dead is rejuvenated. However, it is not necessarily a good thing because you may feel that you sold out to keep the status quo. If you keep holding on to a deteriorated condition you can become exhausted. It may seem that breaking ties is in order but the situation is not hopeless and can actually endure. Everyone has different needs so don't measure what feels right to you against what others have. Commitment makes all things possible.

Line 6 One must go through the water, it goes over one's head = misfortune, no blame. Changes to (44) Coming to Meet. While you had warning that the situation was dangerous, you allow yourself to keep pushing forward anyway. Unfortunately going too deep into danger means you have no choice but learn to swim. The last line of Critical Mass leads to the Abyss or hexagram (29) associated with Danger. Coming to Meet suggests a valuable lesson to avoid this type of situation in the future. You did nothing wrong because you probably didn't know a problem existed. Explore your Shadow or how you might be blaming others for a condition that is uniquely yours.

Hexagram #29
Kan (Abyss)

Action: Relinquish
Hu Gua (secondary influence) 27: Nourishing Vision:
Nurture
Zong Gua: (underlying cause) 30: Clarity: Persist
Received as 2nd Hexagram: The fear of the unknown is
blocking your progress.

If you cannot change the direction of the wind,
adjust your sails and let life guide you.

For the benefit of the flowers, we water the thorns too. —
Egyptian Proverb

Reading at a Glance: Kan reveals how we commit to a
path even when it feels dangerous. Whatever your
question, there is an element of needing to go deep
below the surface to uncover what is really happening
no matter how frightening. In every hero journey, just
when success is on the horizon, the nemesis reappears.
This is similar to the dark night of the soul where life

seems to engulf us in confusion and we give up hope. The situation is highly charged, but like the hero, going through the danger is necessary to discover who you are, what you really need and what you are capable of accomplishing. In hero myths they often discover that the nemesis is actually a teacher, sometimes even a parent! In this case, the dangerous flow of water that has engulfed will lead you somewhere if you just relinquish control. There is great power and realizations to be obtained when confronting fear in the deep waters of the unconscious. The current of events can be overwhelming like a deluge, but there is a benevolent aspect at play which is seeking to set you free. Along with the dangerous abyss you must descend into, we see an image of a cap with wings signifying one who teaches others how to transcend difficulty because of actual experience. You might rise above the danger with the faith that all is unfolding as it should. You can also choose to allow the situation to lead you deeper into your own psyche and emotional dynamics. Using humor or escapism to mask the danger won't work. The winged cap isn't a toy and doesn't magically appear so you can just rise above difficulty. It requires work to achieve enlightenment. However you decide to proceed, after a time of meeting the Abyss, you will become more sincere in your outlook. This is what is meant by 'if you are sincere, you will meet with success.' Kan is a time of testing. Clarity as the Zong Gua can be a message that an old outlook can no longer serve the new person you are becoming. Nourishing Vision as the secondary influence can remind you that even when the way forward seems to threaten your idea of safety, energy is working deep within to transform your confusion into Clarity. Kan is the keeper of the night self and embodies that part of us that knows exactly who we are and where we need to be. Trust the process at play in your situation and pay attention to your dreams. The hidden or Shadowed side of life is every bit as important as what you see by daylight. This is the ultimate hero's journey of self discovery. If you can awaken to how you project the past upon experiences, you will discover that fear is a fertile garden, and once transformed, becomes that place where your dreams become reality.

And the freedom
of dispersion:
life's
energetic elixir.
Scatter your fog.

"The water flows uninterrupted toward its goal." The Abysmal Water is above and below, revealing a flooding ravine that suggests danger. While life coaxes you toward gentle transformation, you can refuse, although events will take you there anyway. If you are swept away by its current, you will discover how life opens you to self discovery.

The master said: *"What is tightly held in the arms cannot slip loose,"* but when the waters are raging, you will let go. Sometimes it is only through the Abysmal that your arms are opened and your hands are set free. Whatever

204

remains, will return you to sincerity, while deepening your connection to life.

Without trusting in the flow of events, the situation becomes threatening, but only in proportion to the disparity that exists between *the necessary transition* and your *fear of going there*. When you recognize the things that you cannot change, you discover life's power to lead you. The path is frightening but a commitment to move forward and jump into the flow leaves no option of turning back.

Faced with the devastation of the old way, you are pulled back into life's greater current. When the storms set in, you will realize how much energy was wasted in worrying about each, and every squall. In the image of a dangerous gorge that draws water downward, Kan also portrays wings and a cap. Your thoughts are given wings that can either trap or release you. Identifying the barriers that you construct to ward off change, recognize how nature's power to dissolve them will come in equal measure. Therefore, discard the need to interfere with something that demonstrates greater wisdom in returning you to balance.

All that is required to achieve wellness is the freedom to move. Kan can reduce all of life to its most fundamental and simple aspects. How liberating!

When the Abysmal pulls you into its flow, the Way is made clear again. You can cling to the floating debris of an outworn way of thinking, but will find that it is useless in your new way of approaching the world. Although it rises in rain, water has a tendency to flow earthward, and is the image of remaining grounded and natural. All that remains after the Abysmal will be your deeply profound connection to life.

Unchanging: Danger repeated = it is the will and not the way. Critical Mass precedes the Abysmal and shows how outer events or inner structures that required renovation end in danger if nothing is changed. With the Abysmal unchanging, an inner attitude has become dangerous but sometimes this is just the energy you put into worrying. You may find yourself in danger time and time again because you are not changing your compulsions. The situation may not be as bad as you think but you are making it dangerous because of an unhealthy attachment to it. It can show unchecked depression that needs to be dealt with if you are always feeling 'down' or 'trapped in a pit.' The message is to stop being a victim and blaming events for your frustration. A change in daily routine which allows even for small accomplishments will work wonders on your self esteem. Once you make changes to the inner world, the outer world mysteriously changes. This is the beauty of allowing your paradigm to flow in the Great River of life. What you are afraid of isn't as frightening as it appears. A dangerous situation has stabilized and won't get any worse.

Line 1 Repetition of the abysmal, one falls into a pit = misfortune. Changes to (60) Limitations. Without changing your propensity for making the wrong choices, you dig yourself deeper into a pit. Playing it too safe and not taking chances can be as debilitating as rushing recklessly into danger. Set healthy boundaries so that you can walk the middle path. Don't sacrifice intimacy because of fear. If what you are doing and thinking is getting you nowhere, set realistic and obtainable goals, no matter how small. The pit is only a cycle of self defeating limitations in thinking.

Line 2 The Abyss is dangerous = strive to attain small things only. Changes to (8) Union. There are many things in life that can appear threatening. The fear is the same whether it is related to romance or job prospects. The message is to recognize the danger but not allow it to overwhelm you in a way that makes you quit. Progress can be slow like water meeting a dam that eventually swells and overflows. Obstacles reveal your sincerity about moving forward. Small advances over time will allow you to overcome your fear and succeed. The change to Union bodes well for any difficulties you may currently be experiencing in a relationship. However, if you can enjoy the simple things, the situation may become more fulfilling.

Line 3 Advancing and retreating, danger everywhere = clinging to a rock so you don't fall into the abyss. Changes to (48) The Well. Escape isn't a possibility when presented with danger in this situation so it is better to wait it out. You may feel that you need to act but that would only increase the danger. Many false starts only undermine your confidence in meeting difficulty. A solution will show itself if you can be patient. However, you must acknowledge the part your beliefs are playing in difficult situations. The Well shows the reservoir of the unconscious and its waters must be clear and flow freely. In the midst of a confusing situation you can rest but you will need to keep pushing forward because turning back is not an option.

Line 4 Wine, food and vessels brought in through the window = no blame. Changes to (47) Oppression/Exhaustion. You are being held back and may even feel imprisoned, but don't make the situation worse by dwelling on what is lacking. A calm and thoughtful approach through clarity of mind will help you overcome all that you fear. Return to the basics and appreciate the simplicity of having your basic needs met. The window suggests getting a clear view of what is going on and then proceeding with calm acceptance and patience. There is an element of gaining assistance at play perhaps through criticism that will help you in your growth. You may be giving in a relationship where what you offer is not being recognized. The simple joy of sharing with others may be all that the situation can offer you at this time.

Line 5 The abyss is not overflowing, it only reaches the rim = no blame. Changes to (7) Army. The danger has passed and the situation will return to normal. However, you might examine whether the danger was created because you attempted more than you were capable of achieving. Follow the path of least resistance and tame your ambition. The Army is a disciplined mindset that allows you to achieve balance.

Line 6 Bound with ropes in a thorny prison = for three years no gains, misfortune. Changes to (59) Dispersion. The illusions that led you into danger have trapped you. In this situation someone has become immoveable and there can be no gain. There may be a disillusioning process required before you will find your true path again. When hurt deeply or ashamed of behavior, one retreats to protect themselves. Dispersion is a positive message that reorganization is already at play. Let go and move on.

Hexagram #30
Li (Clarity)

Action: Perceive
Hu Gua (secondary influence) 28 Critical Mass: Adjust
Zong Gua: (underlying cause) 29 Abyss: Relinquish
Received as 2nd Hexagram: The bond is strong but dependency should be traded for interdependence.

**When you can appreciate nature's power
to break through all barriers,
you will discover that this same power
is inside of you.**

*Life is a pure flame, and we live
by an invisible sun within us.* – Thomas Browne

Reading at a Glance: Li is associated with
enlightenment, nurturing and the idea of serving clarity
of purpose. The judgment says 'care of a cow brings
good fortune.' Should you have the opportunity to care
for a cow you learn about interdependency, a mindset
of being docile, serving another, and the voluntary
dependence you share with life. The more you feed the
cow, the more the cow feeds you. If it stays healthy, you
stay healthy thus 'that which is bright rises twice.' Li
shows your interdependence with others in
relationships and your interdependence with the way.
Life is what you make of it. Clarity and inspiration
abound when receiving this hexagram and the greatest
place to find this is by stepping out of your routine to
observe nature. The plants would tell you how by
sitting still you can follow your inner guidance and
flower. The river would tell you to go with the flow.
Animals might tell you not to make the hunt for
nourishment so complicated, follow your instinct, use
your senses and honor the blessing of your meal.
Wherever you look, you will see poetry. Critical Mass
as the influence and the Abysmal as the cause are both
reminders to be moderate and sincere to avoid having
events crash down around you. When life becomes

complicated, you need only look for the inspiration that reminds you to follow that which keeps your inner light burning. A time of great creativity or a quantum leap in insight is emerging. Clarity teaches you that the only sign post you need can be found by aligning your inspiration to the path you walk. Li is the shining light of inspiration that marries your inner and outer world into Clarity. What motivates you and what are you passionate about? Follow that.

Witness
the unchanging:
cling to
the
firmament.

"The clinging means resting on something. When the waters of the Abysmal flow into the pit, we search for something to cling to." Li is the image of the Clinging Fire, formless except the essence of fuel that keeps it burning. When the changes are underway your only footing is the reference point of the Self. When it too, is undergoing transformation, you must find something more meaningful to cling to.

What emerges from any difficult transition is the discovery of *that thing* which will guide and support you when all else is taken away. This is like a light that is always burning in the darkness. Although events 'out there' orchestrate the changes, they merely lead you to cultivate a shift of awareness 'in here.'

211

The master said: *"The cultivation of the self consists in the rectification of the mind."* The rectification of the mind usually consists of letting barriers go. *"That which is bright rises twice."* Even the most difficult circumstances cultivate your inner fire in a way that allows you to shine more brightly 'out there.'

After the Abysmal waters have receded, we often arrive at the suchness existing at every moment, without the need to look any further. You may discover: 'what is...is,' and stop fighting the very thing that shapes you and reveals your purpose. *"Life is like a flowing river; identify its current to know contentment."*

When life is free to move spontaneously, a beautiful harmony can be observed. Obstruction only emerges because you may classify things in terms of good, bad, right or wrong, but the idea of obstruction is a man made illusion. Nature is blind to the idea of obstacles, except in the way that it tears them down. What you may call difficulty is the tearing away of what is blocking your inner light and movement.

The unnatural things that we build to obstruct life's forward progress will never be a match for its enormous power to break them down. Even water will immediately break down the molecules of whatever substance comes into contact with it. Li is the expression in attitude and behavior of an openness that allows all things to keep moving forward. Whether it is removing the outworn, or building something new, nature is always productive.

This transformative power unleashes inner direction and awakens you to a powerful center that you can cling to.

Li can have a message about fate or dharma where a synergistic meeting offers growth through the challenges it presents. *The master said: "When the mind is like a mirror, it grasps nothing, refuses nothing, receives, but does not keep."* This is an important mindset during any fated encounter where another is your teacher. To approach the gateway, you can use mind as a portal or a prison. When you *"unblock the openings"* you can view a world bathed beneath the power of your inner light.

Unchanging: Is this me when I reach for you = or are we the same? Li unchanging can portray co-dependency or a type of cause and effect dynamic that keeps people together because of the intensity between them. This can be good in creative collaboration. In domestic situations, it can be uncomfortable although separating seems impossible. The synergy that is suggested by Li offers a message to make sure that your relationships are interdependent and not dependent. Fate or dharma brings us together. Interdependence is two whole individuals serving each other's well being. Dependence means someone allows another to be responsible for their welfare, self image or self esteem which isn't healthy. In looking at all aspects of your life: health, work and family, ensure that you find balance. Since Li focuses on what it is that keeps the fire burning in synergy and energy, you may be feeling uninspired or unmotivated. In unchanging form, you are coached to remember that behind all accomplishment and fulfillment is the synergy of motivation and reward. Creative fires can burn out of control and die altogether when you are not aligning intent with action. A sense of reward must follow action or your light will simply extinguish. Machines run on an energy source and we too, need passion and inspiration to keep our fire burning. Everything is unfolding exactly as it should to re-ignite your passion. As a static reading, you may be someone who is always inspired so cherish that gift. If you are not satisfied with the results achieved through your inspiration you may need to re-evaluate your motivation. If a wheel is set on fire, the energy makes it turn and it won't stop until the fire burns itself out. Another may be looking for your encouragement or confirmation before proceeding.

Line 1 The footprints run criss cross = if one is sincere, no blame. Changes to (56) Wanderer. It is normal to make mistakes when first trying to manifest your desire. There is no blame because you are sincere in your attempts. If the situation appears overwhelming, go back to your original intention. What is it that you wanted? If you can align your actions with the sincerity to follow through, you will succeed. The greatest gift of the Wanderer is knowing that the home is within.

Line 2 Yellow light of the sun = supreme good fortune. Changes to (14) Great Possessing. You are fully comprehending what needs to be done and you are inspired about doing it. This can be a new situation or a new outlook that comes from the desire to follow your inspiration. All lights are green to move ahead. Great Possessing reinforces the good energy at play in this situation.

Line 3 When the sun sets, we beat pots and sing or bemoan old age = misfortune. Changes to (21) Biting Through. Worrying about the progression of time can make you feel old or late in terms of life stages. It is better to focus on the here and now and sing. You have the opportunity to view the glass as half full or half empty. While a period may be coming to an end make the most of it. If you would rather complain, that is your choice but not the best use of the time or talent.

Line 4 It's coming is sudden = as if it flames up, dies down to be forgotten. Changes to (22) Grace. There is a need to recognize the synergy of sustainability. You may feel that not taking vacations impresses your employer but it leads to burn out, not longevity. Relationships can burn hot and fast in the beginning with no substance to keep it going. Perhaps you are afraid of where love will lead you so you push it away when it appears. Inspiration can only be sustained if you don't let it consume you. Grace brings something suddenly in a flash of inspiration. What you do to sustain this brilliant fire is up to you.

Line 5 Tears in floods, sighing and lamenting = good fortune. Changes to (13) Fellowship. A real change of heart presents itself although this good fortune may come through suffering. You are reminded that suffering builds character and unleashes depth within you. The superfluous is kept in proper perspective because you have touched that place inside of original sincerity. You may have gone through difficulty but sometimes knowing what you don't want or can't have leads you to realize what you do want. When you are forced to defend something, you realize its importance. The good fortune that comes through a time of suffering is learning how to cultivate what you value so that you don't take it for granted. This can lead to sustainable success.

Line 6 The leader issues orders = eliminate those who do not serve the greater purpose. Changes to (55) Abundance. It is sometimes necessary to eliminate what is deficient or not serving you in order to achieve a state of Abundance. When others are influencing you in ways that bring you down, you might need to let them go, but it doesn't mean they are bad people. However be sure to look at the good and bad aspects to see if discipline or making intentions clear might turn the situation around. The punishment may be too strict and you would suffer from judging in haste.

Hexagram #31
Hsien (Influence/Wooing)

Action: Woo

Hu Gua (secondary influence) 44 Coming to Meet: Encounter

Zong Gua: (underlying cause) 41 Decrease: Evaluate

Received as 2nd Hexagram: One can only attract what is desired through magnetism, not force.

**Wooing is how you attract
those things that you desire.**

*Great hearts steadily send forth the secret forces
that incessantly draw great events. – Emerson*

Reading at a Glance: When the Joyful Lake sits upon the sturdiness of the Mountain, one is ascending and the other is descending. The Lake nourishes the mountain while it is the mountain that causes the rain to fall and fill the lake. Wooing is the idea of seeking win/win solutions where all parties benefit by coming together. In courtship, something profound happens between individuals who feel a mutual attraction.

217

While they may not understand why, they just feel more complete being together. Relationships built around expectations and manipulation can succeed, although true fulfillment comes when nature is simply taking its course. The situation has the effect of pulling you forward because it feels right. Affection attracts affection and obstruction attracts obstruction. The secondary influence of Coming to Meet suggest that you are attracting the experiences of which your mind is currently focused. Woo your experiences the way a suitor would woo another. Focus on the positive, complimenting life for making you stronger and wiser. Cherish the gifts that come to you each day. Smile, it makes you attractive. Where the Zong Gua of evaluation or Decrease was a period to understand loss and how to make the best of it, the time has now come to open to how life is affecting you. Open to how you are affecting life with your outlook.

Experience courts
the
abundance
of the
chaste mind.

"The Lake on the Mountain: the image of influence where the weak is above and the strong is below." Like gravity, you have the opportunity to attract events by *wooing*. Centered in your own power, you will attract those situations that *fortify it*. Therefore, if you are wooing something like fear, you may observe how you

also attract an opportunity to fortify it. Be diligent in thought.

The master said: "When you leave the mind alone and allow it to function in its most spontaneous way, Te will develop *naturally*. Just as there is a driving force behind life's pursuit of excellence, Te is your transformative essence and evolving power *to become*.

The Mountain bows down to the Joyous Lake, and personifies courtship, and the lesson of the strong wooing the weak. In the image of two broken pieces of pottery that fit together perfectly, a partnership with life is formed at the threshold of perception.

To observe and accept things as they really are, you are no longer defending anything. This will allow only the necessary to come forward to guide you. Moving away from the negativity of 'what you should and shouldn't do,' you will attract by virtue of 'what you do.' In this spontaneous and unfettered perspective, your entire being is given expression. You will discover how the pathway always mirrors your capabilities.

Lieh Tzu was trained by Lao Shang: *"For three years, my mind did not reflect upon right or wrong and my lips did not speak of gain or loss. During this time, my master bestowed only one glance upon me. After five years, a change took place, and my mind did reflect on right and wrong; my lips spoke of gain and loss. For the first time, my master relaxed his countenance and smiled. After seven years, I let my mind reflect on whatever it would, but it no longer occupied itself with right or wrong. I let my lips utter whatsoever they pleased, but they no longer spoke of gain or loss. Then, at last, my master invited me to sit on the mat beside him. After nine years, my mind gave free reign to its reflections; my mouth gave free reign to its speech. Of right, wrong, gain or loss, I had no knowledge. Internal and external were blended in unity. I was wholly unaware of what my body was resting upon. I was born this way, like leaves falling from a tree and playing on the wind. In fact, I knew not whether the wind was riding on me, or whether I was riding on the wind."*

To activate the power of te, do not negate the mind, but do not allow it to keep you its prisoner. Being natural and spontaneously yourself, you are always wooing experience because it will always reflect the condition of your inner world.

When you open to the Tao of Nature, spontaneity or a willingness to make mistakes drives inner excellence. Since you do not hold back, you are in a better position to receive; not classifying experience in terms of good and bad, you are freed from thought that can become restrictive.

"Like attracts like; obstruction attracts obstruction." Wooing or *influence* is how you activate this spontaneous attraction that is always reciprocated. You must only be vigilant in romancing experience and not overlaying it with your beliefs. Whether it is the lover, who opens to love, or the farmer, who uses the seasons to plant, it is by virtue of 'what you do' that you reap.

Unchanging: Thoughts change everything = be in mutual rapport with experience. If what you see around you does not satisfy, consider changing your outlook. You may have put too much emphasis on what you think you need and are not seeing that you are getting exactly what you are reinforcing: "I feel empty, therefore I feel needy" or "it feels perfect and it is perfect." If you are empty within – the world looks empty without. Wooing is like a mirror showing the reflection of your inner world. The tranquility of the Mountain with the Joyous Lake above shows how relationships should be mutually beneficial. All that is needed to turn this situation around is opening to the ability to be influenced, to allow life or another to make you smile. Two people are affecting each other in a mutual way and the connection endures even without communication. Since the situation is unchanging, perhaps one is not sure whether they want to act on the attraction because of where it might lead. This can be a message about a dysfunctional attraction that is still sustained. Its message can be about boundaries and interdependence rather than dependence. Because two things come together complete in their nature we see a Lake on a Mountain rather than a mud slide or flood.

Wooing is not commitment however, so give a situation time to sort itself out. Perhaps a focus on play is more important. Give careful thought to what you wish for, because you may get it. In non-relationship matters, the message is that you will get out of something all that you put into it. If you feel pessimistic it will translate into experience. If you are excited about it, chances are others will be too.

Line 1 Influenced in the big toe = a goal without movement. Changes to (49) Revolution. While the influence is being felt it is not yet being acted upon. There is something in the air, and you might have a great idea or attraction but there is more to do to make it a reality. Before movement can occur a time of Revolution or a change in outlook may be required.

Line 2 Influenced in the calves, misfortune = better to wait. Changes to (28) Critical Mass. It may seem like it is time to move, but you don't have all of the facts. To avoid danger, control your response until the time comes when you will know when to act. Critical Mass is a condition of too much of something so your advances might not woo the situation favorably, but appear needy. Waiting will allow natural magnetism to manifest if the situation is correct for you.

Line 3 Influenced in the thigh, humiliation = do not seek low hanging fruit. Changes to (45) Gathering Together. Just because what you desire seems within reach doesn't mean getting it will make you fulfilled. Don't be influenced by compulsions or base urges. The attraction is strong and gathers others to you but it may be an unhealthy way of interacting. Gathering Together shows interdependent roots growing stronger through mutual support, not clinging behavior.

Line 4 Wishes come true, perseverance brings good fortune = companions recognize your dream. Changes to (39) Obstruction. You have the chance to woo others in following your ideas. You need to test it out in the real world, however. Close friends can encourage you but you need to see if it has merit beyond your immediate circle. Influence is effective but it requires perseverance to make it successful. If you are facing an obstacle to unity, slow down and compose your thoughts. If there is sincerity in your wish and perseverance in action you will succeed.

Line 5 Influenced in the back = no remorse. Changes to (62) Small Exceeding. You feel energized and ready to proceed and small boundaries can be crossed in order to express truth in a way that resonates with another. The back is the most rigid part of the body so influence without remorse can mean a feeling shifts at a deep level. If we cannot be influenced ourselves we cannot influence the outer world. Small things done consistently can work wonders. While an unconscious attraction has yet to reach consciousness because of boundaries, something stirs in the depths. It is beneficial to remain correct and proceed in small ways toward your goal.

Line 6 Influence in the jaws, cheeks and tongue = superficial talk. Changes to (33) Retreat. You must disengage from trying to convince others with talk that appears to have no substance. Don't waste energy talking about what you are going to do, prove it with your actions. But first, give more consideration to an actionable plan. Otherwise the situation becomes one of Retreat or withholding.

Hexagram #32
Heng (Duration)

Action: Commit
Hu Gua (secondary influence) 43 Determination: Breakthrough
Zong Gua: (underlying cause) 42 Increase: Expand
Received as 2nd Hexagram: The situation has reached a state that is unlikely to change any time soon.

**Commitment is the force of attraction
that brings all things back to you.**

*Tis not the many oaths that make the truth;
but the plain single vow, that is vowed true. – Shakespeare*

Reading at a Glance: While much changes in life, there are elements that are enduring. Constancy and commitment ensure success in both relationships and career. A person who is committed to achieving a particular goal will persevere until the goal is achieved. They do so because they focus on results and not just tasks. At the end of the day it really doesn't matter how many tasks you accomplished. Rather, did you accomplish your goal? When obstacles appear, it is the commitment to succeed that can turn the obstacle into a learning experience. For someone not committed to success, an obstacle is a reason to give up. If we share a lot of words to tell the story of our failure, it is a good sign that commitment was lacking. Commitment needs no words. In the same way, marriages that operate on commitment weather any conditions. Marriages sought just for benefit or pleasure will break apart the moment difficulties set in. Yet in nature difficulty or limitations are its treasure trove for bringing something to a higher level. This can enhance relationships which explore difficulty as a means of digging deeper into intimacy and understanding. The secondary influence is Determination because breaking through any obstacle requires this constancy and commitment. The Zong Gua of Expansion shows that rather than look at accomplishment out there, we turn within and examine our foundation. Commitment is like gravity that pulls you toward the object of your desire. Once in orbit, there is not much that can pull you from success. You can be sure that there is an element of consistency associated with the object of your enquiry. You can be committed to either failure or success and the end result will always reveal which one it is.

Nature teaches constancy –
in relentless adaptations.
Never complete
and without extremes.

"Relationships should be long lasting; therefore follows the principle of duration." The Thunder and Wind Arouse movement in an enduring portrayal of what remains constant.

The situation requires your commitment to weather the highs and lows in the same way that all successful partnerships are founded in this way. Either you are validating reasons to go or reasons to stay. Observing this validation process will reveal your level of commitment to stay the course.

The master said: *"When you act from benevolence, it will feel good; it will feel like self-realization."* Benevolence allows you to recognize your connection to what unfolds. Nowhere is this more apparent than when you make a commitment to your spouse. Fulfilling their needs is inseparable from fulfilling your own. Only when both of you are fulfilled, do you experience *personal* contentment in the relationship.

The same commitment should be cultivated in following the Way.

The nuclear trigrams of the Joyous Lake and the Creative portray 'firmness in joy.' Firm in joy, you will experience the joy of discovery. The image of two broken pieces of pottery that fit together perfectly suggests the partnership formed at the threshold of perspective. Commitment is the force of attraction that brings all things back to you.

Commitment gives durability to the changes. Nature is composed of phenomenon that arises from the unseen or hidden movement of something deeper. Thunder is the explosive sound of expanding air when heated by lightning. Wind is the movement of air when hot and cold pressure systems collide. Although you cannot see the greater force, you can observe its effects in what unfolds. This is how a commitment or trust in the way gives durability to *that which is to come.*

Benevolence is an unconditional appreciation for *what is,* and keeps you open. Union brings two things together to make them one. In this case, your inner perspective is 'joined' with experience. Whether in relationship to each other or to events, *"stand firm and do not change direction."*

Embodied in Heng is the idea that although things come to a conclusion there remains a quality that is enduring. A torrential storm can pass through a landscape, but what is firm will not only remain, it will be strengthened. The master said: *"It furthers one to have somewhere to go."* Through movement you can you test your unwavering commitment in the face of adversity.

Commitment always unites what was once perceived to be separate. When you *"fix the mind on an end that endures,"* commitment is the unseen, which gives durability to the changes.

Approaching the gateway of perception, strengthen your trust in what remains unseen and unproven. You are carried through life as the image of a boat and a heart between two shores. The two shores are how you travel between good and bad, right and wrong, emptiness and fullness as you classify your journey. In reality, they are merely the banks of one great river. Life is powerful and good; it is profoundly committed to your success, but you must remain committed to meeting events 'half way' with sincerity and openness.

Like the highs and lows and the vicissitudes of emotions spent during courtship, once a commitment is established, the Way becomes much easier. *"Fix the mind on and end that endures. Knowing that which is to come"* is made easier by the simple act of devotion.

Unchanging: Constancy endures = commitment is like gravity. Duration unchanging can show that the situation you are inquiring about is a lasting one. That might be good news if you are looking for constancy in a presently good situation. If the idea of a current situation continuing isn't good news, perhaps because you are single, then you might want to give consideration to what you are committed to achieving. If all of your relationships feel like abandonment or rejection, then examine a possible fear of intimacy that is making you attract the wrong partners. Perhaps you don't realize you are afraid to have a lasting relationship. If you are not achieving success as you would like, examine your vision, perseverance and whether you give up too soon. Heng is about constancy and aligning with the appropriate time. You may be seeking an answer about what you don't understand today, but its 'appropriateness' will manifest as time passes. Its core message is that the result always rests in your mindset. A move toward commitment or the need for examining consistency in outlook is necessary in your present situation. A commitment that is enduring can move mountains.

Line 1 Seeking duration too soon, misfortune = nothing that would further. Changes to (34) Great Power. You are seeing a situation that is in flux as permanent. Don't jump to conclusions or rush in making a commitment too soon. There are elements that are still unfolding so be patient and examine sincerity in the direction you would like to go. Let events unfold before drawing conclusions.

Line 2 Regret disappears = abide in the due mean. Changes to (62) Small Exceeding. Avoid extremes in action and find the middle way between receptivity and action. You may have complicated the situation with too much force and may need a more simple approach. By matching your fortitude to what the situation calls for, regret disappears and things flow more easily. The due mean and Small Exceeding both suggest the middle path without extremes.

Line 3 No duration to character leads to disgrace = persistent humiliation. Change to (40) Liberation. Emotions run between hope and fear leading to inconsistency in character. The result is not only a lack of success but an undermining of self esteem. Calm the turbulent waters of your emotions and hold to your inner consistency. Vacillating with a lack of commitment to success leads to failure. Liberation shows that you need to keep your mind free of fear in moving forward. Hope is not the same thing as commitment.

Line 4 No game in the field = persistence is inadequate. Change to (46) Pushing Upward. If your goals are unrealistic you'll have difficulty achieving them. Therefore you reinforce failure because nothing happens. However, if you examine your desire and set small attainable goals, you can succeed. You are seeking something that cannot be found where you are currently looking. Seeking something in the wrong way is also futile. Pushing Upward suggests patience and rising from the center toward real fulfillment.

Line 5 Duration to character through perseverance = male and female keep to proper roles. Changes to (28) Critical Mass. Logic and the need to act or not act is always changing although emotional responses should be tamed. The feminine sense of following intuition and being receptive should remain constant even while masculine traits of daring and force will be flexible and changing as events call for a different approach. This is the essence of constancy in character. Emotionalism can waste the energy necessary for endurance. Tame yourself and change as the circumstances require.

Line 6 Restlessness as an enduring condition brings exhaustion = misfortune. Changes to (50) Cauldron. The concept of duration teaches constancy but a lack of focus and perpetual anxiety will wear you down. You can rush to conclusions or feel that a decision has to be made instantly when the situation will resolve itself if you leave it alone. Life often makes the decision for you if given time. All the worrying merely depletes your power to succeed. The Cauldron shows that a transformation of thought is in order.

Hexagram #33
Tun (Retreat)

Action: Disengage
Hu Gua (secondary influence) 44 Coming to Meet: Encounter
Zong Gua: (underlying cause) 19 Approach: Advance
Received as 2nd Hexagram: Necessary withdrawal or a time out is at play in this situation.

Content in your power,
you have no need to engage the obstacle.

A quarrel is quickly settled when deserted by one party: there is no battle unless there be two. — Seneca

Reading at a Glance: The idea of 'not embroiling' is a cornerstone of Taoist philosophy. In dreams we see how all symbols and even the characters mirror aspects of ourselves that we are examining and either adopting or discarding. Because the secondary influence is Coming to Meet, we can see that a situation calling for Retreat is a heavily charged one. We give 'charge' to a situation that pushes our buttons but Coming to Meet always brings us face to face with the transformative opportunity of the Shadow. The fact that there is so much charge makes the object of your enquiry an important one. However, you cannot force your will on the situation because it is teaching you something. It is better to step back and reflect on what it is that you are learning. 'Not embroiling' means not to throw more fuel on the fire. Emotional reactions between people stoke a fire that can burn out of control. The Zong Gua of Advance shows the opposite of what you need to do in this situation. Now, it is time to Retreat or disengage. When you engage an obstacle you only give it more power. The same holds true for negative thinking because you give these ideas credibility due to the charge you carry with you. You can actually stalk adversity by looking for it. Backing down does not mean you fail because it can create greater success. If you can step back, perhaps you can discover a win/win solution. Retreat is not a sign of failure but of a well thought out pathway to success.

The joy of stillness:
Nothing held.
Nothing lost.
The ease
of transparency.

"Things do not remain forever in their place. Therefore follows retreat." Retreat means withdrawing and when difficulty arises, you can observe how retreating from a situation cultivates power.

This is movement in stillness and allows you to conserve energy and fortify strength. *"Content in your power, you have no need to engage the obstacle."*

The master said: *"Mountain under the Creative: the image of retreat. The wise keeps the inferior at a distance, not angrily, but with reserve."* Even while you are firm in te, compassion allows you to continue in your growth. Life has a reason for bringing two strong types of energy together. Since two things that are firm do not deviate much, the chances increase that they will eventually meet in the river of life. If you are content in your power, you will have no need to engage firmness or contention in another.

"Retreat means success. In what is small, perseverance furthers." This is not a time for grand demonstrations of power, but requires care and an appreciation of your integrity. Tun is an image of a pig, representing contentment and well-being, combined with the idea of walking away. Do not be rude and indifferent; if you do

233

not become defensive, the other party cannot pull you into a confrontation. They meet with no resistance and therefore, do not contend. This captures how *"when you open, all obstacles disappear."* If you are correct, there is nothing to be defended.

In martial arts, one is taught 'economy of movement.' By holding to a specific position, the opponent is kept at a disadvantage, enabling one to maximize strength. In this case, you hold to your character or integrity. As a principle of movement in stillness, Tun is the image of purposeful withdrawal. Retreat does not mean giving up, but allows you to further strengthen your ability to remain open, while firm in your character.

Coming up against any barrier, engaging the obstacle always gives it more power. *"The wise meet all opposition with a quiet mind and open heart. Then all opposition naturally disappears. Without doing anything, nothing is undone."* When you do something, you may create action that can trigger endless reaction that may need to be undone. This is the great power of not doing. Purposeful withdrawal can disconnect you from a charged situation that might deplete you of your integrity. *"Perseverance in small matters brings success."* In the small matters that take place within, integrity fortifies character so that your nature remains incorruptible.

Observing nature, you may sometimes feel that things are not what they should be. Yet, eventually you recognize how nature too, turns back to regenerate, rather than always displaying obvious forward growth. Even while you are open to growth, turning back is also a pathway forward. *"The sheerest whiteness seems sullied. The great vessel takes long to complete."* The great vessel holds your Te as you travel through the river of life.

Unchanging: Pushing too hard = life responds by pushing back. The idea of inflexible thinking or hard headedness can be associated with Tun unchanging. There is not much you can do in this situation but step back and give the situation or person breathing room. If your enquiry involves a relationship, you may have pushed someone into a corner. If you are examining whether or not to move forward the message can be 'no.' Either the situation isn't right for you or your thinking is too rigid and requires flexibility. Because it is unchanging, a lack of positive response can go on for a long time, possibly permanently. On a softer note, the message can be to just step back and think about what you are asking because your reasoning isn't sound. In most cases, the message is that you need to withdraw from an inferior situation, way of thinking or questioning.

Line 1 Hiding the tail from danger = do not undertake anything. Changes to (13) Fellowship. An animal hides its tail in an act of submission but that type of compromise can only leave you vulnerable to attack. Because you are not too deep into the situation, you can calmly withdraw avoiding danger. Don't trade integrity for a quick solution.

Line 2 Held fast with yellow ox hide = no one can tear it loose. Changes to (44) Coming to Meet. The situation is dangerous but you are holding tightly to your integrity and can succeed. Knowing that there is something valuable to be achieved, you are correct in holding fast to your desire. By examining how you approach a sense of danger and why, you will learn much about yourself.

Line 3 A retreat is blocked with strings attached = sentimental attachments that can nourish. Changes to (12) Standstill. You are embroiled in a situation that does not allow for retreat. Examine what has brought it to an impasse and see if honest communication and mutual respect can solve it. The strings attached show that retreating is not something you wish to do so open to the opportunity for growth it presents. You may feel obligated in some way and can certainly learn a lot from the situation, but without the freedom to ensure your needs are met the situation can lead to Standstill.

Line 4 Voluntary retreat good for spirit not the ego = retire. Changes to (53) Development. The strong appreciate the opportunity for retreat as a way of reinvigorating one's center, but those emotionally inferior are frustrated and want to hold on to some sort of attachment. One should not be tempted to stay in an unhealthy condition because the other wants them to stay. However, if negativity or emotional immaturity retreats, the spirit is served through higher interaction. A gradual and well thought out retreat lifts spiritual goals but frustrates ego's desire to hold to a specific outcome. Let go and allow the gradual Development to occur.

Line 5 Friendly retreat = perseverance brings good fortune. Changes to (56) Wanderer. Withdrawal is achieved in a friendly matter because everyone is in agreement. Any loss is recognized to be necessary for future growth. This is an example of cutting ties because it is known to be 'for the best.' Letting go of the past happens with no ill will. However, if people are free to come and go or to fulfill their individual needs, persevering in this attitude will lead to good fortune.

Line 6 Retreat without guilt or doubt = everything serves to further. Changes to (31) Influence/Wooing. Withdrawing with the sense that it is right to do so. By letting go or retreating one is able to live abundantly. This line can be associated with retirement or taking a retreat from the daily grind in order to recharge or refresh your perspective. Sometimes we need to step back so that others have more of an appreciation for our contribution. Retreat leads to a magnetic attraction even while that is not our intention.

Hexagram #34
Da Zhuang (Great Power)

Action: Invigorate
Hu Gua (secondary influence) 43 Determination: Breakthrough
Zong Gua: (underlying cause) 20 Contemplation: View
Received as 2nd Hexagram: Don't be afraid to push or assert your ideas.

If you are steadfast in your power,
you cannot be thrown from your center.
A suppressed resolve will betray itself in the eyes. – George Elliot

Reading at a Glance: The Creative moves below the Thunder in an image of one who has achieved great power but does not move until certain that events call for movement. Even while you know you are in a position of superiority, don't be arrogant or pushy. When exerting force, we find resistance but power shows a willingness to adapt with being centered and firm. Therefore the Power of the Great is activated for those who know that the greatest strength is the ability to overcome themselves and their insecurities. Persisting in this outlook will lead to success. The secondary influence of Determination shows that a breakthrough in thinking has changed a landscape of obstacles into opportunities to prove the strength of your inner character. The Zong Gua of Contemplation shows that after a period of surveying the playing field, you are ready to move forward. Invigorate your sense of resolve because success is in sight. By restraining emotions and instincts the Power of the Great is similar to the concentration of force necessary to chop a block of wood with the hand. One remains calm and focused. The inner certainty of knowing that the hand will go through the wood without any doubt allows it to happen. Align the intention to succeed with the certainty that you will and nothing can stop you.

> *The thunder*
> *startles wakefulness.*
> *A vigorous stroke*
> *self-realized*
> *in the sleeping seed.*

"Things cannot retreat forever. Hence follows the idea of the power of the great." Firm in openness and character, you expand inward and develop your power. This leads to greater outward movement or an opportunity to shine. The Creative is strong as it pushes upward, toward the Arousing Thunder. This union of movement and power reveals how stillness and not aggressiveness activates the power of the great.

239

The master said: *"The meaning of the power of the great shows itself in the fact that one pauses."* Ta Chuang is another aspect of movement in stillness, where one steadfast in Te is never thrown from their center when confronting events. This is the 'constant virtue' that ensures that you will act benevolently. *"Mysterious virtue is far reaching, but when things turn back, it turns back with them."* What cannot be accomplished through force will be fortified through stillness.

Many myths describe a hero, abandoned or separated from the parents, and forced to grow up as an ordinary child. You too, can feel abandoned and thrown into a world that does not understand you. Heeding a call from within, you embark on a great journey and ultimately discover *your real identity*. Although you travel across dangerous terrains in the journey of a lifetime, once you arrive, you realize that this discovery could have taken place in our backyard. Yet, the actual journey 'out there' had the effect of changing you 'in here.' It opens you to the understanding that 'your way' was only one way.

"If you are a valley to the empire, then the constant virtue will be sufficient." To be a valley to the empire is to be composed and willing to bow down in every situation. Your constant virtue does not require that you defend it: *it is just so.*

When strength surpasses the turning point, there is a danger that one may rely on power heedless of what is right, yet *"without rightness, there can be no greatness."*

240

You are always activating the power of attraction. Sincerity keeps your experiences real so that you have no need to defend. One willing to bow down or concede in the face of opposition is demonstrating ultimate power. Vigilant in te, you will find yourself on a pathway where nothing needs to be undone. *"Lay hold of this truth and you can be master of your present existence."*

The germinal nature of Te blossoms from the foundation of sincerity and benevolence. *"The penetration of germinal thought into the mind promotes the workings of the mind. When this working furthers and brings peace to life, it elevates one's nature. Whatever goes beyond this indeed transcends all knowledge. When one comprehends nature and understands the transformations, one lifts the character to the level of the miraculous."* One who is on the pathway of greatness has no need to demonstrate force. Great success is how benevolence allows you to transform the obstacle into an opportunity to fortify your authentic power.

Movement in stillness becomes the image of bowing down with the knowledge of a power that cannot be threatened. This is the Power of the Great. This power does not need to be demonstrated or proven; it is always sufficient. Just as you gather and tame your passions for productive use, you compose your Te in the same way. Doing nothing out of the ordinary, you again achieve great movement. Success happens naturally by virtue of applying your constant te, or character.

Unchanging: Limitations that nourish = respect the time. You can stand your ground in an effort to succeed but you must also respect the customs and rituals that have historically worked. Respecting the limitations or expectations of others might be key to getting beyond any barriers you face in communication. You may need to tone it down a notch. Like a weight lifter, you can't just press heavy weights without starting small and your aggressiveness isn't winning you friends. You can feel like you have the energy to achieve something but the timing may not be right. There are established rules or needs of others that you may have to work within. This would be similar to a race car that must wait for the signal to go. Moving too soon or too late would only lead to failure. It doesn't matter how fast or powerful your car is. You still need to act with propriety and at the right time. Unchanging, the Power of the Great is about more than exerting your will although you may be tempted to act aggressively. In fact, not considering another's perspective may be the obstacle currently keeping you in a holding pattern. Obstacles can also be helping you to develop your resolve to succeed. Check arrogance and frustration with a willingness to develop your inner strength. In this case the strength to control your aggression.

Line 1 Strength in the toes = undertakings bring misfortune. Changes to (32) Duration. While you may feel you are ready to proceed, it is not time. There is not enough of a foundation yet in this situation so don't jump to conclusions. A strong urge to act is meaningless if the time is not right to   do so.

Line 2 Persevering brings good fortune = moderation leads to lasting success. Changes to (55) Abundance. The way is clear to achieve growth and progress. A lack of resistance should not make you overly confident. Proceed, but be moderate in all you do.

Line 3 Weak people use force while the strong do nothing = a ram butts against a hedge entangling its horns, danger. Changes to (54) Subordinate. When you have the power to bring about change you can meet resistance, entangling your horns. It is better to conceal your power and work quietly so you are not forced into danger, even if it appears that you are in an inferior or Subordinate position. Don't force anything but allow events to develop.

Line 4 Power like axle mounts, the fence breaks = remorse disappears, good fortune. Changes to (11) Peace. The persistence of pushing forward and attracting others to your cause leads to success. Obstacles are no match for your inner strength and persistence. Leveraging Great Power with repetitive action allows you to break through what seemed stuck. There are no regrets because you know your course of action is correct. Peace shows how events can begin to flow easily again.

Line 5 Losing the goat while using force = no remorse but not appropriate. Changes to (43) Determination. While trying to change the situation with force you lose what you were seeking. You can't push too hard because the situation may call for a period that allows others to reflect and come to your way of thinking. You may have been out of place with your actions because your idea of how things must happen isn't flexible enough. Rather than have regrets, find a less excessive approach while remaining Determined.

Line 6 A ram butts against the fence and cannot go forward or back away = nothing furthers until the difficulty is identified, then good fortune. Changes to (14) Great Possessing. A different approach is required because what worked in the past has now led you to become stuck. Stop pushing and reflect on the impasse because all further action will only complicate the situation. Compose yourself and allow your inner light to shine with an attitude of abundance and acceptance. What cannot be gained through force may succumb through gentle penetration.

Hexagram #35
Chin (Progress)

Action: Enlighten
Hu Gua (secondary influence) 39 Obstruction: Innovate
Zong Gua: (underlying cause) 5 Nourishment While Waiting: Patience

Received as 2nd Hexagram: A more vigorous approach may be needed.

A foundation without prejudice
is the first step in how the weak progresses.

To regard all things as one,
is to be a companion of Nature. -Chuang Tzu

Reading at a Glance: When a person possesses great power with an ability to sense the seeds of genius in others, expansion is assured. In this way your inner sun or Clarity shines over the earth for others. The secondary influence of Obstruction becomes a lesson in innovation, where obstacles are simply opportunities to learn and grow stronger. The underlying patience developed through Nourishment While Waiting now allows for an opening where you can apply your expanded consciousness. If you are feeling stuck, all that is required is a shift in consciousness since Chin focuses on attitude. The idea of not striving but simply doing is at play. Remove the anxiety and ignite the power of stillness and certainty so you can flow with Tao. You might imagine all sorts of scenarios and outcomes but if your mind is focused on progress and gratitude, the outcome will always be positive. It may be that you accept that whatever happens is always for the best. The idea of innovation is also a cornerstone in this situation. If you explore the many ways that nature achieves innovations through evolution you will see that limitations were its breeding ground for developing strengths. Chin is the image of the sun

245

rising over the earth in expanding brightness and clarity. The morning fog and mists evaporate as you achieve progress through discovering your Tao as a way of illuminating the Tao of others.

Illumination
grows by day.
Innate knowledge
received
as truthfulness.

"Beings do not stay in a state of power. Hence follows progress, which means expansion." To progress without the outward demonstration of force is how you expand outwardly, by activating *'a power that is sufficient'* in any situation. This is true enlightenment.

The master described one of extreme power: *"When a drunken man falls from his carriage, no matter how fast it is traveling, he is never killed. His bones and joints are no different from other men, but because he did not know that he was riding, he does not know that he has fallen out."* Unruffled by the changing scenery, power is not a measure of the force that you exert; it is the measure of your connection to the profound germinating power within. *"Only when you stop trying, will you discover that you are simply doing."* Be natural, that is all.

We tend to measure strength in the same way that we view force. Force moves bodies and is always creating a reaction. If we push on something and cause it to move, we will also be propelled *backward* by the force we have exerted. Strength is the power of the 'weak' or yielding, when energy radiates without force. Force can exhaust energy, but strength grows exponentially.

If you can become yielding, all energy that is no longer wasted in defending yourself against events *out there* fortifies strength *in here*. Becoming supple and strong, you achieve progress.

Strength is not measured in how you overcome others, but in how you overcome yourself. *"Those who master others have force; those who master themselves have strength."* Cultivating inner strength, the weak progresses to unprecedented heights in the image of outward expansion.

Once a pupil of Lao Tzu settled in Wei-lei and hired servants that showed no intelligence and handmaidens who were selfish. The botchy and bloated shared his house; the dithering and fumbling waited upon him. After three years, the crops in Wei-lei began to flourish. The people said, "When he came, we thought him stupidly eccentric but now the day is not long enough to count our blessings." In time, the people wanted to treat him as ruler, but he refused and said: "When the breath of spring comes, the hundred plants begin to grow and during autumn, we harvest its treasure. So long as the Way works unimpeded, spring and autumn cannot fail at their task." He was unaware of the discriminations that the townspeople placed on each other. *"Spring never fails in its task;"* that was all that he observed. Without the need to pass judgment on the things around you, your steadfast virtue and trust in the Way unleashes success where others are crippled by negativity. You tap the seeds of genius in others because you know they are there.

Chin is the image of birds taking flight as the sun begins to rise. It happens naturally, day after day, without great ceremony; *it is what they do.* The spider portrays the proper relationship to life. They build their web and simply wait for life to bring them nourishment. They do not contend with anything, and are unconcerned with what has not landed on their path.

Tiny seeds too, portray the progressive power of the weak that is accomplished through movement in stillness. It is their nature to grow intricate spikes that will attach to the fur of passing animals. Observing the myriad of ways nature achieves reproduction shows a tapestry created without prejudice.

To follow life, you build your foundation by cultivating whatever unique qualities life has given to you. You can then embrace the wondrous things that life brings to nourish your uniqueness. You have the opportunity to bring light to others in their time of darkness. Regardless of the situation, all things are progressing as they should.

Unchanging: Progress unseen = is still progress. Chin unchanging can show a situation that is stable and growing even while you may not see the progress. Much has been developing underground long before the plant opens its leaves to the sun. Because of this germinating work, the situation can be founded upon stronger roots and a higher level of understanding. It may take some time to work out the kinks of ensuring that the goals of everyone are met. What makes the situation difficult is that you have to recognize progress even in the face of opposition. Because of the opposition, the truth is arrived at and therefore, an opening occurs. You just have to trust the process to arrive at progress. Keep nurturing your vision with optimism while you wait.

Line 1 Progressing and turned back but don't lose confidence = no mistake because perseverance brings good fortune. Changes to (21) Biting Through. You seem to be making progress when suddenly you are rebuffed. Perhaps you have not gained the confidence of others or the path is not the right one. Stay calm and persevere anyway with generosity and warmth without frustration or anger. Give the situation time and you will recognize that you will be returned to the proper path. Like a bolt of insight, the obstacle gives you time to look deeper into the situation. Allow others to develop trust in you by remaining kind hearted. This enables you to achieve your desire.

Line 2 Progressing through sorrow, perseverance brings good fortune = one is favored by the Queen Mother. Changes to (64) Before Completion. The path seems difficult because of a lack of communication. This can lead to sadness but great growth is achieved so persevere because there is a last step to be taken toward Completion. Approaching with sensitivity and feeling leads to happiness because others open. The lack of selfish aims leads to mutual attraction. Great insight achieved through suffering.

Line 3 All are in accord = remorse disappears. Changes to (56) Wanderer. Previous disagreements or misunderstandings are cleared up through clarification. You need others to succeed in your aims and shouldn't act independently. You are able to gain the support of others to achieve a cooperative advance. The Wanderer is a message about the need to respect others because you depend on them. It suggests how 'absence makes the heart grow fonder.'

Line 4 Progress like a squirrel = perseverance brings danger. Changes to (23) Split Apart. You don't have the necessary skills to accomplish something in this situation. If you try to push forward with questionable means you will not succeed. Additionally, your ethics will be in question. There can be manipulative tendencies associated with the situation so step back and identify what is wrong with it. You may be getting into something over your head in an effort to keep the situation from Splitting Apart.

Line 5 Remorse disappears without thought of gain or loss = undertakings bring good fortune and everything furthers. Changes to (12) Obstruction. While you may be focused on what is gained or lost as you meet Obstruction, don't worry because everything will work out. There is something more fundamental of value than appearances. Make a commitment to remain gentle and reserved without thought of failure or success.

Line 6 Progressing using horns is beneficial but presents danger =, no blame although perseverance in aggression will lead to humiliation. Changes to (16) Enthusiasm. There is a careful balance of how much force is needed in this situation. You may think you need to apply punishment but if you push too hard, it will be you who is humiliated. It may be that you need to curb your own power and be Enthusiastic rather than alienating others by pushing them too hard.

Hexagram #36
Ming Yi (Brightness Hiding)

Action: Reignite
Hu Gua (secondary influence) 40 Liberation: Untangle
Zong Gua: (underlying cause) 6 Conflict: Let Go
Received as 2nd Hexagram: Don't sweep issues under the rug, but don't allow obstacles to break your spirit. Difficulty is simply testing your sincerity.

When the world grows dark,
your inner light is given definition.

I prefer winter and fall, when you feel the bone structure of
the landscape,
the loneliness of it – the dead feeling of winter.
Something waits beneath it – the whole story doesn't show. –
Andrew Wyeth

Reading at a Glance: Ming Yi is often associated with
castigation or feeling that you are being misunderstood.
You've made great progress up to now and might have
been enthusiastic, but for whatever reason, the walls
have begun to close you in. Others are not speaking
your language and often, Ming Yi is associated with the
dark night of the soul. In Taoism there is no such thing
as punishment or retribution. Nature merely seeks to
turn something back when it is in excess. There is
always a balance of traveling inward and outward
according to fixed rhythms. This is not the time to begin
anything new or to continue pushing forward. The only
way your inner light can be kept burning, is if you turn
within and stoke the flame. The secondary influence of
Liberation promises that relief is in sight. The situation
may have become entangled or your actions have
moved toward embroiling. This is what happens when
emotion and illusion override stillness and strength.
The Zong Gua of Conflict "out there" has now led to a
period of examining the root of conflict "in here." You
have a period to understand the beliefs you defend to
yourself. This can be an extremely illuminating period
but it doesn't come without a little soul searching and
perhaps loneliness. Like winter, much needs to grow
under the cover of darkness before it is strong enough
to return to progress in the outer world. For the time

being Clarity has been wounded or obscured. Often we are initiated into the hero's journey of individuation when the ego has been wounded. Whatever comes during this time should not be viewed negatively. Once this period passes you will have a stronger sense of Clarity about who you are and where you belong. Brightness Hiding is a message to keep your own counsel while you go through a difficult change or transformation.

This light
that shines
in darkness:
it cannot be concealed;
it illuminates the eyes.

"Expansion will certainly meet with resistance. Therefore follows the darkening of the light." As the Clinging Fire sinks below the Receptive Earth, Ming Yi is the image of being forced to operate in darkness. Like the time of winter, the situation requires that you turn within to stoke your inner fire.

Even while you are growing in power, you still experience the friction or life's natural tension that keeps all things evolving. If this power is real, it will endure.

The master said: *"Face adversity as if life is asking you a question 'is it real?' as it tests the sincerity of what you are doing. You may answer: 'yes…it is good…it is real, and nothing can threaten it.' If this is true, it will endure. In this, 'the way that is bright seems dark.'"* Darkness gives definition to brightness and since sincerity aligns with intent or Clarity *'that which is bright rises twice."*

Regardless of the circumstances, your inner light is cultivated so that it may shine upon your footsteps. Keeping the fire of Te burning, Brightness Hiding is an image of the sun and moon, and a threat by an archer, who is no match for these great luminaries. The sun is your inner light and clarity, while the moon represents how it reflects upon experience. Although the light may appear dim outwardly during darkness, it still burns brightly within like the sun below the earth.

What you cultivate grows like a seed beneath the soil of this inner light. *"We tend to hide what we dislike about ourselves and display the beautiful. In this way, what is good is put on parade and wasted, while we nurture and hold tightly to what is ugly."* Outwardly searching for acceptance and appreciation will lead you to become a mere reflection of what you believe the world expects of you. Instead of the flowering of your beautiful nature, a weed takes root within and grows.

"One that is born beautiful and not given a mirror or told of their beauty will not know that they are more beautiful than others. Beauty will simply be a part of their nature. What happens of its own accord is like the leader who simply loves the people. Without fame or being told of their graces, love is their nature. We do not hide away in the woods and hills. What we hide is our Te. One can interact with the world without losing the self."

When the environment grows dark, the sun is reflected by the moon. It captures the sunlight which remains hidden below the earth but always remains bright. Sometimes, the light within can only be revealed in contrast to the darkening of the light outside. Movement in stillness is how you stoke your inner fire, regardless of the changes. Veiling the light becomes an image of protecting your vital force and keeping it sacred.

If others are not supporting you, don't take it personal. Often people are simply jealous and want to knock you down a peg or too. That is why it is important to hide your light. Stoke the fire of certainty and keep your strength fortified. Soon you will have the opportunity to make your debut and return to the light.

Unchanging: In the depths of darkness = sunrise is coming. The greatest gift you can give yourself is your inner light that shines regardless of the weather outside. Sometimes you hide your light in somebody else's pocket, hoping one day they'll discover you when doing the laundry and pat you on the head. Sometimes you hide it the pot of gold at the end of the rainbow if you can just find that one thing that eludes you. You hide it in cookie jars and at the bottom of a pint of ice cream. You hide it in the valley and bury it with moss so nobody discovers you are hiding. The obscurity of your brightness is not serving anyone because you have misplaced the reason for your existence. You are not a victim and life is eagerly awaiting your sunrise. If you don't let the real you shine, how can life reinforce your goodness? Only you know what it means to be fearlessly yourself but you need to look within to discover who you are. This is a lesson life continuously teaches because you are one of its unique variations and it celebrates your Liberation. Open to whatever you are so afraid of because there is no longer any reason to hide. Brightness Hiding unchanging suggests that whatever is unfolding is allowing you to tap this inner light and knowing. Without taking time to connect with your inner world you may continue to experience conflict around you. This hexagram can come when sharing your wisdom for the benefit of others without needing to focus on what you get in return.

Line 1 Darkening light during flight and lowering wings = fasting and wandering among those who gossip. Changes to (15) Authenticity. At the first sign of difficulty it is natural to seek advice from others, but how can anyone tell you who you are? This was the reason you chose a different path; because what you experienced did not resonate as truth for you. Flying under the radar is necessary because others may not understand what you are doing and why. If you are in a subordinate position, watch your step so you don't outshine a superior. This line can show the beginning of difficulty and a bit of mis-stepping where neediness can make you lost to yourself . Being humble and moderate is the best course of action, but be authentic. Don't fly too high just yet, it is better to lower your wings and hide your light.

Line 2 Darkening of light injures left thigh = strength in aiding others like a horse. Changes to (11) Peace. A sense of being injured does not stop you from proceeding because you are inspired to share what you learn to carry others in their times of darkness. You have the good fortune that comes from turning adversity into an opportunity to learn. The wound to the thigh is like Chiron of Astrology, who is half horse/half man. He is honored as the greatest healer even while he is injured. The 'flow' suggested by Peace shows how we forget our suffering when in the service of others and are therefore healed ourselves.

Line 3 Hunting the darkening of the light the enemy leader is captured = perseverance after a period of waiting. Changes to (24) Return. While you hunt for the cause of your suffering you capture the enemy in your sights. However, can another possibly hold the power to change what your life looks and feels like? Your life is your own. Because of the difficulties that you face, you have time as a gift to re-connect with the foundation of who you are and to become empowered. The period calls for a period of patience where you will discover that what you can't change 'out there' is a source of great enlightenment. Don't hurry the time because it is spaced in a way that allows for the echo of your sincerity.

Line 4 Darkening of the light in the left belly revealing the very heart of the matter = one goes beyond the gate. Changes to (55) Abundance. If you are fearless enough to face the fact that you are not a victim but the

257

orchestrator of your destiny, you might encounter your own darkness and transform it into light. While you may feel that you have uncovered the source of darkness in another and are prepared to run, the situation just may be opening you to your own internal prison. However, the situation may offer more transformative pain than you are ready to face. You choose whether you own the power or give it away. At some point on your journey you will need to face the inner wound and heal, why not now?

Line 5 Darkening of the light like the Prince Chi = perseverance furthers. Changes to (63) After Completion. Prince Chi had to feign insanity during his imprisonment by the evil tyrant Chou Hsin. The light is alive within you but you may need to shelter it from those who would wish to exterminate your flame. In this case the goal of enlightenment is achieved as you learn to watch the signs and continue the work of keeping your inspiration burning. The time will come for success because you do not allow oppression to exhaust you and tap it to make your light shine even brighter.

Line 6 First light then darkness = sometimes we climb to heaven and fall to the earth. Changes to (22) Grace. The threat we face during enlightenment is in believing this is a destination. We forget that it is a constant perspective of openness. We are always rising in inspiration and falling back to reality when our spiritual longing or emotional extremes become burdens. The highest form of Darkening of the Light comes when we see light and dark as merely hues that give life depth and dimension. Enlightenment comes when we move beyond judgments of good and bad. From an earthly perspective, we cannot understand heaven's flow of spiritual enlightenment and it can feel like the sky is falling. Too much of the spiritual and we come to fight the flow of what we learn on the earth so we lose our home. It is better to walk the middle path of openness and become a guest of the Great Unfolding. Uncover your Shadow as power. Stop judging so that you are not judged. You are here now and whether awake or sleeping, you are learning. The way of Grace is constantly revealed to those without preconceptions. In this way darkness is no longer hidden. Life goes up and down only in proportion to what you cling to. On the middle path life is always unfolding perfectly.

Hexagram #37
Chia Jen (Family)

Action: Support
Hu Gua (secondary influence) 64 Before Completion: Prepare
Zong Gua: (underlying cause) 40 Liberation: Untangle

Received as 2nd Hexagram: The situation requires the same sacrifices and clearly defined roles as are found in the family.

In the contrast of your differences,
life reveals your deepest color.

To put the family in order, we must cultivate our personal life;
and to cultivate our personal life, we must first set our hearts right. —Kung fu tzu

Reading at a Glance: When facing any type of difficulty, returning to the family allows us to feel unconditional love and acceptance. Sometimes the family is nothing more than the circle of friends who 'get us' and offer unconditional support. When we return to a place in which we relax into our authenticity, we discover that part of us that is unchanging over time. Perhaps a period of battles must give way to a period of rest and sharing meals with loved ones. The Judgment says it is the care of the woman that brings good fortune. Men and women alike must nurture their sensitivity and need for comfort. When all the people sharing a household understand their roles the family thrives. When all the characters and aspects of the psyche are functioning without repression, the individual thrives. However, just as evolution ensures that each offspring is a unique variation of the strengths and weaknesses of the parent our siblings will not be like us. This means that the family will not be without some stresses of non compatibility. Accept your differences with gratitude because the family is a perfect place to see your real face in their mirror. The wind excites the flame and we see the hearth fire stoking one's individual nature. The secondary influence of Before Completion also underscores the idea of incompletion even in what appears to be a safe environment. The home can be any structure where each individual is supported in their unique needs. While it remains a platform for growth, it is a home. When it becomes a prison the walls will never hold us. The Zong Gua is Liberation which is something that sets us free. Therefore, while the family of any type including work and friendships creates a communal space we must never forget that life will continue to prod our authenticity forward. Only when our heart is right can we enjoy the communal space we share with others. We fall into our roles because of our strengths and gifts, not because of other's expectations.

> *You seek a haven*
> *and find a stone.*
> *But the stone will shape you*
> *of your own likeness.*

"During times of adversity, we turn back to the family." The Gentle Wind stirs above the Clinging Fire, fanning it and sustaining illumination. Chia Jen is the hearth fire, kept burning during times of trouble. It is a place where we find safety and nourishment during difficult times.

"The perseverance of the woman furthers," the master said. *"Know the male, but keep to the role of the female and be a*

261

valley to the empire." Where the father may inspire children toward conformity and placement in society, the mother recognizes a child's uniqueness and loves them unconditionally.

The Clinging Fire reveals how you are shaped by the family in this way. Within this small circle, you can observe your character active in the larger aspect of society. You may think you are only different in family dynamics, but this is not true. Heat creates energy. The Wind stirs it up and is excited by it. The truthfulness of the family circle simply has a way of activating dynamics *more quickly.*

All things that your family holds sacred endure for you throughout life. Chia Jen is the image of a pig and a dog, protected under a dwelling, while someone prays. The pig represents what you value while the dog is your faithfulness. Even as the Winds of experience continue to shape your character, the root of your inner light emerged when you were young. Chia Jen suggests the dwelling, which protects all that you hold sacred.

Natural selection drives divergence in character traits because the more diversified we are, the better will be our chance for survival. Even among family members within a particular species, each are endowed with variations. This ensures that competition for short supply in a shared environment is always minimized.

The master said: *"There is no greater joy than to examine oneself and be sincere."* There is no other pathway than to cultivate what is real for you. You often seek encouragement from the family and do not find it. You believe that they will provide a haven and instead, they offer a stone. Yet, this stone becomes your gift, because it will shape you in your own likeness.

The family can be a source of support, even while their dynamics shape you in the same way that the wind carves a mountain. In the contrast of your differences, they often reveal your deepest color. You stand in the present as life's best example of *one variation* of the line you carry forward. As the Wind and the Flame glow brightest near the hearth, you will discover just how unique you are.

As a message about supporting others in a team dynamic, open communication is necessary. Everyone should understand the role they play and each should be encouraged to achieve their highest potential.

Unchanging: Establish structures = define roles. Chia Jen unchanging shows the illumination of Clarity rising from careful penetration. As we move from neediness, we discover what we are seeking is actually our unique gift to give. Establishing structure and defining roles may be the key in ensuring a situation remains stable. Without ground rules in the communal space, it loses its effectiveness in ensuring all parties are supported. Liberation is only a response when a situation becomes like a prison. Since the hexagram is unchanging it can indicate that the situation has or will achieve this stability as long as everyone is free to have their needs met. If stability is lacking, a return to being more receptive and offering support is required.

Line 1 Firm seclusion within the family = remorse disappears. Changes to (53) Development. When forming relationships with others there is a need to define roles so that each understands what is expected. In this way we offset conflict, confusion and arguments because the ground rules are established in the beginning. This Gradual Development of expectations and observances is required when union of any type is being considered.

Line 2 Constancy in providing nourishment = perseverance brings good fortune. Changes to (9) Small Restraint. Gentle submissiveness in fulfilling the basic needs of the group prior to establishing larger goals brings good fortune. It may be necessary to not step outside the bounds of propriety in the situation. Before the group can achieve its higher aims, its most basic needs must be addressed. If the foundation isn't created at a basic level, the welfare of all suffers.

Line 3 Deliberating punishment or over obliging is exhausting = good fortune nonetheless. Changes to (42) Increase. In close quarters dynamics can turn into the exhaustion of real growth when the focus is based on judgments and expectations. Sweeping issues under the rug or being overly bearing leads to distress. If you can transform any conversation that begins with 'I want' or 'you should' to 'we can both benefit if..' the relationship prospers.

Line 4 Providing care for all = good fortune. Changes to (13) Fellowship. Family and Fellowship are both aspects of a relationship that transcends emotional neediness. Both focus on how people best interact by fulfilling roles while finding support at the same time. Working toward common goals is the only way good fortune manifests for all.

Line 5 The sovereign corrects deficiencies = a tough beginning but a good end. Changes to (22) Grace. Nature corrects deficiencies without extremes and shows no favoritism. Because the one who guides the gathering can be trusted, all prosper. While there are things that at first appear out of place, the situation has the proper foundation for successful union. Just as Grace shows its benevolence over time, the relationship is one of mutual care and support. When deficiencies are transformed the beginning can be tough but it leads to greater fulfillment for all.

Line 6 Relationship founded on mutual respect = in the end comes good fortune. Changes to (63) After Completion. If you lead others by example, everyone does their part and the entire team prospers because nothing artificial exists. A relationship will always be a reflection of your inner world. When you have done the work in achieving authenticity and are complete in yourself, respect leads to good fortune. Your heart and mind reflect sincerity and it shows itself to others. You remain in contact with those you respect and your call to join is well received. There is a house and the people are happy living in it.

Hexagram #38
K'uei (Opposition)

Action: Accommodate
Hu Gua (secondary influence) 63 After Completion: Renew
Zong Gua: (underlying cause) 39 Obstruction: Innovate
Received as 2nd Hexagram: Opposition doesn't mean giving up; you may need to consider a win/win solution.

**Life's natural friction is the force
that shapes your individuality.**

*He that wrestles with us strengthens our nerve,
and sharpens our skill. Our antagonist is our helper. –
Edmund Burke*

Reading at a Glance: When Clarity is rising over the Joyous Lake we see fire and water which can extinguish each other through interaction, thus they remain apart in the image of Opposition. To make matters worse, Fire burns upward while Water flows downward so any flowing connection has been lost. Opposition shows a situation where people are not seeing events from the same perspective. This mutual alienation reveals how an impasse can stop union. Nothing major can be accomplished because the situation is one in which all must acknowledge their unique natures while arriving at accommodation. Unlike Obstruction as the Zong Gua where the innovation of change and merging of unique qualities leads to growth, in K'uei the incompatibilities are actually given greater definition so that Clarity and Joy can be mutually strengthened in all. People are drawn together who might be incompatible in every way and yet, nature uses polarities to deepen individual definition. We join groups because of the way we are similar but discover who we really are in the ways that we are different. Union should not come at the expense of giving up your individuality. Because stagnation never endures in nature, there will be a meeting of the minds but it must come without concession. A good example can be found during courtship where we struggle to change some opposing or strange quality in another only to discover this characteristic is exactly what endears us to them. Opposition is a fertile breeding ground for creative transformation because we stop attempting to make our way the only way. When we can accept that there are many expressions of the right way, polarity gives way to a condition where Clarity can illuminate Joy.

Therefore, honor

267

the evolutionary tension
that keeps
all of life evolving.

"In family gatherings, we find that misunderstandings arise from habitual behavior, thus we see the principle of opposition." Habitual behavior can lead to stagnation, while nature appears to work against this tendency. Your conditioning can best be observed in family dynamics where you can see a snapshot of the defensive tendencies that you carry forward in life. Regardless of the opposition, life gives definition by bringing opposites together.

K'uei is the movement in stillness that allows you to observe what happens when opposites meet. It is not the pleasant exchanges that you remember, but the unpleasant ones that can stay with you for days, months and years. While you may cherish the times of harmony, it is through difficulty that real growth occurs. Even when someone seems to be challenging you, they are also helping you to further define your individuality. Opposition further defines your strength.

When you can move beyond the idea that the world is a place of polarities, you will begin to see opposition as life's movement toward a higher unity. The Clinging Flame burns above the Joyous Lake as an image of clarity being reflected upon the vicissitudes of experience. Nature explores variety and change through contrast; at the same time, it achieves harmony by releasing accumulating energy in the bound up things that crash together.

In the natural world, opposition is the universal face of changing phenomena. When you open to its creative and regenerative pull, you discover life's pursuit of novelty, not its polarities. At all levels of life, friction always releases and disperses energy.

The master said: *"opposition is a prerequisite for union."* Two people who would prefer to sweep issues under the carpet will never discover *authentic* union. Confucius taught that opposites are merely two different aspects of a higher unity.

While we clash, we identify our differences that give form to our unique qualities. As we bridge our differences, we honor our separate wills and move toward a common purpose. Through this blending of wills, a higher unity takes form. Yet, this transformation could not take form without the diverging energy that is released through friction. Any type of union requires that we not sacrifice our individuality.

In the species, when the masculine and feminine meet, there is reproduction. Opposite elements that retain their unique nature in coming together, eventually sharpen and define each other's individuality. In life's movement toward contrast, whatever is dormant is excited to the surface to be applied for productive use.

Unchanging: Show your real face = judging others makes one feel judged. K'uei unchanging can be a message about holding to your vision or unique nature in the face of strong opposition. Circumstances can make you wonder if you are crazy or missing something but your unique perspective and authentic nature should not be sacrificed for union. We often feel more severely judged when we are judging others. If we can celebrate the joyful quirkyness in others, we are more fearless in expressing our eccentricities. The situation can only thrive if everyone is allowed to be themselves. Perhaps the opposition you feel has roots in your own judgment of others. A change in mindset can work miracles in transforming a tapestry of conflict or opposition. Acceptance and a lack of prejudice gives way to tolerance. Eventually tolerance opens us in a way that we learn something new and therefore open to joyous discovery. If you are meeting with unchanging Opposition you need only become accepting of other's points of view.

Line 1 A lost horse returns of its own accord, contention in another is best examined within = remorse disappears. Changes to (64) Before Completion. Since Opposition is a lesson of honoring differences, don't attempt to chase or change another. Accepting those for who they are can attract their return. In meeting contention one always does well to examine one's prejudices and judgments. To cross to the other side of Opposition requires that you honor differences while staying true to oneself. You need only go half way, so don't sacrifice your uniqueness.

Line 2 One meets the master in the street = no blame. Changes to (21) Biting Through. Life brings us together propitiously to meet those who can teach us something about our own hidden nature. Those who push our buttons the most are often our teachers. Our meetings with these types of teachers are never accidental. This line carries the essence of Kung fu tzu's comment: "when meeting contention in another, we would do well to examine the self." The attraction leads one to discover deeper knowledge about the self. In a relationship there can be a deep affinity but not an easy way for it to achieve expression. Allow the situation to teach you what it is attempting to become.

Line 3 Wagon and oxen halted while one's hair and nose are cut off = not a good beginning but a good end. Changes to (14) Great Possessing. Sometimes the truth can be humiliating and the way forward is blocked until we learn the valuable lesson about 'what is'. In dreams cutting the hair is releasing ideas while cutting the nose removes our intuitive ability to sniff things out. The challenge in the situation is to recognize how past ideas or misconceptions need to be released without abandoning one's individual integrity or intuition. Great Possessing can only be achieved through openness and honoring different perspectives and needs. Although the situation has an uncomfortable start, enlightenment is assured even though the union and forward movement is difficult.

Line 4 Isolated and alone one meets an associate = high risk but no blame. Changes to (41) Decrease. While the situation creates isolation, you find someone in which you share an intimate connection and affinity. The isolation or opposition was necessary to open you to this new connection which can lead to great accomplishment.

Line 5 A companion discovered behind the wrappings of an enemy = to join them is not a mistake. Changes to (10) Treading. We meet someone who initially appears like an enemy or completely opposed to our expectations. Like all Shadow work or stepping on the tiger's tail of Treading, if we stop projecting the past and look deeper at the reason we meet those we do, we discover that often our enemies become our best friends. The quality that attracts and binds is holding integrity and individuality above all else. Your similarities are hidden but once the defensive wrappings come off, there is great shared affinity.

Line 6 Isolated, one sees companions as pigs and devils, drawing the bow and then laying it aside = there are no enemies only love. After the rain all rejoice. Changes to (54) Propriety. Disagreements may cause you to look unfavorably upon others but misunderstandings are resolved. The steps to union can only be achieved by allowing uniqueness, opposition and then acceptance to flow in its natural cycle, like rain. Authenticity is not sacrificed so that deeper affection can grow. Opposition revealed differences that are now appreciated for what they are, and thus good fortune.

Hexagram #39
Jian (Obstruction)

Action: Innovate

Hu Gua (secondary influence) 64 Before Completion:
Prepare

Zong Gua: (underlying cause) 38 Opposition:
Accommodate

Received as 2nd Hexagram: Before you can proceed
you need to honor the obstacle for what it is teaching
you.

**Adversity is how life
unleashes your excellence from within.**

*You cannot teach a man anything;
you can only help him to find it within. – Galileo*

Reading at a Glance: Jian is composed of the Mountain
and the danger presented by the Abysmal. Keeping Still
on the Mountain doesn't mean wisdom and
enlightenment are a destination or a place to hide from
life. Enlightenment is a perspective of openness as the
world changes around us. Also, the path ahead will
always pose threats and dangers so it does no good to

believe that conflict or difficulty can come to an end. Conflict is the driving force of change and how you approach it determines your success. The secondary influence of Before Completion also suggests a similar message. Obstruction suggests preparing in advance for Innovations. The Zong Gua of Opposition revealed how diversity and uniqueness were kept intact during union. In Jian we must bring diverging energies together so that both are transformed. In a world that is not stagnant and always growing, evolution is the rule. Regardless of the Obstruction it has come to teach you about a new approach or a new perspective. The image of someone limping with cold feet reveals how we fall out of circulation with the path or the constant flow of change. We may have a sense of danger and get cold feet, but the feet only grow cold because we stop moving. Sometimes the Obstruction is in the mindset and Keeping Still to observe what events are revealing, you can see the situation differently. Sometimes the Obstruction is on the path because we have wandered away from ourselves. During a time of Obstruction the only real blockage is an unwillingness to change. Anything that comes to block your progress is simply life's pursuit of a better way. Yes, circumstances may be frighteningly unfamiliar, but there is also great promise of excitement as the old way transforms into a new way.

Danger, opportunity
and the cracking of ice.
This path
of closed eyes -
fulfillment falls like rain.

"Through opposition, difficulties arise in the form of obstruction." Behind you is the Mountain of Keeping Still while ahead of you is the Abysmal Water. Without delving below the unknown aspects of this situation, you cannot proceed.

Opposition is the universal face of change. It leads to innovation and harmony, although union will eventually give way to renewal. Life brings elements together to explore a higher unity, but in time, it also comes to separate what leads to stagnation.

Whether in your personal or professional life, all that appears to block your forward progress is life's pursuit of a better way. You can curse circumstances and apply your will in a futile attempt to ward off change. On the other hand, you can allow the obstruction to reveal how you might achieve movement in *more innovative ways*. If you want to get across the Water, you must explore a new way of doing so. Like anything else in the natural world, the path of your evolution is only limited by your unwillingness to move with the changing time.

"Acting from knowledge of the constant, keeps one impartial;" you meet with no difficulty because you do

not see it as such. You can observe a world that is becoming, where everything must become stronger. Adversity is simply how life unleashes your excellence from within: something 'out there' will make you grow 'in here.'

You may encounter difficulty, although by remaining still, you will discover the 'new way' where the obstacle becomes an opportunity to expand. *"Obstruction means difficulty. The danger is ahead. To see the danger and know how to stand still, that is wisdom."*

Keeping Still, the obstacle is transforming and you need only learn to see it differently. Jian portrays someone limping, where cold feet have impeded circulation. Cold feet suggest fear and impeding circulation indicates that something is causing a blockage to the natural flow. Rather than flailing about in the waters of stagnation, allow the current to lead you.

The master said: *"The path that leads one to encounter further obstruction becomes the only danger."* Obstruction is always a clue that change is necessary. You may be limping along a path of extreme resistance, when a different route might be more appropriate and *easier.*

Like the Chinese image of crisis, which combines danger with opportunity, there is always the danger of continuing, or the opportunity to change direction. You may perceive obstruction as a barrier to your forward progress, but it is also an opportunity to regenerate your ability to climb higher.

In Jian, wisdom rises from stillness and the obstruction leads you away from the path of danger. It is only dangerous because it is unnatural to believe that anything can withstand the forces of change. In this situation, you will discover why *"those who go against the Way meet with constant difficulty."*

You can change direction, do what is expected of you, or become still to explore if proceeding on your chosen pathway is correct. If the path before you remains blocked, seek the help of someone knowledgeable enough to guide you.

Unchanging: Obstructions that paralyze = movement is necessary. Because the Mountain of Keeping Still refers to a mindset and Difficulty as the Abysmal remains unchanging before you, the Obstruction you face is something that can't be changed until you change the way you approach it. Chances are the Obstruction is specifically appearing insurmountable because it isn't real. In nature Obstruction gives way with time, but if time hasn't loosened it, this is all the more reason to turn within and examine how your thoughts are the only real Obstruction. Is the path a correct one? Is your own fear operative as Obstruction? You can remain frustrated or step back and see what the Obstruction can teach you about yourself.

Line 1 Going leads to obstruction = coming meets with praise. Changes to (63) After Completion. The difference between going and coming is expectation. Coming feels like an invitation where going can be associated with fear, assumptions, escape and sadness. After Completion suggests knowing the cycles and how to wait for the proper time to advance. In this way Obstruction is a timing indicator showing that the time is not right. When meeting obstruction invite dialogue without being defensive. Your willingness to see all sides of a misunderstanding meets with praise.

Line 2 The king's servant is beset with obstruction = it is not his fault. Changes to (48) The Well. The Obstruction is a perfect opportunity to pull deeper from your inner resources which couldn't have happened otherwise. It may seem like there is no choice in the matter but to confront the obstruction head on. The situation is not easy but the cause is greater than just personal ends and your integrity is at stake.

Line 3 Going leads to obstruction = therefore one comes back. Changes to (8) Union. You may need to wait to see if the situation will reverse itself because pushing forward is futile. Coming back allows those who depend on you to recognize their value in your life. Use this time to fortify unions and alliances. Revisit the goal to see if a change in strategy might allow for advancement.

Line 4 Going leads to obstruction = coming leads to union. Changes to (31) Influence/Wooing. Going leads to obstruction while coming back brings union. The idea of Wooing is how we attract people because of who we are not by chasing or selling ourselves. Going through difficulty shifts something within that allows others to recognize it is good to follow you. Perhaps you realize the importance of a relationship because of the threat of loss.

Line 5 In the midst of the biggest obstructions = friends arrive. Changes to (15) Authenticity. It is normal to feel alone when first pioneering change. Often others don't understand why you would change the status quo. The closer you come to success, the more it seems opposition and competition become overwhelming. Because others begin to see the importance of what you are building they come to your aid. Getting to this point may have been the greatest challenge you have ever faced but once helpers and supporters rally to your cause the way forward moves towards a successful outcome. It you need help, don't be too proud to ask for it.

Line 6 Going leads to obstruction, coming leads to good fortune = it furthers one to see the great one. Changes to (53) Development. The master said: *"When great responsibility is about to befall one, life appears to confound all undertakings. Thereby it stimulates the mind, toughens the nature and improves all deficiencies."* By proving one's tenacity in the face of Obstruction one becomes a vessel for distinguished service. You have the choice to give up or to become the great one. By joining forces or examining what is working for someone else you may find a solution to any difficulties.

Hexagram #40
Jie (Liberation)

Action: Untangle

Hu Gua (secondary influence) 63 After Completion: Renew

Zong Gua: (underlying cause) 37 Family: Support

Received as 2nd Hexagram: Forgiveness allows you to untangle your neediness so all parties can find the freedom to be.

**There is no real difficulty
that requires outward movement.**

*Within yourself deliverance must be searched for,
because each man makes his own prison. –Sir Edwin Arnold*

Reading at a Glance: Thunder over the Abysmal water shows a sudden storm meant to release tension. This type of natural phenomena happens when the leaves need to be removed from the trees during autumn and again when the protective husks sheltering spring's rebirth are also removed. In either case something is being loosened so that rebirth is Liberated. Whatever is blocking your ability to move effortlessly and joyfully through the world of events will be no match for the situations that unfold to help you let go. The secondary influence of After Completion also underscores a need for renewal. The Zong Gua of Family suggested a time of nurturing and protection. Defensive ideas meant to protect anger or a lifestyle of hiding will be brought out into the open so that you can find Deliverance from yourself. Forgiveness is not something we offer others but something which leads to our freedom. The upper trigram of Arousing hits like a bolt out of the blue to lead us from the Abysmal danger. Whatever is transpiring will bring renewal and calm to the inner landscape. It is important that you return to a place of calm and renewal. Jie releases tension and stress and is a time of letting go so that you don't drown in your own quagmire of negativity.

> *To arrive -*
> *return*
> *without going.*
> *Find the medicine*
> *of forgiveness.*

"Things cannot remain permanently obstructed, therefore follows deliverance and the release of tension." The Arousing Thunder stirs over the Abysmal Water presenting the idea of a sudden storm, which relieves atmospheric pressure.

Jie is the image of a sharp instrument, which loosens knots. You can be *"worn and newly made,"* when you release the unproductive energy that remains connected to anger. Anger becomes a stone upon the measure of tomorrow; if you cannot let something go, you are forced to carry it with you. Jie is another principle of movement in stillness, where you can find deliverance in the liberation that comes from releasing your hold on the past. In the case of forgiveness, you give nothing away, that you really needed anyway.

By holding onto anger, it becomes your burden and dissipates as unproductive energy. *"There is no real difficulty that requires outward movement."* All of the principles of movement in stillness teach how there is no real difficulty that requires action 'out there,' only a shift of awareness 'in here.' It is said that change only happens when the pain of holding on is greater than the fear of letting go.

Through forgiveness, you can move freely, unhampered by unnecessary baggage. This is how anger becomes a shackle on the pathway of your freedom. Liberation is how life moves to free us - even when we unwittingly become stuck in complicated dynamics.

As clouds gather, electricity generates moisture, and you can feel the unproductive heaviness accumulating in the air. The ensuing storm releases the tension and cleanses the earth, where all things can breathe freely again.

Forgiveness releases you from the burden that keeps you a prisoner to the past. *"When Thunder and rain set in, the seed pods of all fruits, plants, and trees break open."* The deliverance that comes from pardoning mistakes and forgiving misdeeds, allows new life to flourish. Whatever the storm, it has the sole purpose of ensuring wellness below.

Unchanging: Abundance or scarcity = you create your world from the inside out. In its unchanging form you may be so stuck in your own negativity and anger that you don't realize the life of scarcity you are creating for yourself. Any type of behavior or addiction that is unhealthy must be released so that you can return to abundance and optimism. Events on the outside continually challenge us to let go and find the freedom to open within. If your own mental energy is consuming your attention in a negative way, events will continue to challenge you until you let go. You think life is pushing back against you but it is pushing you out of your prison. This is the way of nature as it seeks growth and freedom at every level. Liberation unchanging can show a major breakthrough or release of what had previously been a strong barrier.

Line 1 Without blame = there is no error. Changes to (54) Propriety. In the course of human affairs Propriety is how we judge whether something is correct or not. However, seeing something as wrong when it isn't can lead to disagreements. No error has occurred and nobody is to blame. Let it go and return a sense of freedom of movement to the situation.

Line 2 Killing three foxes and receiving a yellow arrow = perseverance brings good fortune. Changes to (16) Enthusiasm. Deceptive obstacles appear and your suspicions need to be investigated as truth or illusion. The yellow arrow is discernment and you must uncover the truth so that you can clear the way and succeed. You may be using force in an innocent situation because your Enthusiasm has run away with you. If others are not demonstrating the same level of integrity as you, it may be wise to move on.

Line 3 Carrying a burden and riding encourages robbers = perseverance leads to humiliation. Changes to (32) Duration. It is difficult to move forward freely if you are holding onto ideas meant to protect your ideas of the past. A mindset of defensiveness leads one on a road of many battles. An attitude of haughtiness invites others to knock you off your perch. Life is what you make of it so you can either be in the present or allow a bag full of weapons to make every moment an improper response to the situation in front of you.

Line 4 Deliver yourself from your big toe and the companion will come = it is someone you can trust. Changes to (7) Army. The big toe can relate to the need to always put your foot down or behave defensively as suggested by Army. If you release any attitude of mistrust you will find companionship. While you may feel the need to be wary of persons or situations, there is no need. Lao tzu said: "if one doesn't trust how can they be trusted?"

284

Line 5 Delivering yourself from yourself brings good fortune = you prove your earnestness. Changes to (47) Oppression/Exhaustion. If you can release yourself from the ideas that are binding you to an agitated outlook and the distrust of others, you will find liberation from yourself. An attitude of defensiveness will always attract you to situations that seem Oppressive as life mirrors your mindset. Earnestness is how you show depth and sincerity. If you believe others aren't sincere it may be because you aren't being sincere. Clear your mind of negativity.

Line 6 Shooting the hawk on the high wall, killing it = everything serves to further. Changes to (64) Before Completion. Kung fu tzu saw the hawk as the promoter of rebellion or undisciplined and dangerous thinking. By eliminating this defensive guardian from the high walls that serve to protect you from intimacy – the way becomes open for more joy in your life. To resolve difficulty begin with your own ideas.

Hexagram #41
Sun (Decrease)

Action: Evaluate

Hu Gua (secondary influence) 24 Return: Go Back

Zong Gua: (underlying cause) 31 Influence: Woo

Received as 2nd Hexagram: Regardless of the importance you have put on the past, whatever is lost allows for greater authenticity.

What is unobservable in this world
is gestating in unseen form.

For everything you have missed, you have gained something else;
and for everything you gain, you lose something else. –
Emerson

Reading at a Glance: It is said that Tao appears to move backward. Life moves inward and outward in fixed rhythms and it is time to turn back and evaluate. There is a period a flowering followed by decline although what appears to be turning back is really turning inward as life continues to move forward. Decrease is the only way to Increase because what is full cannot be filled anew. The Zong Gua of Influence revealed a time focused on the world around us. However, the secondary influence shows this to be a time for Return, gestating, planning or turning inward. Trees are made stronger through pruning where over watering a plant would kill it. Decrease can still be a principle of growth even when the message is to do less or remove. You may need to cut back on one area of your life in order to direct more energy toward another. The message of Decrease suggests finding strength by removing the superfluous. Sun is the image of offering something freely in a ceremonial vessel to make a sacrifice in some way. Amazing benevolence is how you let go to discover what is rightfully yours. You may need to give up something you feel is important as a commitment to conscientious growth with another. Businesses often use a time of Decrease to expand. If sales are down, distribution channels can become an opportunity to market new products. Those who understand the cycles know that Increase will follow Decrease and will use the time to fortify the foundation or to examine what is working and what is not. Whatever you may lose during a period of Decrease will pave the way for something else. Nature shows us that Decrease is not a negative event. It is simply how it continues in its forward movement even while appearing to move backward.

Harvest
comes
from pruning and drainage -
by what
is taken away.

"Through the sudden release of tension, something is sure to be lost. Hence follows the image of decrease." Just as there is a beginning to the time of flowering, there is also a beginning, which ushers in a time of decline. At the height of summer, autumn is imperceptible and yet the decline has already begun. The sage is aware of the moment when phenomena begins to change, and knows that *"what ebbs outward flows inward."* When you model nature, you will discover how life's energy remains constant.

The idea that 'nature abhors a vacuum' comes from the conservation law of physics. It states that *the sum total of matter and energy in the universe cannot be destroyed; it can only be transformed.* Einstein showed how mass could be converted to and from energy. Like the particle collisions that transform energy into mass, we see how what is *unobservable* can still exist in unseen form.

The master's skill in forecasting impending events often made their followers think they were magicians. The great master had merely *followed* long enough to trace the outline of change apparent in all transforming phenomena. During winter, life dissipates in the observable world to bring new life to the unseen world below. Decrease is not a negative event, but merely the shifting of life's energy.

Whatever you may lose paves the way for you to open to something else. It is the natural order of the universe to return to a starting point or cyclical beginning. If something develops in its extreme, it will revert into its opposite condition. Sun is the image of offering something freely in a ceremonial vessel. As the Lake rests below the Mountain we discover how stillness or a thoughts without striving makes the universe surrender. There is nothing pushing back on us to make us open. The unseen potential of Yin becomes accessible when you recognize decrease as pathway to increase, or new growth.

The master said: *"Things are sometimes increased by being diminished and at other times are diminished by being added to."* In viewing experience, try to see that all things are equal. What may be decreasing will open you for new opportunity. You cut away unnecessary growth and the plant grows stronger, while over-watering would destroy it. There are times when decrease or 'letting go' is necessary for healthy growth. Observing the shifting of energy in the natural world, if something is receding in its observable manifestation, it is because unseen energy is gathering somewhere else.

When you *"approach the shape that has no shape,"* you move away from judging experience by the obvious. Someone with riches may have lost their ability to appreciate the simple things; another faces loss and discovers the treasures of rebirth in the face of death. Whether it is phenomena transforming energy on the earth, or the closed doors 'out there,' which lead to an awakening 'in here,' in the great circle energy is always conserved.

In both the inner and outer landscape, "what ebbs outward flows inward" and "what ebbs inward flows outward." When you disown energy 'in here,' it takes shape as an opportunity to discover it 'out there.' When you encounter a barrier 'out there,' it will give definition to the rising wall 'in here.'

The conservation of energy takes form in the image of snow on a mountain. During winter, snow is conserved in the hills above, so that the snow pack can sustain the population throughout the coming year. The flowing water or energy of future rivers remains in an inanimate condition that demonstrates how nature does not destroy, but conserves and transforms. Sun asks you to begin to discern the subtle way that this is occurring around you.

"There is nothing constant in the universe. All ebb and flow and every shape that's born, bears in its womb, the seeds of its opposite." This is the fundamental way that the Yielding becomes Firm and the Firm becomes Yielding. To follow the way of nature, when you yield you become strong; when you are strong, you are more able to yield.

The vast majority of life forms are insects and their longevity on this planet suggests that they will outlive us. Their profound ability to *adapt* is what makes life's most fragile creatures it's strongest. Life never leads you into crisis; it leads you into a season of change. When decrease appears, recognize how life turns you back to fortify you. In this, you will discover abundance and joy even during a period of decrease.

Unchanging: To the mind that is still = the entire universe surrenders. The Joyful Lake is repressed by the weight of the Mountain of Keeping Still. This can show that emotional responses are out of balance to the changing events. By increasing what is below one exacerbates what is above. Frustration, anger or blind enthusiasm will not change the situation. You may need to find the stillness suggested by the Mountain and find the grace to let go. Imbalance is usually the reason that Decrease would appear unchanging. However nothing in the situation will change until your attitude changes. Being resentful, expecting something different or holding onto the past will only blind you to emerging opportunity. Perhaps you are not realizing that you are spending beyond your means or that you generosity can lead to overspending. In unchanging form, Sun is a message that Decrease of some sort may be necessary in this situation although you are pushing blindly ahead. Remember the master's words: *"To the mind that is still, the whole universe surrenders."*

Line 1 Finishing quickly and leaving without blame = examine its effects. Changes to (4) Youthful Folly. One is in a hurry to complete something to move forward. It is important to examine what is left undone, diminished or left behind in this haste. Sacrifices between people need to be a balanced give and take. Consider what may need to be decreased in this situation and whether you are actually taking by giving. Ensure that giving to others does not diminish their power or merely fortify your power.

Line 2 Without decreasing oneself = one increases others. Changes to (27) Nourishing Vision. Consider whether sacrifice for another diminishes your dignity or compromises your principles. The situation allows you to hold to your integrity while still giving to another. Sharing with others brings real fulfillment.

Line 3 Three people journey and lose one = one alone finds a companion. Changes to (26) Controlled Power. You may need to examine companionship to arrive at a proper synergy. Three can create a triangular dynamic of jealousy and intrigue. Even if you have to go it alone you will find those of like mind.

Line 4 Decreasing one's faults = others come and rejoice. Changes to (38) Opposition. Anytime you meet contention among others, it is good to examine the part you play in the conflict. If you can look within and see a heart that is not tainted, others will joyfully join you.

Line 5 Others are benefiting one = Ten oracle readings don't lie, supreme good fortune. Changes to (61) Inner Truth. Because of your steadfast integrity, the way opens and great fortune rewards your Inner Truth. This is a very auspicious line showing that the work you have done to be honest and generous to others will be rewarded. A time of good fortune is emerging after testing.

Line 6 Increase the self without depriving others = one takes a job but loses a home, auspicious. Changes to (19) Approach. You move forward knowing that balancing your own needs with those of others sometimes requires a sacrifice. In that, you are of service but lose the safety of your home or paradigm. This line is auspicious because you are in service to the truth of the moment. This openness leads to great opportunity and others Approach you with trust. Sometimes this line appears when moving because of work opportunity.

Hexagram #42
Yi (Increase)

Action: Expand
Hu Gua (secondary influence) 23 Split Apart: Regenerate
Zong Gua: (underlying cause) 32 Duration: Commit
Received as 2nd Hexagram: While it may not be apparent, something meaningful is growing.

**The law of compensation shows how
'what is' springs from 'what is not.'**

*As there is no worldly gain without some loss,
so there is no worldly loss without some gain. –Francis
Quarles*

Reading at a Glance: Like Springtime, a cycle is
beginning in which new growth will continue its
forward march toward the apex of summer. Increase is
a message about expansion and fullness. Like Decrease,
Yi is simply another cycle of life as it flowers, decays
and achieves rebirth. Since the time suggests Increase
the universe is supporting growth while opportunities
emerge to support your expansion. The Wind is moving
and dispersing the enormous creative energy of
Thunder below and a time of flowering is at hand. The
Zong Gua of Duration can show that after a period of
commitment and planning, it is time to put your plan
into action. The secondary influence of Split Apart
shows how Regeneration requires the ability to expand.
Therefore a time of Increase may also be associated with
releasing any self sabotaging thoughts that undermine
forward growth. There can be a balancing that is
necessary where being too conservative is no longer
working and you may need to take a chance on the
unknown. The opportunity for growth and expansion
is surrounding you and you need only take advantage
of it while it is here.

*The wise detect
and prepare for*

294

the sun's march
across
the empty sky.
"If decrease goes on and on, it is certain to bring about increase." When the moon's waning has reached its zenith, it begins waxing. *"Increase moves gentle and mild; daily progress without limit."* Because change is universal in all regularly recurring processes of nature, all things will reach a stage in which they begin to move toward their opposite condition. This principle suggests a transition toward fullness.

We only give credibility to observable phenomena, although more than 90% of our universe is comprised of the unseen, and scientists call this the 'missing mass problem.' When you can begin to discern the movement of nature's unseen aspects, you can prepare for the opportunity that always arises after a period of decrease. The darkest and most silent hour is always right before the dawn of activity. The 'void' is often frightening, although it is pregnant with enormous possibility.

The law of compensation shows how *"what is, springs from what is not."* A blind person will develop a more acute way of hearing. Another will compensate for a real or imagined deficiency by overdeveloping other character traits. A cold pressure system in the north will draw warmer weather into the southern regions. Regardless of where you look, you will find nature filling in its vacuous spaces to improve 'what is not.'

In the mountain snowmelt of spring, you can observe stasis transforming into movement. Sustenance conserved is now release to flow where it is needed. An empty sky can suddenly fill with clouds and rain. You observe events as they happen, but fail to acknowledge the enormous potential of the unseen that brings about increase. As a lesson about patience, what had appeared stationary or deficient is actually the changing of direction that brings about fulfillment. Compensation is how energy is transformed at all levels of life. Energy rises, but when it is trapped or repressed, it must find another outlet for expression. This can happen in a volcano, earthquake, or in the quaking of your inner landscape.

Adaptation shows how 'what is' springs from 'what is not,' as new traits emerge when required for survival. Increase shows the unacknowledged potential of the unseen that is already taking form. Increase and decrease are natural processions that are mutually dependent upon each other and cannot be separated. Embracing the unseen cycles of potential Yin allows you to prepare for the successive Yang that will emerge on the horizon. You can await the sunrise where others see only an empty sky.

Unchanging: With every awakening = a sunrise comes. As Thunder stirs below the Wind in stagnant form you may not be getting the message about the abundant opportunity that is presented in this situation. This can be the classic message about the silver lining in any difficult situation. To balance the enthusiastic Thunder with the Gentle and Penetrating efforts of the Wind above, you may need to be more sensitive or patient about the object of your enquiry. Perhaps you are so much in a hurry to obtain what you desire that you move too fast or out of step with the time and miss the opportunity presented. The Thunder is powerful but its effects can only become lasting and understood when applied with the Gentle influence suggested by the Wind. When Wind and Thunder move in unison the power is unstoppable. Find a balance between enthusiasm and patience. Consider how abundance is fortified when it is shared with generosity to those below.

Line 1 One is in a position to accomplish something great = supreme good fortune. Changes to (20) Contemplation. The situation is allowing for a greater ability to understand your own issues, even when it is challenging. Contemplation of increase means that blockages that lead to decrease or withholding are eliminated through self examination. After a period of retreat and observation the time becomes ripe to implement your plan. Because you actually lead through experience and by example, you can accomplish great things.

Line 2 Someone increases one and ten oracles agree = from heaven comes this great good fortune. Changes to (61) Inner Truth. Your connection to others is deeply felt and shared. You resonate from clarity and the inner certainty that everything is unfolding as it should. This is an example of a mindset of abundance rather than scarcity. Because you are open to sharing abundance grace shines down upon you in the image of heaven's blessing. However, it is your attitude of acceptance that has created abundance.

Line 3 Enriched through misfortune, no blame in being sincere = walk the middle path. Changes to (37) Family. As life moves in cycles of increase and decrease it may appear that not getting what you desire is bad but it actually is a blessing in disguise. The Family reminds us of life's cycles and what remains constant about us. To walk the middle path is to avoid extremes in judgment. Accept that what is unfolding is purposeful and will lead to greater fulfillment. Discovering sincerity is one of life's greatest lessons in following Tao.

Line 4 Walking in the middle while abiding by rules brings favor = one can move the capital city. Changes to (25) Innocence. The middle way is a mindset of patience and innocence in meeting unfolding events. Innocence is a way of approaching life without expectation but also ensuring that one is not selfishly hoarding out of a sense of scarcity. To bring about increase or to achieve your desire may require ground rules that serve more than just your needs. Moving the capital city is a metaphor of extending your responsibilities to serve the greater good.

Line 5 If the heart is true, no need to ask = supreme good fortune from kindness as a virtue. Changes to (27) Nourishing Vision. It is said that those who go against the Way end up being called unlucky. What is really happening is that fighting the flow or having a negative mindset interferes with the purposeful unfolding of events. To make benevolence and acceptance your virtue, make the most of all situations with a kind heart and a willingness to share. Because you do not use counting rods to measure experience in terms of good and bad, the situation unfolds favorably. When in doubt, follow the heart.

Line 6 Increasing no one and therefore reprimanded = one's heart is not steady. Changes to (3) Difficult Beginnings. The lines of this hexagram show the appropriate way to ensure that increase continues but in this case, there is only confusion. The middle way is an attitude of acceptance but the heart is not committed to this approach. In this situation there can be vacillation and uncertainty which creates false starts. In order to succeed it is important to examine commitment and steady the heart. A purely selfish approach does not benefit others which can lead to a lack of support in achieving your desires.

Hexagram #43
Guai (Determination)

Action: Breakthrough
Hu Gua (secondary influence) 1 Creative: Initiate
Zong Gua: (underlying cause) 23 Split Apart:
Regenerate
Received as 2nd Hexagram: Someone has taken a hard
line in this situation and is not easily swayed.

Success comes when you
untangle the knots and soften the glare.

There is a great deal of unmapped country within us which
would have to be
taken into account in an explanation of our gusts and
storms. – George Eliot

Reading at a Glance: One of the most difficult lessons
we learn in life is how to balance a resolute attitude of
Determination with the openness required to keep
growing. Often the obstacles that we face around us are
merely showing us the condition of our inner world. In
fact, obstacles only show themselves if we are looking

for blockages. If we are determined to see our success manifest, this commitment to vision is often all that is needed to obtain our desires. However, we sometimes need to examine the story we tell ourselves. Is life a place to be feared or is it a tapestry of joy? What is it that you are stalking? Is it the proof that you can discover abundance or is it the reinforcement of scarcity? The secondary influence of the Creative is at play so growth is on the horizon and ready to take manifestation. The Zong Gua of Split Apart or a period Regeneration must now be given concrete form in the visible world regardless of the challenges.

Determination suggests that a Breakthrough in thinking can eliminate any walls to your forward progress. We see an image of looking at an obstacle and discrediting it. This means that whatever is holding you back is of your own making. Like a hero being tested in their sincerity, obstacles are not a reason to give up and if you know you will succeed you will. The master said: "untangle the knots and soften the glare."

Determination can be recognized in the eyes. But there is no need to approach life with a wrinkled brow or a sense that life is fighting you. Life has been committed to your success since the day you were born. Any challenges you face are meant to deepen your resolve and fortify your strength. This is the time of year when the fiercest weather prepares the landscape for rebirth so remain undaunted. You may need to make a difficult decision or share information that is sensitive but important in clarifying your vision and expectations of others. In the current situation a Breakthrough in thinking can transform a closed door into an open door.

Fear stalks
its own reflection -
Remove
the window dressing
of the prison.

"When increase goes on unceasingly, there is certain to be a break-through or a resolution." Kuai shows the type of break-through that comes when a river bursts through a dam in the image of the Lake rising to meet the Creative. The Water opens new pathways through what appeared to be a barrier by the simple fact that it is *constant*. At the same time, pushing unrelentingly through obstacles can lead to an uncompromising will. Turning inward to question the power of the obstacle fortifies strength; forcing your will upon it will always generate more resistance.

The resoluteness required to achieve success, must combine vigor with openness. In the image of approaching an obstacle by discrediting it, you can refuse to acknowledge it as having power over you. To demonstrate anger and emotion can only validate the power of the obstacle and waste your energy.

When you *"untangle the knots and soften the glare,"* you eliminate the gusts and storms of the inner landscape. Softening your belief that nature would ever come to obstruct your forward progress, you will discover that it is always committed to developing the strength of its species. Know this and you will know *constant virtue.*

"The ruler of the South is called Dissatisfaction. The ruler of the North: Revolution. The ruler at the center of the world is Chaos. Dissatisfaction and Revolution met from time to time in the territory of Chaos, and Chaos treated them very hospitably. The two rulers planned how to repay Chaos's kindness. They said: 'Men all have seven holes to their bodies for seeing, hearing, eating and breathing. Our friend here has none of these. Let us try to bore some holes in him.' Each day they bored one hole. On the seventh day Chaos died."

The chaos created from the misunderstandings in your relationship with life, will dissipate when you untangle your beliefs and soften your glare. A breakthrough is achieved by becoming open. You can observe how events are teaching you about achieving this *powerful peacefulness.* All that you believe will eventually come to meet you as *"the Way goes round and round."* When you transform the wasted energy of defensiveness into an inner shifting of openness, you will discover wellness, balance and success in all you do.

This hexagram is also called Deciding because the time calls for resoluteness in moving forward. The goal is in sight and you may need to discuss sensitive matters with others to ensure that all understand your goals and expectations. Between unhappiness and the changes needed to bring about transformation, the way can become tumultuous. In this you have an opportunity to reinforce your resolve or simply give up.

Moving forward in strength is supported while moving forward because of fear may simply bring you back again to a similar situation in the future.

Unchanging: If you are tired of the battles = lay down your weapons. When the Creative is stirring below the Joyous Lake in unchanging form, attitudes can block a breakthrough in thinking. One can be operating so defensively that they don't even realize how they are protecting a past way of thinking. Defensiveness always leads us in circles because we are somewhere other than the present. You may not be seeing that the Creative is generating opportunities to discover something that will make you very happy. Determination and Breakthrough should lead to an attitude of Joyousness and a sense of harmony. If that is not occurring then the unchanging nature of this hexagram can bring up the issue of clear communication. You may need to state your truth in a difficult situation and face the fallout. You can't force your opinions on others but you do need to remain true to yourself. Difficult decisions must be made as you can no longer maintain what worked in the past. Something may need to be said that has nothing to do with compromise and may lead to eventual separation but the truth is the truth, so speak up. If you inspire Joy in others, they will naturally want to be around you. If what you have to say makes another defensive or makes them retreat, there is not much you can do about it. If you are waiting for some type of answer from another, they may be undecided at this time.

304

Line 1 Strength in the toes but not equal to the task = one makes a mistake. Changes to (28) Critical Mass. Your first attempts to change the situation may have been premature. You may be impatiently pushing forward when the time is not right to instigate action. There is more examination and preparation needed in this situation. To just push forward means you may bite off more than you can chew which leads to collapse. Proceed carefully.

Line 2 A cry of alarm and ready to attack = but there is nothing to fear. Changes to (49) Molting/Revolution. It is said that "dragging the adversary about when there is no adversary will cost you your inner treasure." Being overly defensive in this situation you discover that your approach is of a personal nature and not related to the events unfolding around you. Once you 'lay down your weapons' you will see that expecting difficulty or expecting to be attacked is precisely why others appear to attack you. Molting shows the need to let go of your armor as a type of Breakthrough in thinking.

Line 3 Strength in the jaws and walking out into the rain = ridiculed but resolved to go. Changes to (58) Joy. In this situation someone may feel that dignity is kept intact while leaving, regardless of what is left behind or what difficulties might arise in going. Strength in the jaws is a hard line approach when something becomes unacceptable and leaving can lead to Joy. Others may not understand your decision to go but the pursuit of Joy is the Breakthrough you are after.

Line 4 No skin on the thighs makes walking difficult = better to be led like a sheep without blame but these words are not believed. Changes to (5) Nourishment While Waiting. Some sort of negativity or punishment has the effect of traumatizing one but the situation can become one of enlightenment if you allow it. During a heated exchange or times of difficulties with another it is hard to see the Teacher in the Adversary. At such times it is hard to listen to the voice of reason because a Breakthrough in thinking is still creating blockages. Therefore, acquiescing may be viewed as punishment. Patience and receptivity can lead to success.

Line 5 In weeding the garden determination needed = walking in the middle is without blame. Changes to (34) Great Power. The best way to achieve Breakthrough in this situation is to carefully consider what needs to be changed. Without going to extremes of judgment you might learn something new that you hadn't considered. Don't come to any conclusions just yet and give the situation time to evolve. In this case a Breakthrough in patience leads to Great Power.

Line 6 Nothing said – in the end misfortune comes. Changes to (1) The Creative. When a situation requiring a Breakthrough of some sort is ignored, or if you allow issues to be swept under the carpet, they will fester into decay. Not speaking up can only lead to demise where a new beginning is all that can be achieved. In attempting to maintain the status quo or to hold to your pride, you lose that which you desire. Speak up, you have nothing to lose.

Hexagram #44
Gou (Coming to Meet)

Action: Encounter

Hu Gua (secondary influence) 1Creative: Initiate

Zong Gua: (underlying cause) 24 Return: Go Back

Received as 2nd Hexagram: Whatever the situation, it is highly charged and will teach you about your Shadow projections.

**Hope is like a flower
forced to grow without sunlight.**

Most of the shadows of this life are caused by standing in one's own sunshine. – Emerson

Reading at a Glance: There is no other hexagram with so much controversy surrounding it. The only consensus is the intensity of feeling inherent in it. The powerful feminine energy of rebirth is at play because of the single yin line emerging at the bottom of many yang lines. Some see it as the emperor's first wife's child who becomes the heir. Gou can be important in creative readings as suggested by the secondary influence of the

Creative. Others define it as a temptress who may lead a man astray. If we look deeper into the transformative power of the entire I Ching we find room for all images. As the Shadow or Anima in a man's dream, the Trickster temptress is actually allowing a breakthrough of his feeling nature. For a woman, the Shadow shows how her own power may need to be resurrected after being forced underground because it was misunderstood or thought to be bad. The Zong Gua of Return shows how the present can be overlaid with unacknowledged images of the past. Return is a message about what is going on inside and you may be judging a situation subjectively rather than objectively. Therefore, Gou can symbolize any type of encounter that leads to Shadow transformation and putting misunderstandings under the proper light. This may be why Kung fu tzu said: "when meeting contention in another it would be wise to examine oneself." The Shadow is always portraying the opposite of what we believe about ourselves. Just as hate is the Shadow of love and fear the Shadow of trust, something is on the horizon that will teach you a great deal about transforming difficulty into meaning. Look at the things you want to judge harshly or that you avoid because they can teach you much about your Shadow. Coming to Meet shows an unavoidable encounter where opposites fund powerful creative growth just as the heir depicted in a royal marriage. There are many challenges in the individual lines but nothing inauspicious. Tread carefully but go. Revisit the past to forgive yourself or others. Only by overcoming fear and pain can one move from a period of Return or introspection into healthy interaction. The penetrating Wind is below the Creative, and together they unleash what is hidden to reveal your authentic power. The situation won't be anything like you expected but it is important that you move forward to see what you can learn.

The unexpected
draws the breath in -
It is a wind that tugs
with a million teeth
on the uninhabited.

"Through resoluteness, one is certain to encounter something. Hence, follows the principle of coming to meet." Gou embodies how you can waste much energy fighting against imaginary foes. *"Riding and hunting make the mind go wild with excitement."* Expecting difficulty can be a way of ensuring that you meet with constant difficulty. A negative outlook ensures that the outcome is relentless. Life is attempting to break you out of your self-made prison.

"Some things are distinctions made by the senses, others are distinctions made by the mind. Discard the one and you will lay hold of the other." Resoluteness can sometimes cost you the inner treasure that remains at home with the possibilities of the unknown. The master said: *"To know yet to think one does not know is best."* This hexagram can bring up a past experience so that you might understand it differently.

Gou is associated with the idea that inferior forces are on the rise. But just as nightmares are a positive sign that repressed power is become available in the psyche, meeting the Shadow or confronting contention in another is best approached by observing what the situation may teach you about yourself.

A student asked: *"If nature creates all things, then is evil too, its creation?"*

The master replied: *"What need has nature of thought and care? When the sun goes, the moon comes; when the moon goes, the sun comes. Sun and moon alternate, thus light comes into view. When cold goes, heat comes; when heat goes, cold comes. Can one be any different from the other? Suchness is neither pure nor impure."*

"What about the cruelty in the world?" The student continued: *"What about crime and suffering?"*

"In the absence of seeing, you wander in the darkness in search of light. Yet, darkness comes every night without fail. One who excels in understanding uses no counting rods. Why struggle like beating a drum in search of a fugitive?" Whatever you have hidden away as bad may actually be passion that gives flame to your inner light.

If you think of yourself as a victim and blame events for your sense of failure, you might never discover life's fundamental goodness. To *"beat a drum in search of a fugitive,"* is to attract others that can share in your misery. Fugitives will come, but it will be those who are also hiding.

Psychologists agree that people who commit atrocities are conflicted by inner compulsions. Coming to meet reveals how you trade validation for discovery, while you beat your drum to attract all that you believe. A hardened perspective will be made pliable: *"when the people lack a proper sense of awe, it seems that an awful visitation descends on them."* Too much hardness of thought and experience comes to carve away your shackles. Coming to meet is how you create your own misfortune and an opportunity to discover freedom at the same time.

"Thus the good transforms the bad, and the bad is the material that the good works on. Not to value the teacher, nor to love the material, betrays great bewilderment."

Opposites give contrasting symbolism meaning: up/down, sound/silence, order/disorder. Although they stand in relationship to one another, they fail to capture the real essence of *what is*. One variation is simply a degree of the other and therefore, *"suchness is neither pure nor impure."* You can become attached to the *things* that generate a response in you, when in reality the actual value resides in your response. *"Take the one and discard the other."* Once you have been moved by the experience or the 'carved block,' you must let it go.

311

The greatest thing Gou can teach you is how to move away from extremes of judgment and feeling to see that life is *just so*.

The master was having tea with two students and tossed his fan to one of them. *"What is this?"* The student opened it and began fanning himself. The master nodded because the student had transcended the need to give the object a name.

"Now you," he passed the fan to the other student. This one closed it and began scratching his neck with it. He opened it, and placed a piece of cake on it, offering it to the master. Beyond the need to classify the present in terms of the past, real vision begins. You may need to train yourself to see beyond the limitations that you are placing on experience.

Walking around knowing that *"when there is frost underfoot, solid ice is not far off,"* you tread with care because the first sign of danger makes you defensive. Yet, there is a fine line between avoiding danger and stalking adversity; danger is often the *first phase* of *emerging opportunity. "The more taboos there are in the empire, the poorer the people. The conflict between right and wrong is the sickness of the mind."* Hope is like a flower forced to grow without sunlight. It is a blindfold, which keeps you from discovering the beauty of what is. Acceptance of what is in order to see life's harmony is your elixir.

Gou is the image of intercourse and how you can be made whole by integrating 'that thing,' which is completely opposite from everything you believe about yourself. Kou demonstrates both the danger and opportunity presented when opposites first approach each other.

The great image of what you believe will eventually come to meet you. *"Coming to you and meeting with no harm, it will be safe and sound."* When you observe, reflect and own your experiences as a reflection of your beliefs, you come to recognize the profound harmony at the root of life.

Unchanging: All that you attract = a reflection of the life unlived within you. The situation is charged with energy that may feel addictive or destructive in its unchanging form. We may give someone the power to push our buttons but the response is still our own. In fact, this power is ours to do with as we like and we might as well own it. There may be an obsessive attachment to the situation where you are not seeing the transformative opportunity it presents but would rather stay in your comfort zone as a victim. You can be attracted to a powerful partner and then fall back into a sense of unworthiness when you feel outshined. There is a fated encounter unfolding that is simply the meeting of opposites to give birth to something new. If you are brave enough to see the situation or person as a teacher, you will discover that your inner core can be shaken out of its self perpetuating story of woe. If you'd rather run each time an opportunity for growth shows itself through conflict, you will miss this enormous Creative and transformative opportunity. The situation won't be anything like what you have known but if you can overcome your fear, it will teach you a great deal.

Line 1 Persevering in stopping something from taking its course = a tied up pig will seek freedom from rage. Changes to (1) The Creative. There is a sense of dominance versus passivity at play in this situation which is not allowing for more natural interaction. In providing for another you may actually be causing them to feel restricted or restrained. Even with the best of intentions this lack of balance in give and take can lead to resentments. In the beginning of any fated encounter it is wise to not rush forward. However, not allowing for the natural unfolding of events can only leave one stuck in their own story of being a victim.

Line 2 There is fish in the tank = does not benefit guests, no blame. Changes to (33) Retreat. A new insight or perspective is emerging although you may not know exactly how to describe it. Without being defensive, you may need to hold your cards to your chest and wait for the appropriate time to share your feelings. It is wise to recognize an inferior response or reaction and keep it to yourself. Blaming others is inappropriate as this situation has personal significance for your growth. In this case, Retreat is an opportunity to sit with the feeling to better understand its cause.

Line 3 No skin on the thighs and walking comes hard = mindful of danger, no mistake. Changes to (6) Conflict.

Through the blending of opposites or incompatible outlooks creativity is heightened. Do not allow another difference of opinion make you feel misunderstood or like an outcast. There is much to be gained in this situation if you recognize that the only danger is in not meeting the challenge. In nature when opposite forces come together all are lifted to a higher level.

Line 4 No fish in the tank = leads to misfortune. Changes to (57) Penetration. Give the situation time to evolve so you can understand its newness. What appears to be empty is actually the potential for discovery. All creativity begins with a blank slate. Inspiration is the faith that something is there that can impregnate you with vision. Penetration allows you to recognize the difference between discernment and judgment. Where judgment creates polarization and is based on past assumptions, discernment allows for compassion and realizations without criticism. If a shift in thinking always remains a possibility, you can make more conscious choices.

Line 5 A melon covered with willow leaves = what drops from heaven remains hidden. Changes to (50) The Cauldron. You may need to keep your light burning when feeling misunderstood. The Cauldron promises transformation and the call to something deep and profound if you open to it. While the time may not be right to realize your desire, by keeping faith you will succeed. You know the importance of what you are doing and that will see you through.

Line 6 He comes to meet with horns = humiliation but no blame. Changes to (28) Critical Mass. All encounters are propitious in that something valuable can be learned. Meeting with horns shows a defensive posture that can only block the potential for transformation. One can only be humiliated if they are upholding something that is not true or no longer relevant. It is better to approach the situation with openness and a willingness to learn. Critical Mass is the condition of upholding beliefs that can no longer serve you.

Hexagram #45
Cui (Gathering Together)

Action: Network
Hu Gua (secondary influence) 53 Development: Flower
Zong Gua: (underlying cause) 26 Controlled Power: Amplify
Received as 2nd Hexagram: Be sure you are associating with those who will lift you up ~ not bring you down.

Success is allowing your lot
to reach its highest degree.

It is while you are patiently toiling at the little tasks of life
that the meaning and shape
of the great whole of life dawns on you. – Phillips Brooks

Reading at a Glance: Gathering Together is a hexagram that shows interdependency and people coming together because of a shared ideal. The secondary influence of Development reveals the natural exuberance generated in grass root efforts where people of like mind network and become a strong voice. It can appear when there will be meetings or events where you find people with common interests. Where the Zong Gua of Controlled Power was a time of fortification of vision, the time has come for increased social interaction. The image of grass multiplying in nature shows how the individual root is strengthened and multiplies because other roots are joined to its cause. There is great magnetism created in this situation which brings others to share your vision. In business it is important to network in whatever way allows you to expose your product or services to others. In relationships, Gathering Together is more about shared interests and enthusiasm rather than romance and intimacy. In this situation it is not as important to focus on outer events as it is to keep fortifying your vision in a way that others understand and can participate in it. There is a cliquish quality to this hexagram that focuses more on similarities rather than differences. By fortifying order the group assembles around a shared goal and this gives the situation a shared sense of purpose.

Wearing
a cloak
of woven grass,
become a rainmaker
for the living.

"*When creatures meet one another, they mass together.
Hence, follows the principle of gathering together.*" Over the
Earth, is the Joyous Lake in the image of crowds
drawing together. "*The strong stands in the middle,
therefore others mass around it.*" The nuclear trigrams
suggest a character that emulates the movement and
influence of the Wind, while remaining steadfast like a
Mountain. "*When you have in your hold the great image,
the empire will come to you.*"

The mind forever travels in search of success to be
achieved 'out there.' Yet, to be still, while "*in silent
harmony with one's ultimate capacity, means allowing one's
lot to reach its highest degree.*" This is using each moment
as an opportunity to blossom. The master said: "*Nothing
exists but the present. If one cannot live there, one cannot live
anywhere.*" You must not make *where you are going* more
important than *where you are.* "*If one allows their nature to
follow its own course, there will be no place for joy and
sorrow.*"

"*Only when you stop liking and disliking will all be
understood.*" Your journey is not in the pursuit of
perfection; seek only the authenticity that unfurls from
within. Like the performer who discovers self-

318

consciousness as a barrier to their craft, being authentically yourself is what draws others to you.

"This is why the sage puts themselves last and finds that they are in the forefront; treats the self as extraneous and it is preserved. Is it not because one is without personal desires that one is able to fulfill one's desires?" Discard the extraneous and open to the cultivation of your real essence.

Te is not a virtue that develops from moral rectitude; it is the creative power of authenticity that comes from spontaneous and natural expression. If the character is authentic, one becomes, quite naturally, effective. *"Because this power is most true, within it there is confidence."* This confidence creates the magnetism that draws others to you.

As the image of grass growing and multiplying, life drives the strength of the individual through interdependency. The strength of the one root relies upon the growing strength of the collective root, while the collective thrives on the power of the individual. You may gather in places because of the ways that you are like others, but your Te is revealed in the ways that you are different. This contrast allows you to hear your drummer on the pathway to your destiny.

Authentic in the moment, you can detect the greater shape and the larger meaning of life's interdependency. *"That is why the sage concentrates on the core of things and not the husk. They let go of the 'that' to lay hold of the 'this.'"*

When you remove your outer covering that brings you together with others, you discover that *'this'* is the person you are meant to be.

In life, you take your part in the group by serving others with your unique way of giving. In this way, you are not taking but giving; and through giving, you will strengthen the core of who you are.

Unchanging: To find your clan = open the door. If you are spending too much time alone, Gathering Together unchanging can be a message that it is time to become more sociable. There is great potential to expand and even achieve greater happiness, which is something that cannot occur until you open the door and go outside. Often when people feel listless or depressed, joining some type of activity can work wonders in invigorating enthusiasm or inspiration. You may be part of a group and feel out of place when this hexagram appears unchanging. The focus is on finding similarities and shared interests. In relationships there can be stark differences in social standing that must be considered. In business, the message can be to network in a way that allows others to find you, such as creating an identifiable brand or social media presence. You can only remain an outcast if you keep hiding. Your clan is out there. You need only go in search of it.

Line 1 Seeking union with confusion and indecision = without sincerity to the end and alone. Regret not, offer the hand again and re-establish joy. Changes to (17) Following. Initially there can be confusion which can creates difficulties in achieving union. Yet by offering a handshake and moving deeper in understanding the situation leads to joy. Following is a message about making your intentions clear so that others can follow. In order to re-establish union, you may need to reach out your hand.

Line 2 Letting oneself be drawn brings good fortune and remains blameless = if one is sincere it furthers one to bring even a small offering. Changes to (47) Oppression/Exhaustion. The situation is not what you expected and you are drawn to those you do not understand. Even while you feel you do not belong, be open to the differences of others because providence is at play. If you sincerely want union, you may need to sacrifice the known and open to the unknown. One can only be exhausted through giving if there are strings attached. Trust where the situation is leading you and how it will change you.

Line 3 Gathering together amid sighs does not further = leaving is an option though does not satisfy. Changes to (31) Influence/Wooing. In a gathering of many differences, the situation is highly charged and may leave you feeling frustrated. Communication may be suffering and you feel that leaving is the only option. However, Wooing is a message that shows attraction and the desire to achieve union. You may need to work through the difficulties rather than abandon the situation. Wooing can also be a message that you get more bees with honey. Strive to listen rather than to just be heard.

321

Line 4 Great good fortune = no blame. Changes to (8) Union. The situation is moving forward favorably and will lead to a meeting of the minds. Union is achieved after meeting and gathering in discussion. There is nothing wrong in this situation and all are in accord.

Line 5 Established position over a gathering = yet others are still unclear so persevere to gain trust. Changes to (16) Enthusiasm. You have achieved a connection with others yet there still may be issues related to trust. It is important to persevere in enthusiasm so that others recognize your loyalty. Don't take the union for granted because it can only continue on a foundation of mutual trust and the enthusiasm to continue.

Line 6 Lamenting and sighing, floods of tears = no blame. Changes to (12) Standstill. Gathering together under difficult conditions can lead to frustration because the situation comes to an impasse. There is nothing wrong with voicing your frustration if you are sincere in achieving a meeting of the minds. Simply being critical can only lead to further obstruction. The sense of loss in losing this connection may be what it takes to reveal its importance to you.

Hexagram #46
Sheng (Pushing Upward)

Action: Ascend

Hu Gua (secondary influence) 54 Propriety:
Subordinate

Zong Gua: (underlying cause) 25 Innocence: Open

Received as 2nd Hexagram: Interdependency is at play
in this situation so ensure that all parties are getting
their needs served.

**If you pay respect to the great,
you pave the way for your own greatness.**

*It is always better to fail in doing something
than to excel in doing nothing. – Chinese Proverb*

Reading at a Glance: Sheng describes a situation
requiring an extended amount of sustained effort and
results that may not be readily visible. It is like a small
tree taking years before it ever provides shade. At the
same time it is focused on growth so unless the
situation is one of growth, it cannot move upward. It
can also be a message about patience and authentic

interaction. Generally events happen so fast that we lose touch with the flow of what we are doing. We can become a part of routines that have nothing to do with fulfillment. Situations unfold that are the result of past actions that are forgotten. Like the patience that would be required to observe the growth of a tree, you need to get back to the moment in conscious awareness of what you are doing and why. Therefore, Pushing Upward can be a message to slow down and become mindful. The secondary influence of Propriety or subordination aligns the will to the way. If we nourish an authentic approach to each day, keeping in mind our intention while opening to the nurturing events that unfold to hone us, we can create a sense of fulfilling opportunities that lead to success. If we are neglectful or caught up in routines, nothing can flourish. The Zong Gua of Innocence sought a perspective without intention but now you are asked to give form to intention and provide it with the conscious care over time that will allow you to realize your ambition. Sheng focuses on purposeful action and asks that you examine the situation to see if real growth is occurring. Pushing Upward can also be a message about the need to leave a deteriorating situation if it is no longer serving growing. The emphasis should be on healthy growth and not ignoring deterioration. A promotion or other opportunity to expand outwardly is also indicated.

The rain comes
and what bends
will rise.
It is a purposeful journey.

"*Massing toward the top is called pushing upward. That which pushes upward does not come back.*" We sometimes believe that successful people get 'a lucky break,' but more often than not, it was the heaping up of small efforts that led to their success.

You can be successful, but if it came at the expense of your authenticity, success will leave you feeling empty. When you model nature, you will see the progression of how big things have their beginnings in the small. In the atom, molecule, cells, tissues, organs, people or nations, big things emerge from the heaping up of small things. To create a type of success that generates fulfillment, you must build your foundation from the inside - out.

The Gentle Wind becomes the Wood that pushes upward through the Earth, and Sheng is the image of something growing with an emphasis on expansion. "*One generation plants trees; another gets the shade. What grows upward does not come back*" because the flowering usually occurs much later than the actual effort.

The master said: "*In time, you carry on your back, the Yin; In time, you embrace in your arms, the Yang.*" This captures the idea of how you carry on with your efforts, even while the results may not be apparent. Ascending vertically suggests the rise from obscurity to a position of power because of your sincerity. "*One who pays respect to the great paves the way for one's own greatness.*" You tend to the small with the knowledge that everything is a part of the great whole.

When work displays immediate results, you are gratified, but because you cannot see the result, you may question what you are doing. To *"shine and not dazzle"* is the sense of holding to your sense of inner purpose, without the need for recognition. Only you know the importance of what you are doing. If it is real, it will endure. All effort is consequential because even small contributions are important. Like the principle of waiting, there is no immediate response. Sincerity is strengthened when you do the small things that make you qualified to do even greater things.

Through convergence, you stand in the collective to find your core. Pushing upward alone, you achieve success through perseverance. Thus, you can transform the devotion of following your inner drummer into greatness.

There are many cases where executive leadership in major corporations rises from the mailroom. To achieve great things, do not measure your efforts in terms of big and small; all effort is meaningful. Like the Gentle and penetrating Wind, if you consistently do even the smallest of things, you will ascend. Without obvious results, you can understand a deeper meaning of gratification: it is your devotion to the work that makes you great.

Unchanging: Devotion is one part patience = and an equal measure of sincerity. While you may think that a quick fix or short term effort will lead to long term success, you are mistaken. Shun unchanging is a message about the sustained dedication and effort that is required in this situation. Responsiveness and receptivity need to be blended with small steady efforts. There is no easy way to success in this situation so unless you are in it for the long haul, you may want to change direction. A stable foundation and daily nurturing is required in the same way you plant corn in the spring but do not eat it until autumn. Are you committed to the long term picture? Is it possible that you have outgrown the situation or that things have changed in a way that will make it different? Those grappling with a curriculum of patience may pull this hexagram unchanging because patience is not their strongest quality. If you want to enjoy the harvest, you have to be willing to nurture the garden. Know that nothing will change any faster than the seasons. Slow, steady progress is the only way to success in this situation.

Line 1 Pushing upward meets with confidence = brings great good fortune. Changes to (11) Peace. As you advance toward the object of your enquiry you are well received. There is nothing blocking your way and others appreciate your approach. Peace shows a time of harmony in advancing.

Line 2 If one is sincere it furthers one to bring even a small offering = no blame. Changes to (15) Authenticity. Because of your sincere and humble approach you are well received in your advance. The mention of no blame is because that while you may not be suited for the position or lacking in experience your ethics and sincerity make up for it. Being authentic in advancing a sacrifice of some sort may need to be made to show your sincerity.

Line 3 One pushes upward = into an empty city. Changes to (7) Army. Whether you have advanced too soon or into the wrong situation, there is nothing there to receive you. You have set your sights on something and are eager to obtain it but the timing isn't right. Discipline and rules may need to be established prior to moving forward. The empty city can be literal, as in moving into a new house that is unfurnished or making a move that will not happen until later. Have patience because you are moving too fast and putting the cart before the horse.

Line 4 The king offers him Mount Ch'i = good fortune without blame. Changes to (32) Duration. Because you are supported in your advance you receive a promotion. Whatever your objective, the advance forward is based on commitment and will be long lasting.

Line 5 Perseverance brings good fortune = one pushes upward by steps. Changes to (48) The Well. Because you have taken the preparatory steps to advance, nothing blocks your way. The Well shows that others benefit by your objectives. This can be a message about receiving a promotion. In relationships, the message of the Well is that the situation doesn't really change even while it looks like progress is occurring.

Line 6 Pushing upward in darkness = it furthers ot be unremittingly persevering. Changes to (18) Dec Both the darkness and the image of Decay show proceeding even while the way forward is uncertain or fraught with difficulty. In times such as these it is solely your vision and unquestionable ethics that allow you to advance. It won't be easy but if you are sincere and dedicated you will succeed. You may not have all of the facts so don't blindly rush forward.

Hexagram #47
Kùn (Oppression/Exhaustion)

Action: Adapt
Hu Gua (secondary influence) 37 Family: Support
Zong Gua: (underlying cause) 22 Grace: Accept
Received as 2nd Hexagram: A sense of exhaustion is at play which means the old way will no longer do and some sort of new approach is required.

Success is a pathway of self-completion
and the seed is always within you.

Perfection is reached, not when there is no longer anything to add,
but when there is no longer anything to take away. – Antoine de St. Exupery

Reading at a Glance: Kùn is an image of a tree growing within an enclosure and offers a lesson about remaining cheerful and abundant in the face of confining situations. Tranquility in Disturbance is one of Tao's greatest lessons to overcome the extremes of responses. Whatever unfolds might simply be a lesson to cultivate patience and to become less reactive. Great frustration can mount when you feel hemmed in or when your words are not believed. However, sometimes you have to be backed into a corner to discover your inner truth or real capabilities. The secondary influence of Family can show dynamics at play when you feel your buttons have been pushed. At some point you have to take responsibility for your condition and stop looking around for blame. The Family provides an environment that shows us the responsibility of caring where giving is not exhausted because it is done with no strings attached. We care for others because they are a part of us. Nature shows how adaptation mechanisms evolve to help species overcome adversity. These mechanisms are not external. They are inborn, and in the same way all that you will ever need to survive blossoms from within. The Zong Gua of Grace offered a message to accept what you cannot change. Now Kùn offers a lesson about adapting and changing to the present circumstances. After a time of Pushing Upward, it is normal to meet with resistance. Sometimes Oppression rises when you are most successful as healthy competition emerges. The greatest thing Kùn presents is that while you may feel weak within, it is exactly those Oppressive situations that reveal your inner strength. It cannot be exhausted because it is not dependent on external conditions.. "Keep knocking and the joy inside will eventually open a window to look out and see who is there." (Rumi) Allow this time of Oppression to reveal the abundance within you.

> *Life's gentle prodding*
> *whittles away*
> *the unnecessary -*
> *until only the necessary*
> *remains.*

"If one pushes upward without stopping, there is sure to be oppression. Hence, follows the principle of oppression and exhaustion." The Joyous Lake is dispersing water into the Abysmal Water below. Since both bodies of water tend to move downward, eventually the Lake is drained. *"There is no water in the Lake"* and when oppression appears, you can lose your joy and consider giving up.

The Lake represents a sense of trying to contain fulfillment, while the Abysmal Water suggests a source that is inexhaustible. Kùn's message is that while you tend to attach yourself to what can be held within the hand, you cannot know today what will come to fulfill you tomorrow. Like an ocean that cannot be depleted because all streams lead back to it, you access a source within that is inexhaustible. It is inexhaustible only when you do not try to contain it. In giving it is only when there are strings attached that we become exhausted. The secondary influence of Family shows us the proper way to support others as if everyone is our Family.

When you model nature, observe how all life forms follow instincts or an inborn pattern of development. Adaptation reveals how oppression 'out there' acts as a mechanism to unleash your capabilities 'in here.' To measure success only by outward accomplishment, you may fail to see how adversity pushes you back to discover your real capabilities. When you explore your value in the mirror of the unknown, you are 'just so,' living the life that you are meant to be living, here and now.

Oppression pushes back against you and has a way of whittling away the unnecessary that leads to exhaustion, until only the necessary remains. The master said: *"When great responsibility is about to befall one, life appears to confound all undertakings. Thereby it stimulates the mind, toughens the nature and improves all deficiencies."* Without friction, the unnecessary cannot be carved away. Its message is that *"great fullness seems empty."*

To believe that life is working against you will lead to exhaustion and manipulation. That is why the judgment says *"there are words that are not honest."* Feeling confined, we may serve base desires with a type of neediness that is not healthy. Success comes when you can approach all of life without prejudice. *"With gentle compassion, I can be brave. With economy, I can be liberal. Not presuming to claim precedence in the world I can make myself a vessel fit for the most distinguished service."* In the image of a tree growing within an enclosure, you can be hemmed in and still grow. Success takes root when *"you are abundant and yet, not reactive."*

Bamboo symbolizes great virtue because its leaves droop, portraying how one can bow down to the changes and still be content. When the winds of change blow, it moves too, and simply bends in shimmering laughter. Great fullness comes when you recognize success as a pathway of self-completion, and that the seed is always within. *"The power that is most sufficient looks inadequate."* When you do not contend, nothing contends with you: that is real power. When there is no longer anything to be removed, you are rich.

Unchanging: If you are abundant but not reactive = nothing gets exhausted. Oppression unchanging can show the long term effects of dealing with a deteriorating situation that you have been unsuccessful in changing. Even with the patience of a saint this can only lead to exhaustion. It may be time to throw in the towel because unchanging, the Oppression is simply confining you in an unhealthy way. This can happen when you are feeling depressed but doing nothing to get out of your rut. The definition of insanity is to keep doing the same thing while expecting a different result. "There are words that are not believed" can mean that you have stopped trusting in your intuition, in another or even in the purposeful flow of events. Perhaps you have even begun to lie to yourself? Another may no longer trust what you say as the truth. In this situation somebody feels hemmed in, trapped and movement or communication has stopped. There can be a clash of interests or the exhaustion that comes from not being heard. Perhaps stepping back or changing course is the only way forward. If you feel isolated, talk to someone who can be objective in helping you find your way forward.

Line 1 One sits oppressed under a bare tree and strays into a gloomy valley = for three years one sees nothing. Changes to (58) Joy. Even while the situation clearly shows that nothing is growing, one remains in it. In this case Joy can be a self deluding or escapist approach to ignoring how bad things really are. The only pathway to authentic Joy is in admitting that you may need to face the truth about the situation.

Line 2 One is oppressed while being nourished = a sacrifice for real fulfillment. Changes to (45) Gathering Together. It is not uncommon for even the wealthiest of individuals to feel depressed. This is because no amount of possessions can take the place of real fulfillment. In this situation instant gratification or the search for pleasure has become more important that obtaining lasting fulfillment or making the sacrifice needed for real happiness. You may have gathered a lot of companions but are lacking in real friends.

Line 3 Oppressed by stone and thistles = entering the house and not seeing the spouse, misfortune. Changes to (28) Critical Mass. The situation is one that is severely limiting and some type of change is required. Critical Mass shows how the roof collapses because the foundation is not strong enough. Even while you'd rather not face the need for change, the situation is not sustainable and will collapse. Not seeing the spouse can be a message that you are attempting to make someone something they are not.

Line 4 Being quiet while oppressed and going in a metal carriage = humiliation, but the end is in sight. Changes to (29) Abyss. The situation is one that is not easy but the end of difficulty is in sight. Because of the danger presented the situation can be humiliating although you protect yourself from its affects and remain silent. In fact, the power of silence and the resiliency of spirit can be at play in a way that actually allows the situation to correct itself.

Line 5 Nose and feet cut off, the oppression ignites spirit = it furthers one to make offerings. Changes to (40) Liberation. During a time of oppression or punishment all you can do is to learn from the situation and ensure that your spirit is not broken. The offering can be allowing the ego needs to fall away so that you connect with a spiritual perspective. Liberation suggests freedom although there is not much you can change in the situation. Therefore, Liberation in the face of Oppression can mean acceptance.

Line 6 Oppressed by creeping vines but sad to leave = if going leads to remorse, make changes to achieve good fortune. Changes to (6) Conflict. The situation is unpleasant and does not provide any comfort. However, leaving may not be an option. Perhaps there are changes that can be made that you haven't considered. Conflict is a condition that asks that you meet opposition half way. Don't be cynical or overlay the present with negative images of the past. Perhaps the Oppression you feel is merely an illusion.

Hexagram #48
Jing (The Well)

Action: Inspire

Hu Gua (secondary influence) 38 Opposition: Accommodate

Zong Gua: (underlying cause) 21 Biting Through: Discern

Received as 2nd Hexagram: While you may believe the situation will change, something fundamentally continues to remain the same.

**You can spend a lifetime
and still never come anywhere close
to exhausting the resources
that are inside of you.**

*Your vision will become clear only when you can look into
your own heart.
Who looks outside, dreams; who looks within, awakes. – Carl
Jung*

Reading at a Glance: The Well is associated with the reservoir of unconscious activity like fear and inspiration and also symbolizes elements of life that do not change. *"The town may be changed but the well cannot be changed."* This hexagram can also appear as a representation of complex situations that are unfathomable and can only be understood over time. The beginning of any relationship opens a depth of feelings in a way that can be overwhelming. In work, the Well can show that you possess the deep inner resources to meet the challenge. The secondary influence of Opposition asks you to accommodate the needs of others by nourishing. During a time of Biting Through you had the opportunity to discern or use the mind to comprehend events. Now you are asked to reach deeper within your reservoir of spirit to activate intuition. Observing the guidance presented by your dreams can reveal much about your life path. The object of your enquiry is something that is enduring and not easily changed. It can suggest a relationship that remains vague and undefined. Over time it can appear to be changing or moving forward yet it always seems

337

to come back to the same issues. When people are learning from each other under the influence of the Well, the connection goes deep and can give definition to the spirit. However, it is important to realize that all relationships require that the life sustaining waters are kept clear. This can mean that communication needs to be honest and open so that assumptions and misunderstandings don't dilute the purity of interaction. Whether the message is about the enormous creative gifts at your disposal or the abundance of feeling associated with the situation, the Well promises some type of inner journey of sustenance. As inexhaustible nourishment from the deep source of the psyche, the Well can be an initiation into intimacy and authentic expression.

Untie the rope,
discard the bucket.
The inexhaustible source
is the water
of an endless stream.

"One that is oppressed above is sure to turn downward. Hence follows the idea of the Well." When oppressed outwardly, you eventually turn inward. *"The town may be changed but the Well cannot be changed."* Circumstances change, although the root of experience always leads to the same place: *within.* You can change what your experiences will *"look and feel like"* by traveling inward to look at life's reflection in the great reservoir of the heart.

The master said: *"That is why the sage is concerned with what is inside and not what is seen outside. One abandons the 'that' to lay hold of the 'this.'"* The difference between 'this' and 'that' is ownership.

This resides in the Well, and Ching is the image of accessing the unknown depths of your mysterious nature. The Gentle symbolizes wood, embodying how a plant stalk finds nourishment from the wellspring beneath the earth. *"Discover the Well before you are thirsty."* You are coached to delve into the inexhaustible resource within to find your unique pattern of development. You could spend a lifetime and never come anywhere close to exhausting its resources.

At the same time, there is danger of being overly focused on knowledge or what is correct, which will disconnect you from what can be gained by experience. In this, your self-development can be arrested.

Ching is the state of mind that bubbles from the great reservoir of the heart. In the image of nine fields with the well at the center, each family farmed their individual fields, but collectively worked the ninth field at the center, since it housed the well and belonged to the lord. The eight fields represent daily routine but the ninth field required a sacrifice if one would draw from its contents. To access your undiscovered potential you need to sacrifice the *known* and travel into a strange territory.

The master said: *"Penetrating under the water and bringing up the water: this is the Well. If one goes down almost to the water and the rope does not go all the way, one has not achieved anything."* You sometimes only discover this pathway, and reach this inner sustenance because events throw you back upon yourself.

Symbolically, water has always personified the unseen and unknown. In dreams, water embodies how we approach change, and its behavior reflects how we feel about these changes. Many myths present water as the powerful reservoir, where the hero must solve a mystery before receiving a great treasure. The Abysmal appears dangerous only to those afraid to test their inner depths.

The Well holds the unseen or unrecognized potential that you can draw upon as power. *"Look within and discover the world; look without and discover the self,"* the inner and outer cannot be separated. *"The Well shows the field of character, abiding in its place, yet it has an influence on other things."* Any changes to what you experience 'out there' must first be cultivated 'in here.' What remains hidden is actively seeking expression and experience will always brings it forward.

When you look into your heart, you discover the seeds of your destiny. Composure within will always reflect itself upon experience. This is the rope that goes all the way down to the water. When you awaken sincerity, you discover the Way.

Unchanging: The well is deep = and flows from the waters of an unending stream. The Well unchanging is usually associated with deep fears we would rather not face. In a relationship, someone might be unable to make a deeper, more intimate connection because of doubts and fears. This hexagram can symbolize how you have much to share with others as an inexhaustible and nourishing soul. Since the Well is unchanging and the hexagram appears in unchanging form, whatever your object of enquiry you cannot expect the situation to change. The situation is deep, profound and not one that can be easily described. Since the Well is associated with the inspiration of dreams or intuition, you might need to look deeper into this aspect of yourself for guidance. Perhaps the Well has been there all along and yet you have not yet learned how to access it. Whatever you are sharing – the Well stays put and you need to encourage others to come to it. It is deep and profound. The Well can portray a highly inspired individual such as an artist or spiritual ally. Of course, as with anything associated with the unconscious, it is important to ensure that you are not operating in illusion or fantasy.

Line 1 One does not drink the mud of the well = no animals come to an old well. Changes to (5) Nourishment While Waiting. Some aspect of the situation has not been maintained and is no longer providing nourishment. Even while it has been neglected, Nourishment While Waiting suggests that through patience and diligent work, the source can renewed. Since the water is muddy, renewal will take an overhaul in how the situation is structured.

Line 2 At the well hole one shoots fishes = the jug is broken and leaks. Changes to (39) Obstruction. The situation is old and worn out yet does provide some nourishment. You may not have everything you want but you do get what you need. Obstruction like the broken bucket can show that all is not hopeless. However, the situation has been neglected and may be in decline.

Line 3 The well is cleaned, but no one drinks from it = leads to heart's sorrow because it could be very nourishing. Changes to (29) Abyss. Because of the fear of danger, a valuable resource is not being put to use. In a relationship, someone may be fearful and holding back. This can be heartbreaking for the other who has feelings that run deep. Only fearlessness can transform your ability to obtain your desire.

Line 4 The well is being lined = no blame. Changes to (28) Critical Mass. After a situation reaches a breaking point, it deteriorates. However since the source of this nourishment is being restructured, there will be an opportunity to enjoy it again. In this situation establishing foundational agreements may be necessary to ensure a healthy balance supports it.

Line 5 In the well there is a clear cold spring = one can drink from it. Changes to (46) Pushing Upward. The situation is robust and provides nourishment for all. Knowing how valuable something is, you are careful to keep communication clear and focused on growth.

Line 6 One draws from the well without hindrance = it is dependable, good fortune. Changes to (57) Penetration. Over time a situation proves to be a dependable source of constant nourishment. You are appreciated for the wealth of resources or insight you provide others. Supreme good fortune is suggested because you are open to sharing what you have with others. Penetration shows small efforts sustained over time.

Hexagram #49
Ko (Molting/Revolution)

Action: Transform

Hu Gua (secondary influence) 44 Coming to Meet: Encounter

Zong Gua: (underlying cause) 4 Youthful Folly: Try Again

Received as 2nd Hexagram: There is a strong need to transform your perspective, your sense of self or your approach to this situation.

**Unhappiness is the first sign
that something powerful stirs within you.**

*A mind once stretched by a new idea
never regains its original dimension. – Oliver Wendell
Holmes*

Reading at a Glance: Ko describes a situation that has
come to a point where a revolution in thinking or action
has become necessary. The Joyful Lake has a Fire
burning beneath it which brings the situation to a
boiling point and it transforms in the same way water
can be vaporized. At the same time, Ko is the image of
how animals and reptiles shed their skin in cycles.
There may be nothing familiar left about the situation
after it goes through Revolution. The Zong Gua of
Youthful Folly showed a situation where repeated
attempts can transform it. However, Ko suggests that
sustained effort will be futile because a complete
transformation is necessary. The secondary influence of
Coming to Meet can embody the fear that accompanies
the change because the new path is unfamiliar. There is
always some element of increased self knowledge
available when the hexagram of Coming to Meet is
influencing it. Molting or the changing of the skin or
hide can show that you may have conformed to a
situation that did not tap who you really are. As you
open to the transformation, you can make your debut
into authenticity. Whatever worked in the past will no
longer do and you must open yourself to deep and
powerful change. Unhappiness is usually viewed as a
negative feeling but it is the heart sending messages
about the need for change. Therefore, even while the
previous type of Joy evaporates, like rain, it will return.
There can be excited energy generated once you make

the commitment to change. In life we don't always know what we want until we discover what we don't want. Ko is a hexagram purely focused on truth, authenticity and the discovery of real fulfillment.

Shed your skin
in cycles
and reflect
your power
to renew.

"The setup of a well must necessarily be revolutionized in the course of time. Hence, follows the idea of revolution. Revolution means the removal of what has become antiquated." The Well connects you to your inner direction, although Molting is nature's sacred ceremony of renewal. Over time, the waters of the Well must flow clear to keep its contents purified.

In the old days, we used ropes and buckets, while the Well remained at the center of all social interchanges. Today, we simply turn on a faucet and barely speak to each other. Experience will always have more meaning when life revolves around the Well. Old ways of detaching from experience will no longer work and a Revolution in how you approach experience is required.

"In the landscape of spring, there is neither high nor low" because during spring, everything is *in a state of becoming.* Shedding the old skin allows you to express your full potential. Fear or the need to conform will

keep you from natural expression; only you can know what it means to be fearlessly yourself.

As the image of an animal skin stretched on a frame, you can work the hide, or outer covering to make it pliable for use. Shedding the skin of the past, you are made ready for your debut. Molting is how animals renew their outer covering as the seasons change.

Like an animal, you can fearfully take on the appearance of the landscape through conformity to hide your real self. You have a tendency to remain faceless in a crowd, although as you molt, your individuality comes to skin awareness. During the season of rebirth, you will discover that unhappiness is the hunger pain for change: it is the first sign that something powerful is stirring within you. Where the old way of approaching experience allowed you to remain hidden, you must peel away the layers that hide your real nature.

Being self-actualized and spontaneously yourself is the only way that you can remain connected to life. When civilization held mysticism and religion above reason, the world grew dark. Turning back to appreciate the principles of nature, they circumnavigated the globe, and discovered that the world was indeed, round. The great turning always creates balance. The master said: *"One is how life unites the duality of two."* Three becomes the image of an unnatural condition, and a lack of balance that generates this turning.

When you separate yourself from life, you create two ways of viewing the world. 'This is who I really am, but that is what the world expects me to be.' Somewhere in the middle of 'this' and 'that,' your real life has taken on a protective covering. To prepare for your revolution, shed your protective skin. You will discover that *this* is the person you were meant to be and you must cherish it.

Unchanging: The only constant in life is change = shed 'that' and embrace yourself. The situation is calling for some type of transformation even while you think it can remain the same. Clarity or truth is burning like a fire beneath the appearances of Joy that may not be fulfilling. There is much changing around you that you may not be recognizing. You may not know what to do although some change in thought or action will be necessary. Look at the situation to understand what has grown unproductive. How can determining what you don't want lead you to discover what you do want? You may be wearing a protective covering to hide behind while your authentic nature remains unexpressed. Perhaps you are shy or afraid to be who you are? How can life celebrate your unique qualities if you keep them hidden? Metamorphosis and molting are natural occurrences, so set yourself free. You have the opportunity to create systematic change in your life but if you choose not to, circumstances beyond your control may transpire to lead you back to your authentic path.

Line 1 Fastened and bound = in the hide of a yellow cow. Changes to (31) Influence/Wooing. Although the situation is going through a transformation, you are in the early stages and the time is not appropriate to act. Someone can be operating in fear and still in the chrysalis stage where they do not open to you. Rather than force their change, approach the situation in the way you get more bees with honey. You may need to win someone's confidence before the change can take place.

Line 2 On your own day you can begin a revolution = starting brings good fortune, without blame. Changes to (43) Breakthrough. The situation requires change and you are in a position to bring it about. Through careful planning and a resolute attitude you have the ability to make lasting changes. Because you know that the old way cannot endure, rocking the boat is in order. Others eventually recognize that the changes are indeed for the better.

Line 3 Starting brings misfortune, perseverance brings danger = when talk of change occurs three times, commitment brings the trust of others. Changes to (17) Following. After convincing others that your plan for change will be beneficial, they follow your lead. Change should not be sudden or without careful planning and foresight. It may take several attempts to achieve your desire. While your first attempts may have not worked, careful communication reveals your commitment to others and brings trust. Don't be hasty in initiating change.

Line 4 Remorse disappears and you are believed = a change in command brings good fortune. Changes to (63) After Completion. Because the rules have changed, initially the environment can be one of mistrust or sadness. The changes have already occurred and now you must regain other's trust. Your words are believed and any feelings of remorse, sadness or regret vanish. You may be forced to make changes even while not initially being supported. It may be that a changing situation seemed unfortunate at first but you realize it has changed for the better.

Line 5 The great change like a tiger = even before questioning the oracle you are believed. Changes to (55) Abundance. Whatever the object of your enquiry, the changes you are contemplating will improve the situation and are supported. Because you are fearless in letting go of the old, this attitude of Abundance leads to success. It may be that the answer is so obvious that no oracle reading is necessary.

Line 6 The best of all change like a panther while others only change their face = beginning brings misfortune but to remain persevering brings good fortune. Changes to (13) Fellowship. You are undergoing a deep transformation that others may not understand. While attempting to conform to the needs or expectations of others you lose your way. Because you persevere through change eventually success is achieved. The change in other's faces is their expression. It doesn't really matter what others think of you as long as you are being true to yourself.

Hexagram #50
Ting (Cauldron)

Action: Refine
Hu Gua (secondary influence) 43 Determination: Breakthrough
Zong Gua: (underlying cause) 3 Difficult Beginnings: Persevere
Received as 2nd Hexagram: Have patience, something is still cooking.

**You hold the power
to become the master of your existence.**

*Everyone is a moon, and has a dark side,
which he never shows anyone. – Mark Twain*

Reading at a Glance: Ting is associated with the alchemical process of transformation where the distance between spirit and ego must evaporate. On the hero's journey to fulfill one's destiny, you are first called into initiation. You can choose to ignore the call or follow it. Generally the initiation begins when the ego has been wounded or a path suddenly ends. Therefore, the Ting

350

or Cauldron is often about the deeper, spiritual and more all encompassing aspects of your journey. This is a powerful hexagram with a message about fulfilling your destiny and the enormous inspiration you possess to accomplish your aims. The cooking pot can show a situation in its beginning stages such as taking a job to receive training or the early part of a relationship that is as yet undefined. The preceding hexagrams all describe change. The Well is your access to the unconscious where its inspiration leads to the necessary change described by Molting or Revolution. While the Zong Gua of Difficult Beginnings suggested persevering or pushing onward toward your goal, the Cauldron is a complete rebirth and reconnection with your life path. In other words, most of the hexagrams are reflecting the mundane or daily experiences you encounter. When you receive the Cauldron, the perspective has broadened into a more omnipotent view of your life. If you are asking about work or relationships and receive the Cauldron as an answer, you can be certain that fate or karma is infusing the answer. There is enormous power in the situation. The secondary influence of Determination or Breakthrough can only work if you are on the right path. Life can seem to be pushing back against you as a way of ensuring you get where you need to be. With the proper Determination to succeed on your authentic path, success is assured. Since the Cauldron is a spiritual vessel, this hexagram can portray enormous talent, creativity or spiritual insight that you can tap. In a sense, YOU are the Cauldron and your inspiration is boundless.

Initiation.
A sacrifice made
for the unlived life inside.
Balance your basket
on the winding path.

"Nothing transforms things so much as the ting. Therefore follows the idea of a cauldron." The ting was cast of bronze, with three legs and two carrying rings on each side. Like most cauldrons, it served as a ritual vessel where sacrifices were made.

A ritual is how you validate the unknown, unseen or unspoken through ceremony. On a mundane level, you tip your hat, shake hands, or kiss on the cheek as each culture prescribes. This leads to the habitual behavior, which becomes common within the empire; it is also the image of how the inner empire can become a wasteland.

"Inner and outer, it matters not" they cannot be separated. Famine within, will always project itself upon the outer world. When you do what is expected of you, authenticity is lost and famine grows within and without. The Cauldron asks you to approach the invisible with a sense of reverence and sacrifice. The Well is the source within, but the Cauldron reveals how this source nourishes you in the same sense as food. The work you do 'in here' will be powerfully reflected into events 'out there.' This is how you can become the master of your present existence.

The Gentle Wind becomes the wood used to inspire the fiery flame beneath the cauldron. Unlike the image of the Well, which uses the Wood to draw from the Abysmal Water, the Wood now gives life to and feeds the Fire of transformation. The Cauldron suggests that you are ripe for your debut.

The nuclear trigram of the Gentle Wind seeks upward penetration, while the Creative remains firm at the center. It captures the image of how you are gathered toward the center of Te, where *"thirty spokes share one hub."* At its rim, you surface to call experience fortune or fate in the random turning of events. Events are not random, in that what is full becomes empty; what is still begins to stir as the Way goes round and round.

Connected to Te or your authentic center, where the center of the wheel moves the least, you are no longer buffeted by outer events. You stop traveling in circles, reacting to each event, as if you are not connected to it. Everything you will ever become takes root from within. Yet, sometimes you must traverse the wasteland to resurrect your real voice.

Exploring the power of your inner drummer, you will find a meaningful pattern unfolding in daily events to exercise your growing power. The Clinging portrays how you can move toward an awareness of the synergy existing between the inner empire, and how it takes shape in the outer world. Like the incense and smoke that is burnt during spiritual offerings, the burning Fire brings the visible to meet the invisible. At the same time, approaching the invisible can shed light on the visible.

Observing experience, you may fail to see how it mirrors the unseen world within. As the seen and unseen interact, what is called fate is how life moves to unleash your real nature. You must question what you hold to be sacred, and learn to let it go. In a world of change, the idea of sacred holds little relevance.

The master said: *"At dusk, the cock announces dawn; at midnight, the bright sun."* What is visible in one realm is only a portion of what remains unseen in another. Transcending the distinction between 'in here' and 'out there,' the Cauldron becomes a ritual vessel that offers you a deeper understanding of how you participate with life. It always responds to lead you back to the center of your Te.

Unchanging: Te is the bubbling of instinct = at the prospect of your coming-to-be-real. The spiritual associations with this hexagram describe a deep connection to your life path. In unchanging form, you may not be recognizing how profoundly life is leading you toward your destiny. At the same time, you may feel like fate allows you to just sit back to see what unfolds. The Cauldron combines enormous personal resources with the idea of destiny. This means you may need to combine Determination and action with your outlook on destiny. Your Te holds your blueprint like the image of a tree that resides within the seed. Events will unfold to peel away all protective coverings and to provide you with the nourishment that will give your destiny form. However, the seed doesn't just sit back and hide in the earth. There is a self actualizing energy at work in all living things that pushes it toward growth and to make it strong. Examine your path and connect with your inner drummer or vision. Then take the steps necessary to place yourself out there where the sun and rain can nourish you. As the image of a boiling pot that remains unchanged, the message can also be that something is still in its 'cooking' phase and you need to give it time before it can nourish you.

Line 1 A ting with legs upturned to unclog it = care of a concubine for the sake of her son, no blame. Changes to (14) Great Possessing. There is a saying about removing the 'residue of red dust from your journey' meaning to cleanse yourself of past experience or all things that hamper your forward movement. It is important to meet each day openly and without judgment. The 'heir' or result of transformational work can come from a concubine so classifications are unnecessary. As the first step toward achieving your ambitions, throw out preconceived ideas and begin with a fresh perspective. Great Possessing is a sign that your talent will be recognized.

Line 2 There is food in the ting, my companions are afflicted but they cannot harm me = good fortune. Changes to (56) The Traveler. Whatever the object of your desire, it has merit. However, you may be surrounded by negativity or jealousy. The Traveler is the ultimate hero on a solo journey of self discovery.

Follow your heart and don't allow conformity to cast a shadow over your spirit.

Line 3 The ting handle breaks so it can't be moved and one is impeded = the meal is not eaten, but once rain falls, remorse evaporates. Good fortune. Changes to (64) Before Completion. You are temporarily impeded from achieving your goal because the situation requires some type of mending. Even though you have something valuable to share it is not recognized immediately. However, all things change like the rain and after some difficulty you achieve your aim.

Line 4 The legs of the ting are broken = the prince's meal is spilled, soiling him. Misfortune. Changes to (18) Decay. This is a delicate situation requiring great care. Even with the best intentions you cannot share what you have if it is not based on a solid foundation. You are lacking in either energy, knowledge, commitment or support so without remedying what is inherently weak, doing anything can only lead to disaster. It is better to examine what has decayed in this situation and reinvigorate it or start over.

Line 5 The ting has yellow handles and golden carrying rings = perseverance furthers. Changes to (44) Coming to Meet. Because what you have to offer is recognized as valuable and nourishing, it is well received. Others can provide critical input that might actually be important. Everything is in order for you to keep pushing forward.

Line 6 The ting has rings of jade, great good fortune = nothing that would not act to further. Changes to (32) Duration. Beyond the trials that challenge and eventually lead to success, you show a suppleness in your outlook that combines talent with integrity. While you are able to achieve your aims, you have also stayed true to your life path. There is a valuable spiritual lesson that you have mastered.

Hexagram #51
Zhen (Shocking)

Action: Arouse

Hu Gua (secondary influence) 39 Obstruction: Innovate
Zong Gua: (underlying cause) 57 Penetration: Permeate
Received as 2nd Hexagram: The situation is serving the purpose of unearthing old and buried feelings so that your inner garden grows anew.

**Success comes when you
achieve tranquility in disturbance.**

*The gem cannot be polished without friction,
nor man perfected without trials.* – Confucius

Reading at a Glance: When children ride roller coasters, they discover that allowing fear to have expression is energizing. If only we could always remain joyous in approaching our fears as we move along our dusty road. Unfortunately we grow complacent and seek security and stasis. Anything in nature that becomes stagnant will be re-energized by the unexpected. *"Shock brings success. Shock comes – oh oh! Laughing words – ha ha!"* Whether hurricanes balance ocean temperatures or tumultuous autumn and spring storms invigorate new growth, nobody can hide from nature's power to keep all things thriving. The Shocking can symbolize the unexpected things that generate emotion and wake us up. It can symbolize the fear of intimacy that is suddenly awakened as stirrings of unexpected love. It can represent changes you didn't ask for but are good for you. The Zong Gua of Penetration showed a period of rest and concession, but now it is time to stir things up. The secondary influence of Obstruction is always a call to innovate. What worked in the past will no longer do. The two words most associated with Zhen is 'uh oh!' However, it should be viewed in the same laughing sentiment as children riding a roller coaster. Something is coming that is unexpected but is meant to awaken you to how you hide. Each day we witness the mutability of nature and fail to recognize it in our own life. No matter the event, the pace may quicken and you may suddenly find your heart racing and a smile on your face.

Thunderstorms
and rainbows
are born of the same
rattling sounds -
and promises.

"Among the custodians of the sacred vessel, the oldest son comes first. Hence, follows the idea of the Arousing or shocking Thunder." The Arousing means movement that disengages you from complacency. *"Shock brings success. Shock comes – oh oh! Laughing words – ha ha!"* Like a clap of thunder, sudden and spontaneous events ensue where you will observe how *"that which goes against the Way comes to an early end."*

"The shock terrifies for a hundred miles, although one does not let fall the sacrificial spoon and chalice." The sacrificial spoon and chalice carry the idea of the Well and Cauldron as the utensils used for transformation. When you are stuck in a transformational process, Shocking events come to release you from stagnation, but do not forget that you hold the key and the power to transform.

The master said: *"Everything is in destruction; everything is in construction. This is called tranquility in disturbance. Tranquility in disturbance means perfection."* Wisdom comes in knowing that whatever takes form is necessary. *"The shock terrifies and fear brings good fortune."* In the land of authenticity, fear is aroused from slumber so that it can be transformed into a greater power: *the freedom to move.* Understanding the necessity of what transpires, fear and trembling give way to tranquility and faith in the way.

In the natural world, a baby albatross will leave the comfort and safety of its nest on an island. Before it can fly, it must venture into the ocean like a duck, paddling to achieve the momentum necessary for flight. At the same time, tiger sharks will swarm in the shallows, seeking their opportunity for sustenance. Some of these baby birds will fulfill the destiny of being a shark's sustenance. Those frightened enough to attempt what they have never tried before, *will fly*. That part of you that has remained dormant will resurface in the image of quaking and excited rain.

The shocking always comes as the event necessary to transform fear into new life: *it is fundamental to your survival. "Nothing is worse than struggling not to give play to feelings one cannot control. This is called the Double Injury and of those who sustain it, none live out their natural span."* Closing down, stagnation and fear can turn energy back upon the body. The shocking is the good fortune that can awaken you to self-destructive tendencies. Holding yourself in contempt for harboring natural urges, you may intellectualize taboos that go against your base nature. In proportion to how critical you have become of others, you will recognize the severity of your inner critic. When you believe others are judging you, only turn inward to see how you judge yourself.

"*Precious things lead one astray. A situation only becomes favorable when one adapts to it. The kind man discovers it and calls it kind. The wise man discovers it and calls it wise. The people use it day by day and are unaware of it.*" Even the most shocking situations embody life's drive toward harmony. Whatever is removed makes room for something meaningful to grow in its place.

As the image of an earthquake, the ground gives way to loosen what you held to be solid and precious. In dreams, natural disasters always show how the inner foundation must continuously be renewed. The sound of Thunder is captured in the laughing words 'ha - ha!' You can move like bamboo, bending and laughing in the winds of renewal. Whatever the event, you are released of the structures that have become the tower and prison of your real nature.

Unchanging: You can hide under the bed = but life knows where to find you. Something shocking or reinvigorating is in the air. Because it is unchanging, its unpredictability is specifically what it will take to wake you up from your slumber. One who believes they can ward off love will suddenly find themselves smitten. Another who thinks they can keep lying to themselves about an unfulfilling job may suddenly be forced to switch careers. Fear may go along with the ride but if you trust how nature is always purposeful as it regenerates, you need not worry. This is a situation where you may look back and see the hand of providence with a smile. The fact that someone thinks they can ward off change is exactly why change happens. Life doesn't happen to us, it happens because of us.

Line 1 Shock comes-oh, oh! Then follows laughing words-ha, ha! = good fortune. Changes to (16) Enthusiasm. Change is in the air and while it may at first appear that something bad is happening, you will discover it has reawakened your lost passion. Like children laughing in enthusiastic fear on a roller coaster ride, the amusement park is coming to you.

Line 2 Shock brings danger. A hundred thousand times you lose your treasures and climb the nine hills. Do not go in pursuit of them = after seven days you will get them back again. Changes to (54) Propriety. You may find yourself in a situation that has trapped you because you are doing what you thought was expected of you. Events can transpire in a shocking way to set you free. Whatever you think you are losing will come back to you. The steps you were taking to move in one direction can be suddenly halted as you are swept up and placed on a different path. What is valuable and meant for you is never threatened.

Line 3 Shock comes and makes one distraught = if shock spurs action one remains free of misfortune. Changes to (55) Abundance. An unexpected situation may be causing you concern but it forces you to take action. You may want to maintain the status quo even when feeling unfulfilled, but that won't work. The change to Abundance is a positive message about reconnecting with fulfillment. Whatever is unfolding

362

will lead you to take the necessary action that will lead you from stagnation.

Line 4 There is a shock = it is mired in mud. Changes to (24) Return. You may be stirring the pot in an effort to spur one to some sort of awakening or action but it doesn't work. Some people are so deeply mired in selfish thinking that nothing can wake them from their prison. Return can be a message that rather than focus on others, do what is right for you.

Line 5 Shock coming and going that feels like danger = while nothing is wrong there is work to be done. Changes to (17) Following. This can be a situation where everyone is over reacting. There can be a lot of emotional fireworks and button pushing although nothing is done to improve the situation. Following can show how others react to you and how you react to them in an endless circle. If you want to succeed stop reacting and make the necessary changes.

Line 6 Too shocked to move and unsettled in one's self = the neighbors are hysterical but you are free of blame. Discussion of union brings gossip. Changes to (21) Biting Through. If you are in an anxious condition about a decision then it is probably better not to do anything just yet. Clarity is lost because fear is running rampant. Too much time focusing on how others view you or what they are doing is not a fulfilling way to live. You need to use discernment rather than judgment in this situation. Discernment allows the heart to have a voice while reasoning quietly 'bites through' the conflicting feelings. Once you can settle your fear and return to your own center, you will know which is the proper course to take. One can be overly concerned about what others think of a partner.

Hexagram #52
Ken (Keeping Still)

Action: Meditate
Hu Gua (secondary influence) 40 Liberation: Untangle
Zong Gua: (underlying cause) 58 Joy: Encourage
Received as 2nd hexagram: The idea of remaining still and taking no action is at play in this situation.

> **You will discover the germinating power within**
> **in the silence where a thousand seeds**
> **are becoming the landscape of spring.**

As soon as man does not take his existence for granted,
but beholds it as something unfathomably mysterious,
thought begins. – Albert Schweitzer

Reading at a Glance: "To the mind that is still, the entire universe surrenders." In meditation or yoga people learn to quiet the chatter of the 'monkey mind' which is always focused on need, fear or what is wrong in the world. Using the mind to force the body to do what it wouldn't do naturally is the only way to achieve stillness. The secondary influence of Liberation asks you to untangle the thoughts that have you on the hamster wheel. It is time to get disciplined and learn to control your fear based thinking. In the image of two mountains or two men with their backs to each other, we go into the inner temple and forget about all that is going on around us. This doesn't mean we should always negate experience. It simply means that prior to resuming activity it is sometimes good to take a sabbatical. Where the Zong Gua of Joy or encouragement showed participation in events and interactions with others, you are asked to be still and turn inward. In this situation someone is not doing what you expect them to do. You too may need to stop all the activity and quiet the mind. Whatever your query, now is not the time to act and you need to stop and be still. Perhaps you will discover something you hadn't considered if you can quiet the mind of its chatter and listen to the sound of the breath emanating from the heart.

Travel below
your
obvious foliage.
Turn backwards,
harvest the unseen.

365

"Things cannot move continuously and one must make them stop. Therefore follows the image of keeping still. Keeping the back still, one no longer feels the body." Just as the back is that part of the body that remains invisible to you, the master said: "going into the courtyard, the king does not see the people." Turning within, you can disengage yourself from outer events to re-connect with your inner voice. "Composure will straighten out your inner life," to reflect itself in your outer life.

There are times of advancing forward and times of keeping still. Ken is the image of two Mountains facing each other so the inner and outer can meet in meditation. "One does not permit the thoughts to go beyond the situation." No longer distracted by sensory input and expectation, you can reconnect with the voice of sincerity within. In the image of an eye, looking around to see what has led to the present situation, when you lose your sense of stillness, you lose the self and become lost in your surroundings. "To find the self, you need only recapture your sense of stillness."

When the master asked a pupil why he would sit in meditation, the pupil replied that it was a way to know Tao. The master picked up a tile and began to polish it against a rock. When the pupil asked why he did this, the master replied that it was a way to make a mirror. The pupil asked: "How could polishing a tile make a mirror?" The master replied: "How could sitting in meditation produce Tao?"

You turn inward to reflect on events, where the inner and outer can meet in meditation; not to deny the relevance of all experience. Unlike other types of meditation, the ancient Taoist sought only to release the sense of separation existing between 'in here' and 'out there.'

Ken is a message about recapturing this pure perspective. In the image of birds moving through the sky, they seek their destiny, but leave no trace; they are challenged by circumstances, yet eagerly celebrate each sunrise. *"Continue easy and you are right."*

The master said: *"When the fish is caught the trap is forgotten. You gallop around in search of the mind and are unable to stop it."* When the idea comes, the mind is forgotten. Yet, the mind is the trap, while what you capture is the 'thing event' that represents your passing desires. No mind allows you to connect with a greater movement that is endless. Life speaks to you and you must cherish each opportunity to understand it.

"The fish must not be allowed to leave the deep." The fish is the treasure of Te. It is that place within, which holds you to the center of each experience. You are coached to cultivate an awareness that remains unattached, deep and therefore, becomes profoundly powerful.

The master asked: *"Where is your place of birth?"*

The pupil replied: *"This morning I ate rice and now I am hungry again."* Need is an endless movement without a home.

The master asked: *"How is my hand like Tao?"* The pupil replied: *"Playing the lute under the moon."* Joy comes when you discover yourself emerging upon the tapestry of life.

The master asked: *"How is my foot like a donkey's foot?"*

"When the white heron stands upon the snow, it has a different color." All things will always remain relative to each other…this is all that you can really know.

When you shadow life, you shadow your beliefs. They can become traps on the pathway of true perception. Whatever the trap, you can unseat it by letting go.

"The court is corrupt. The fields are overgrown with weeds. The granaries are empty, yet there are those, who are dressed in fineries." Oblivious to a lifeless inner landscape, you may come to wear the costume of what is expected of you. If you can open to the mystery within, the real journey of individuation begins.

Unchanging: When the outer world stops responding = stop seeking and turn within. The object of your enquiry is currently in an immovable condition. If you are expecting to hear from someone or get an answer, the time is not right. Others may be taking time for themselves prior to re-engaging. Keeping Still unchanging can show a person with their back turned to you, perhaps out of defensiveness or anger. Nothing you can do or say will change this. Just allow time to heal the wounds. If your question involves making a move, it is probably not the right time. There is more information or time needed to understand the situation more clearly before doing anything. In any type of negotiation, make your offer and then step back. They say 'the one who speaks last loses.' If you are feeling frenetic or anxious explore meditation or yoga to learn to quiet the mind. Keeping Still and surrendering to unfolding events will be the easiest way forward.

Line 1 Keeping the toes still, no blame = continued perseverance furthers. Changes to (22) Grace. While you may be anxious to move forward, the time is not right. There is an element of acceptance or looking beyond the façade at the deeper elements of the situation. Keeping the toes still in perseverance is a message not to take action.

Line 2 Keeping the calves still, one cannot rescue who they follow = the heart is not glad. Changes to (18) Decay. You may want to change another's direction because you feel that it is incorrect. This can be a situation of co-dependency where there is nothing you can do, although you feel the sadness it brings. If you are unhappy being swept up in the drama, let it go. There is nothing you can do except create the boundaries where you are not owning another's condition.

Line 3 Keeping the hips and sacrum stiff is dangerous = the heart suffocates. Changes to (23) Splitting Apart. Forcing stillness on natural desires creates inner conflict. Splitting Apart can show a time of examining

369

thoughts and feelings so that you can move forward consciously toward your desire. Keeping Still because of fear is not the same as moving freely while establishing boundaries. Some element of the situation requires more flexibility, rather than repression.

Line 4 Keeping the trunk still = no blame. Changes to (56) The Traveler. While you may be over reacting and frenetically searching for a solution, you are coached to remain still and give the mind a rest. Free from external distractions, you can find a sense of peace within. The Traveler's greatest lesson is finding the home within.

Line 5 Keeping the jaws still = the words have order and remorse disappears. Changes to (56) Propriety. One of the greatest lessons in any type of enlightenment is recognizing how words are a measure of inner certainty. If we are insecure and uneasy, we can talk too much. Keeping Still so that one's speech is orderly and not arguing or selling anything allows the situation to advance. Propriety is a careful and respectful attitude when interacting with others. Silence is a powerful way to truly listen or to allow another the space to organize their thoughts.

Line 6 Noble hearted and keeping still = good fortune. Changes to (15) Authenticity. While something is not shared or held back, it is not because of anger or ill will. The hexagram of Keeping Still allows one to organize thoughts and actions with moderation. There is a friendly attitude and much compassion in this situation, even when it seems you are not receiving the response you desire. By remaining still and avoiding worry, you can accept that what is unfolding will lead to good fortune.

Hexagram #53
Ji'an (Development)

Action: Flower
Hu Gua (secondary influence) 64 Before Completion: Prepare
Zong Gua: (underlying cause) 54 Propriety: Subordinate
Received as 2nd Hexagram: You may want the situation to move more quickly but it won't. It is unfolding at its own pace which takes time.

Success comes
when you pull your nature forward
without pushing yourself into the world.

A man will be imprisoned in a room with a door
that is unlocked and opens inwards,
as long as it does not occur to him to pull rather than push. —
Ludwig Wittgenstein

Reading at a Glance: Ji'an shows the gradual development of how a woman follows a man to become his wife. The secondary influence of Before Completion reveals how all developments must be allowed the time and patience necessary for the course to complete itself in a natural way. In the image of a tree, which grows slowly, something rises from a seed or blueprint within. We too are endowed with Te, or the knowledge within that guides our dreams and holds the design of who we are growing to become. The Zong Gua of Propriety reflected subordinating the will or being placed too quickly in an unnatural situation where you must catch up. Gradual Development shows the opposite as a time of moving forward step by step or patiently waiting for something to unfold. This hexagram has emphasis on living from the inside-out rather than the outside-in. Like a tree nourished by the sun and rain, we may look to the outer world for elements that nourish us, but we do not look to others for answers about who we are. This information is sacred to our Te or internal blueprint. We don't push ourselves into the world, we pull from the core of our inspired center and Permeate our being ness into the world. There is a need for a gentle, adaptable and penetrating approach just as a tree spreads its arms displaying its rich foliage – "this is who I am." A commitment of endurance and the elimination of the 'monkey mind' is required. We must quiet its tendency toward survival, always looking for threats and what is wrong in the environment. Instead, we wake up in each and every moment balanced in the knowledge that we are living from the inside out. By honoring who we are, life celebrates our arrival. The lines refer to the Geese which symbolize a connection between our organic and spiritual nature demonstrated in grace and dignity. They walk on land, float in water and soar through the sky revealing how following instinct and relying on surrounding elements to uplift us, we always arrive exactly where we need to be. This hexagram can show a relationship with a need to allow for patience so that one or the other has time to catch up to the other's feelings.

Plant yourself
in the same silence
where a thousand seeds
are becoming
the landscape of spring.

"Things cannot stop forever; therefore follows the idea of development." The Gentle Wind moves on the Mountain in the image of a tree developing according to the laws of its being. The tree on a mountain benefits all, but must grow slowly in accordance with the seasons.

The seed holds within, all that it will one day become, although it must remain steadfast through the changing climate. The tree becomes a lesson of perseverance in your unfolding as you move forward from the foundation of te. Because its growth is slow and steady, it demonstrates the principle: *"a little then benefited; a lot then perplexed."* Should it shoot up too quickly, or at the wrong time, its roots will never keep it upright when the first storms set in. What you are attempting must be cultivated slowly and   patiently.

Bo Ju ji wrote about trees: *"they are useful friends to me and they fulfill my wish for conversations with the wise."* Steadfast and benefiting those seeking comfort, they are the wisest of the earth's teachers. *"When difficulties come, do not lose sight of the power of life. It is only in the depth of winter when there is frost and snow that we have means of knowing how luxuriant the pines and cypresses are. To be in unbroken contact with the stem of life, the germinating power of nature, and to make Te the door to all wisdom; that is what is meant by being a sage."*

You may push yourself forward into the world to achieve success, although if you pulled yourself forward from the roots within, you will find authentic and lasting success. No two trees are alike and they do not grow well in each other's shadow. *"Only one that is entirely real in each experience will have the power to give full development to one's nature. Realness is self-completing and the Way is self-directing. Realness is the end as well as the beginning of things, for without realness there would be no things at all; which is why the sage prizes above everything coming-to-be-real."*

Development coaches you to observe the gradual way that you cultivate the roots of who you are, rather than searching outwardly for validation. If you merely strive to be real, success will come naturally. Like a tree, you must remain steadfast in your unbroken contact with the germinating power of life. In relationships there can be time needed for two very different people to move forward in tandem. In work, the message is that there are great possibilities for growth but it will take time to develop.

Unchanging: From planting to harvest = many seasons of patience and care. Both the upper and lower trigrams of Development show a tranquil, patient and meditative attitude. When you receive Development unchanging you may be feeling that events should be moving more quickly and you can be feeling impatient. The message is that patience is the only way to achieve your goal. It is not that you need to stop any action. You should work diligently, but know that progress will go slowly. In a relationship, you may need to allow the partner time to understand their feelings and catch up to you. Whatever the question, a conservative and practical approach on a traditional path would lead to success. You can't sell anybody anything. Allow events to unfold naturally and organically.

Line 1 The wild goose gradually draws near the shore = there is danger and talk. No blame. Changes to (37) Family. In moving toward the object of your enquiry, you may have received criticism which can teach you something. Because you are innocent of fault, don't take it personally. Boundaries may need to be established so communication can flow more easily.

Line 2 The wild goose gradually draws near the cliff, eating and drinking in peace and concord = good fortune. Changes to (57) Penetration. As you move forward, a concession may be necessary that allows you to Penetrate more deeply into the situation. This leads

to peaceful sharing and Development reaching solid
ground.

Line 3 The wild goose gradually draws near the plateau
= the man goes forth and does not return. The woman
carries a child but does not bring it forth. Misfortune. It
furthers one to fight off robbers. Changes to (20)
Contemplation. The progress one had is lost because of
differing goals. It may feel like you are being taken
advantage of in this situation but there is a need for
Contemplation. You may be wasting your energy or
attempting to force your will in the wrong direction or
on the wrong person. However, it may simply be your
fear that is seeking to validate its own existence so let it
go.

Line 4 The wild goose goes gradually draws near the
tree, perhaps it will find a flat branch = no blame.
Changes to (33) Retreat. You may need to adapt to an
unusual situation by leveling out your thinking. While
the situation may not be ideal it does provide for a safe
environment while you wait for something better. Being
docile and pliant allows you to find comfort while you
examine your future direction.

Line 5 The wild goose gradually draws near the
summit. For three years the woman has no child = in the
end progress. Good fortune. Changes to (52) Keeping
Still. While you make progress toward your goal this
can bring about jealousy and opposition. You must
continue to work diligently toward your aspiration

knowing that by Keeping Still and doing the work you will reach your goal.

Line 6 The wild goose gradually draws near the clouds heights = its feathers can be used for the sacred dance. Good fortune. Changes to (39) Obstruction. The situation allows you to reach your aims and you can even become a source of inspiration for others. By understanding how Obstruction is just a need to innovate while pushing forward, you have much to teach others. You achieve success like getting a feather in your cap.

Hexagram #54
Kui Mei (Propriety)

Action: Subordinate
Hu Gua (secondary influence) 63 After Completion: Renew
Zong Gua: (underlying cause) 53 Development: Flower
Received as 2nd Hexagram: Someone or something about this situation is currently unavailable to you. You may be in a back up position.

**Instinct is the bubbling of Te,
excited by the prospect of your coming-to-be-real.**

*Not the cry, but the flight of the wild duck,
leads the flock to fly and follow.* – Chinese Proverb

Reading at a Glance: Kuei Mei or the Marrying Maiden is about subordinating the will or the need to accept what cannot be changed. You may find yourself in a suspended situation because of changes another is going through or events beyond your control. At the same time a sudden turn of events can place you in a very unfamiliar environment where you have no experience to draw upon. You can't do much about the situation other than wait to see how events unfold. It is not uncommon to receive this hexagram when you are seeking partnership with someone who is currently unavailable. As the 'second wife' or concubine, you may be the other woman or other man. The secondary influence of After Completion underscores a time of waiting for some type of change or completion to sort itself out. There is no reason to think that you cannot achieve the object of your desire. However the act of subordination is necessary and that is not an easy thing for most people. The Zong Gua of Development showed the slow, practical steps necessary to achieve a desire. In Kuei Mei the situation can appear or change suddenly and you are forced to adapt to uncertainty as best you can. The lines in this hexagram refer to the changes a woman faces when she marries and goes into a new home and adopts a new family. It is not her ancestral home and she will not be immediately accepted. Propriety shows adapting to conventionally accepted standards of behavior. This means that although the situation may not be what you had hoped for, you will learn a lot about your patterns of thought, your defenses and even the wisdom that comes from allowing life to lead you into the unfamiliar. Since it is called The Marrying Maiden, success comes after a period of testing. Often the 'second wife' or concubine gives birth to the heir and rises to become the 'first wife.' Just because you are wandering on a road you have never traveled before, don't be dismayed. Rather than push forward willfully with demands, acquiesce and allow the situation to unfold.

Give your carved block
to the Woodcarver.
Let the cutting
shape
your gift.

"Through progress, one is sure to reach the place, where one belongs. Hence follows the idea of the subordinate." The Arousing Thunder moves over the Joyous Lake, while the nuclear trigrams reveal something profound stirring within. Before moving forward, Kuei Mei asks you to *"understand the transitory in the light of the eternity at the end."* Some things will change, while other aspects remain enduring. To know the difference is something you will only discover by opening and learning from the challenges you face.

Perhaps you feel powerless to change a current situation. You may have been impetuous in actions and are now paying for it. Even while this can be a difficult time for relationships outwardly, there is much you can learn about yourself going forward.

Oftentimes we pursue what we believe we need without giving consideration to whether it is right for us. We can fail to listen or see the signs that might help us shape our desire into something lasting. This is the core of what it means to follow. We need to marry the will to the way and to the needs of others. The message of Subordinate is that you are either facing the consequences of being impetuous or are warned against acting impetuously in the future.

"Some things lead, and some things follow." Like the marriage of man and wife, they are usually brought together by something other than logic: *they follow their heart.* However, sometimes the heart is just the bubbling of desire and need without respecting that this coming together must serve each individual. This is the difference between love and lust. In following the way, we recognize that desire must subordinate to how life guides us.

"Once there was a wood carver. When he first began to carve, he gazed at the wood in front of him. After three years, he no longer saw it as a piece of wood, but as something of shape that merely required the movement necessary to give it form. In time, he no longer saw it with the eyes, but apprehended it with a different type of vision. Decision and action were

simultaneously joined, and as he worked, his sense organs were always in abeyance. By conforming to the structure that led him, he carved deftly and without effort."

Like the woodcarver, something within requires only that you allow life to carve away what keeps it hidden. When you subordinate yourself to life, you will discover that *"the greatest cutting does not sever."* Life merely carves away what keeps you from being authentic and fulfilled.

The migrating bird does not follow because of the cry of the other birds. Each bird follows its own instinctual call for flight. Although you follow the shape of what you believe will become your future, your destiny is given definition in the mirror of what unfolds right now. The master said: *"To understand the transitory in the eternity at the end, release the experience and hold only to the thread."* This will allow you to open to the instinctual pull of your evolutionary journey.

"Go on to the limit of emptiness: hold fast to the stability of stillness. For, all things were made by one process and they all turn back. They may flourish abundantly, but each turns and goes home to the root from which it came. Therefore, to turn back is to reclaim your destiny." When you make peace with life, you will discover its enormous power to guide you. As if it already knows your shape, it carves away only the layers that keep you from coming-to-be-real.

"If your true nature has the creative force of Nature itself, wherever you may go, you will see fishes leaping and geese flying." When you make yourself subordinate to the path, *"the greatest cutting does not sever."* Experience always leads you back to yourself. When you follow life and return to your roots, decision and action are simultaneously joined. What is joined cannot be separated. This is the essence of a commitment to the Way. Instinct is the bubbling of Te, which connects you with the germinating power of life.

Unchanging: Forced into an inferior position = be true to who you are. The subordinating energy of this hexagram when it is unchanging can be a message that another's unavailability is not going to change. There can be power games and manipulation at play rather than healthy subordination. In work you may be feeling like you are not getting the recognition you deserve. The politics may be such that this will not change. You may be asking about a potential partner and there can be a prior entanglement or another person who is really in charge. You would remain in an inferior position. Propriety needs to be examined because you may be interfering in something that is none of your business. The message can be that you are barking up the wrong tree. However, by carefully examining your principles, you may be able to succeed by ensuring you are taking appropriate and ethical actions. The unchanging nature of this hexagram can show that you are in a holding pattern of your own making because you do have the power to either accept your subordinate position and make the best of it or move on. Being true to yourself is the important lesson you are learning.

Line 1 The marrying maiden as a concubine, a lame man who is able to tread = undertakings bring good fortune. Changes to (40) Liberation. There is not a lot you can do in this situation but it does provide some possibilities. Perhaps you walk away from a debilitating situation and achieve Liberation of some type. There can be fear associated with throwing down the crutches and hobbling down the road but it is Liberating.

Line 2 A one-eyed man is able to see = the perseverance of a solitary man furthers. Changes to (51) Shocking. Perhaps if you had all of the details of this situation it might shock you. The good thing is that you are only seeing half of it and this allows you to preserve. Sometimes less is more and if you are trying to uncover a reason to leave you will find it. We are either committed to staying or looking for reasons to go. You may be in a period of hibernation or soul searching and events can change quickly to bring you back out into the open. To be one-eyed is to have the other turned inward and to concentrate on your own happiness and fulfillment without giving much thought to what others are doing.

Line 3 The marrying maiden as a slave = forced subservience. Changes to (34) Great Power. In this situation powerlessness may be an issue. Either you need to take an inferior position with dignity or return to your power and reject the situation so you can achieve something better. A more fulfilling situation may be around the corner because you do not sacrifice your dignity.

Line 4 The marrying maiden draws out the allotted time = a late marriage comes in due course. Changes to (19) Approach. You may need to wait for a more fortunate situation to show itself. Because you hold to your principles, you are rewarded as others Approach you. Rather than selling out for something less desirable, waiting out the situation leads to success.

Line 5 Daughter given in marriage who's gown was not as gorgeous as the serving maid = when the moon is nearly full good fortune. Changes to (58) Joy. One accepts a lesser position to recognize fulfillment later. Appearances are not everything as the grace of one's inner dignity makes for real beauty.

Line 6 The woman holds the basket, but there are no fruits in it. The man stabs the sheep, but no blood flows. Nothing that acts to further. Changes to (38) Opposition. This is a difficult line showing what happens when you remain in an unhealthy situation. You may have sacrificed too much of your own needs to acquiesce and are now feeling unfulfilled. While conflict may have been guiding you toward making changes, the opportunities went unnoticed. Too much of the will has been sacrificed and the unfortunate nature of this hexagram reaches its peak in this line. If you are not feeling fulfilled changes are in order.

Hexagram #55
Feng (Abundance)

Action: Fulfill
Hu Gua (secondary influence) 28 Critical Mass: Adjust
Zong Gua: (underlying cause) 59 Dispersion: Flow
Received as 2nd Hexagram: Too much of a good thing is not necessarily good and letting go is sometimes the only way to receive.

If you make your heart like a lake,
life will continuously fulfill you.

Everything flows and nothing abides;
everything gives way and nothing stays fixed. – Heraclitus

Reading at a Glance: In nature we see how all things flow toward increase and decrease. The zenith or height of fullness is expressed in the hexagram of Abundance. It is a snapshot of you at an apex point and is very auspicious. However, at the zenith of our fullness we must keep positive even when events move toward the opposite condition. Like the sun at noon that begins to move toward decrease, we hold to the expanded awareness of an abundant state of mind, regardless of how events unfold. Because the secondary influence is Critical Mass there is a warning that the current state of Abundance can only be sustained by not hoarding or believing that fullness can be protected. It must flow outward freely and be shared. While this hexagram has a positive message, it can also show a situation that is overwhelming you and you may not be seeing clearly. The Zong Gua of Dissolving shows what happens in the opposite condition. The clarity of enlightenment comes when awareness is activated through this motion of increase and decrease. This can mean finding peace even while a situation is in decline. Operating from abundance means that by expecting that everything is moving exactly as it should, we need not hold onto anything. Because our arms are open, nothing comes to threaten our sense of peace. When operating from a state of scarcity, we are afraid of losing and cling too tightly to what we believe we need. In this condition, life appears to be fighting us. The lesson of this hexagram is to realize that since abundance exists, it will return. Sometimes our arms need to be set free to embrace fearlessly so that we can receive. For now enjoy this period where your success shines brightly. Examine whether you are holding to scarcity or abundance. Make peace with the path and trust what is unfolding will lead you where you need to be. Life's only constant is change.

All of nature
is participation
and the sharing
of each
unique offering.

"*That which attains the place in which it belongs is sure to become great. Therefore follows the idea of abundance.*" In the land of Te, you can operate from scarcity or abundance. Scarcity is a kingdom where all of the people are hungry because they do not know how to grow sustenance. They take what they feel is missing, and conquer others out of a sense of inadequacy. Operating from the root of scarcity ensures that you will discover opportunities to validate its existence.

Abundance is a kingdom with a horn of plenty, where the people cultivate and share in the knowledge of an inexhaustible source. Described as the Land of Te or virtue, "*they know how to make things but do not hoard. They give but seek no return.*" Te is your instinctual endowment where inner promptings help you actualize your destiny.

Feng is the zenith of abundance, where something is so full that it overflows. In the image of your overflowing inner reserves, you are not made empty even while you give; this is the way of a kingdom of abundance. The master said: "*When the sun stands at midday, it begins to set: be not sad. The fullness and emptiness of life wax and wane in the course of time.*" If you make your heart like a lake, life will always fulfill you.

"The wise stand firm and do not change direction. A gusty wind and downpour cannot last all day." The changing climate always brings sustenance to the garden within. The longest day of the year means that tomorrow ushers in decline. Yet, when the days are darker, we spend more time with family, celebrating the ways in which we are thankful.

Although the sun appears to set and the moon appears to wane, they always remain full. Life always moves to fill you, but if you are un-fulfilled, you have allowed yourself to be filled with something else. What you protect within, gives rise to what you encounter. *"Too much holding onto anything will leave you perplexed. Leave your kingdom and its ways; take nature as your guide and travel to the land of Te."* You stand at the threshold of actualizing abundance.

This hexagram can show the expansion of consciousness because the simply joy that comes from trusting in unfolding events is something that can never be taken from us. To understand that everything is a reflection of our growth and perfectly what we need to discover in each moment is the basis of enlightenment.

Unchanging: Too much of a good thing = can overwhelm. When receiving Abundance unchanging the situation can be overwhelming in a way that leads to a lack of clarity or boundaries. You may be overdoing or being over emotional toward the object of your inquiry. Abundance in a static condition is not a give and take arrangement. Someone may be holding back in a type of punishment that has its roots in their own insecurity or jealousy. The only way you can release yourself from a situation that has become unbalanced is to focus your energy elsewhere. This reading can also show the negative side of wealth where one has a lot of possessions but a lack of real fulfillment.

Line 1 Meeting a powerful ally, even if only together for ten days = it is not a mistake, going meets with recognition. Changes to (62) Small Exceeding. In this situation forming a partnership with someone of like mind brings recognition. One party contributes energy while another has vision so great things can be accomplished A valuable arrangement presents itself and is beneficial even if only for a limited time.

Line 2 The curtain is of such fullness that polestars are visible at noon = going meets with mistrust although holding to truth brings about good fortune. Changes to (34) Great Power. Someone has shielded themselves in a way that brings about mistrust. Even while encountering a period of darkness or intrigue, remain sincere and you will succeed. The challenge to your integrity leads you to prove its existence in a way that makes your character more powerful. This invisible influence demonstrates your inner state of abundance.

Line 3 The abundant rain glistens like stars at noon = breaking the right arm, no blame. Changes to (51) Shocking. In this situation you are not in possession of enough facts to proceed and cannot see clearly. Even while attempting to assist someone else, you can only be harmed or misunderstood in the process. Shocking refers to the unexpected or unknown so give the situation more time to develop before making any decisions.

Line 4 The curtain is of such fullness that polestars are visible at noon = one meets an ally, good fortune. Changes to (36) Brightness Hiding. Although you may feel that the situation is less than ideal, the eclipse of your clarity is waning. This line suggests projection and the ability to recognize the Shadow. What we experience is always a reflection of our beliefs. Allowing others to teach you about what you do not recognize within leads to good fortune.

Line 5 A colorful sky after a storm = blessings and fame draw near, good fortune. Changes to (49) Molting/Revolution. Because of your modesty, you are able to tap the talents of those around you. You are recognized for your ability to weather any storm and succeed. Your abundant state of mind allows you to draw on the assistance of others.

Line 6 Having abundance in the house but no connection to others = for three years seeing nothing, misfortune. Changes to (30) Clarity. Due to arrogance or greed, one experiences only scarcity even while appearing wealthy. Abundance that is gathered from a sense of insecurity is not the same as Abundance in thought and action. One can only become isolated and alone if Abundance is really scarcity in thought. Clarity is the ability to transform fear into trust so that the situation can become more abundant by opening to others.

Hexagram #56
Lu (The Wanderer)

Action: Explore
Hu Gua (secondary influence) 28 Critical Mass: Adjust
Zong Gua: (underlying cause) 60 Limitation: Regulate
Received as 2nd Hexagram: Complacency sometimes roots us in unhealthy ways so trust that the path is leading you where you need to be.

And the still deeper secret of the secret:
the land that is nowhere, that is your true home.

He had the uneasy manner of a man who is not among his
own kind,
and who has not seen enough of the world to feel
that all people are in some sense his own kind. — Willa Cather

Reading at a Glance: It is said that the greatest Wanderer does not know where they are going. After the zenith of the previous hexagram, there usually follows an anti-climax where the atmosphere becomes uncertain again. Lu symbolizes the message that it is the journey and not the destination that is important. Something is changing and you will need to be flexible to adapt. Familiar routines and comfort zones will no longer do. The secondary influence of Critical Mass shows the importance of not becoming too complacent where stability can lead to stagnation and even collapse. The Zong Gua of Limitation shows the opposite condition, where we hold to the familiar and abide by rules. For now, the vistas open before you and like the Fool in the Tarot deck, it is time for an adventure. Taking the road less traveled or leaving the ordinary behind is the only way to invigorate your sense of discovery. Wandering or traveling is an opportunity to examine the baggage you carry with you. Perhaps it is time to lighten your load? You may be changing residences or careers and an open minded attitude will serve you well as you approach the changes. You can be a gardener of people and yourself by acknowledging how individual differences can lead you to experience something different about yourself. Your way is only one way so be open to what Wandering into the unknown can teach you.

The greatest traveler
has no itinerary.
When traveling, be a gardener
of each new experience.

"Whatever greatness may exhaust itself upon, this much is certain: it loses a home. Hence follows the idea of the

wanderer." You may follow the path of the Wand mastering the art of living in a place without boundaries: *"This is the deeper secret of the secret. The land that is nowhere, that is the true home. When some people travel, they merely contemplate what is before their eyes; when I travel I contemplate mutability."* When you wander in the land of Te, all of life is a place of discovery. You push onward toward new horizons because *"the greatest traveler does not know where he is going."* If you follow, there are no limits to what you might become.

When far from home, you take your inner treasure and ritual along. *"When the heart is uneasy, we support it with ritual."* Your daily 'ritual' is more obvious when you are forced to pack it for a long journey. To travel with companions, much energy is wasted in fortifying the dynamics of familiar routines. When you are traveling alone, you are more authentic and free to discover your real capabilities.

Some part of you is active during dreaming, where you access an awareness that becomes a postcard sent to awaken the one who sleeps by day. Each night, you travel back and forth from a strange land to understand the real essence of who you might become. When you dream, you access a place *"as though there is no home to go back to."* When morning comes, you travel "across the doorsill where the two worlds touch." Yet, you are always traveling across a tapestry that transcends boundaries. This is the openness required to be a Wanderer.

In the image of people loyal to a home that is far away, the Wanderer points to an endless expanse of sky, and shows you how the horizon is an illusion and that there are no real boundaries to your capabilities. The seed of self-realization is unfolding regardless of where you are. The current situation will not linger, and you will soon travel onward, although you have developed a sense of loyalty to carry with you. Everywhere you go, there you are, in a giant tapestry of your unfolding.

To approach the mystery of Tao, *"you cannot take hold of it, but you cannot lose it. In not being able to get it, you get it. When you are silent, it speaks; when you speak, it is silent. The great gate is wide open to bestow alms, and no crowd is blocking the way."* When you discover the great gate, you may lose a paradigm, but will discover your true home.

Unchanging: The Wanderer is not home = enjoy the road less traveled. Receiving the Wanderer unchanging can show a current lack of commitment or an undecided situation similar to the Hanged Man in the tarot deck. Its message that all things become softer in time shows that if you give the situation time and remain flexible it can change in your favor. The Wanderer symbolizes the unknown period that follows any zenith so while you are seeking a definitive answer there is much that is evolving in the situation. Separations or an unplanned change can be on the horizon. You may have the opportunity to experience an entirely new way of life. Unchanging, the message is to let go of preconceived thoughts and remain open to the unfamiliar.

Line 1 The wanderer is caught up in trivial things = this leads to misfortune. Changes to (30) Clarity. You are in a situation where others may not understand your actions. Respect the needs and routines of others and seek more to understand rather than be understood. Pushing your agenda on others can only annoy them. This is a time of learning from an unfamiliar situation so remain open to how you might change your way of thinking or responding.

Line 2 The wanderer arrives carrying possessions on the back = winning a committed young servant. Changes to (50) Cauldron. Although you are operating in an unfamiliar environment you are respected for being modest and flexible. This leads others to help you. The Cauldron can show sacrifices made for the benefit of the group. In this situation life can be reduced to bare necessities so that your sense of value can go through a transformation and lead to a stronger partnership.

Line 3 The wanderer's inn burns down and the young servant is lost = danger. Changes to (35) Progress. Rather than appreciate the kindness of others in a situation where you are being aided, your behavior is not winning you friends. This line is a warning not to bite the hand of those who feed you. Beware of impulsive responses that burn bridges in a way that you lose the support of others.

Line 4 The wanderer rests in a shelter and obtains property and an ax = but the heart is not glad. Changes to (52) Keeping Still. While you have arrived at a comfortable situation and your basic needs are met, the overall atmosphere is not fulfilling. Respecting others and biding your time leads to greater opportunity in the future. Examine what is missing in the current situation and whether it is just your attitude that requires adjustment.

Line 5 The wanderer shoots a pheasant with an arrow = this brings praise and an opportunity for advancement. Changes to (33) Retreat. There are behaviors required in this situation that you may not be comfortable with but are necessary in establishing a connection. Because you demonstrate a willingness to abide by the accepted norms others open to you. Retreat shows how strength and character can be asserted in a peaceful way. Shooting a pheasant was a customary introduction when foreigners visited new territories and offered it as a gift so a sacrifice may be in order.

Line 6 The nest burns up, at first the wanderer laughs and later weeps = losing the cow in the process leads to misfortune. Changes to (62) Small Exceeding. Through carelessness or selfishness one loses their resting place. In the beginning it may not seem so bad but later one feels remorse and realizes the consequences of their actions. Rather than appreciating what one had and remaining modest like a cow, selfish motives lead to misfortune. There will be plenty of time for regret and repentance.

Hexagram #57
Xun (Penetration)

Action: Permeate

Hu Gua (secondary influence) 38 Opposition: Accommodate

Zong Gua: (underlying cause) 51 Shocking: Arouse

Received as 2nd Hexagram: You are not a victim ~ no lines separate you from the life you create. Breathe into this moment and relax, it is yours.

**Something very profound
is also committed to your success.**

When the oak is felled the whole forest echoes with its fall, but a hundred
acorns are sown in silence by an unnoticed breeze. – Thomas Carlyle

Reading at a Glance: There is gentleness and enormous power associated with the hexagram of Penetration. Like the wind blowing over vast periods of time against a mountain, the smallest influence when applied with a steadfast attitude can break down any barrier. The idea of looking more deeply at a situation in order to understand its less obvious dynamics is also at play. Whether you or someone else has established barriers as protection from intimacy, constancy and demonstrating trustworthy behavior can eliminate them. After the hexagrams about reaching an apex and then moving like a wanderer into the unknown, Penetration is a message about constant and gentle action and is often referred to as the Homecoming. In some ways we need not assert anything because there are other forces acting in conjunction with our efforts to bring to a sense of arrival. The extended time period suggested by Penetration is like hexagram 5 Waiting and hexagram 32 Duration which all require great patience for reflection and the power to influence in a permeating way. The secondary influence of Opposition can show the barrier you are faced with and the message suggests that you become more accommodating. The Zong Gua Shocking showed the opposite behavior where events are jarred suddenly from stagnation. This is not the case in this situation and you are being called to become gently persevering. Like Sita in the Indian myth of Ramayana, she was captured and forced through many trials to prove her loyalty to Rama. In this situation you may feel tested to prove your loyalty over an extended period of time. This hexagram is formed by the trigram of the Wind over the Wind so the message of slow and dedicated effort is doubled. After a period of uncertainty and wandering, this hexagram can show coming home.

Move like
the wind -
its soft lullaby,
sculpting
mountains.

"As a wanderer, there is nothing that might receive you.
Therefore follows the idea of the Gentle and penetrating
Wind." Perhaps you have met an obstacle that has you
moving in different directions. Trying to find a way 'in,'
the opportunity may appear closed. However, you
might seek the help of someone in a position to guide
you. With penetrating effort and remaining still,
you will discover that *something profound* is also
committed to your success.

When life touches you, you may feel that something
profound has moved you. Yet, you must ask yourself
what was happening in your life that made you recognize
its magic at that moment? Life is always touching you
in sublime ways; you sometimes only glimpse it when
circumstances emerge to *slow you down.* The Gentle
Wind is a message about steady progress and
steadfastness in the face of difficulty. It slows you down
enough to look deeper into a situation. You are given
time to see that things are not what you thought.
Through trial you may have to prove your loyalty,
commitment and sincerity to your cause.

The sublimity of life demonstrates a type of wisdom
that continuously wrestles you back to the correct
pathway. When you stop trying to understand life in

your terms, you can open to recognizing *yourself* in its terms: *there is something very unique about you and its potential knows no bounds.* Nature always fortifies those committed to success even when the path appears blocked or seems to go backwards.

"The Gentle shows the exercise of character. One can weigh things and remain hidden." By penetrating to the core of circumstances without *doing* anything, you can influence events and move forward.

The master said: *"What is easy attracts the easy; what is hard will attract the hard."* If you are open, there is no need for life to break away your protective covering. *"The way is easy, yet people prefer by-paths."* If you remain easy, you invite the easy. The Way is easy because all it asks is that you remain supple enough to be led.

This is how you can gently influence events. Success comes when you no longer *"contend and yet are be able to conquer; do not declare your will and yet, get a response; do not summon, and still have things come spontaneously to you."* Te, as the 'power in me,' when tapped as nature's drive toward individuation, does not fight the very thing that gives it definition. When you are *just so* all that you need always comes spontaneously to you.

Steadfast and open, *"life leads the thoughtful person on a path of many windings. Now the course is checked, now it runs straight again."* In the image of items arranged on a table, something is needed to support them. After each experience, you will discover how life supports you to *keep growing*. The Wind is invisible and yet influences everything upon the earth. You can find a sense of contentment where others experience only frustration by trusting that everything is unfolding as it should. Adjusting your sails to harness how life moves you, 'one who never fails' is the mark of one devoted to the Way.

Penetrating experience with the same effort as the gentle Wind, you will discover too, that *"when the decision is made, all things come to you."* This is steadfastness. Embracing nature's pursuit of the best of what it might become, you awaken into a world that always meets you half way to bring it forward. As *"a mirror that receives, but does not hold,"* know that whatever you are seeking, you will find. In the suchness of life, you will discover that something very profound has been committed to your success since the beginning.

Unchanging: When the way forward is blocked by rocks = climb up for a better view. You may be pushing too hard to alter a situation that is very complex. Any blockage may require that you examine your sincerity or prove that another can trust you. This is a hexagram of Homecoming so a period of wandering can be followed by returning to an environment of comfort and peace. Penetration unchanging can lead to success if you are patient enough to remain dedicated to your cause regardless of what obstacles are presented. In fact, it may just be this type of testing, where your sincerity is defined over time that will allow you to achieve your desire. Nothing will happen quickly when you receive Penetration unchanging but over time a lasting commitment can be made. Allow any barriers or obstacles to your forward movement to become a source of enlightenment. Constancy in gentle action and allowing for deeper penetration or understanding are keys to your success in this situation. Any barriers to intimacy or union will eventually erode in the same way the Wind will chisel away a mountain over time. Actions speak louder than words and you may need to prove to another that you can be trusted. This may take some time so be patient and persevering.

Line 1 Advancing and retreating = the perseverance of a warrior furthers. Changes to (9) Small Restraint. In being gentle in your actions, it can appear as indecisiveness. At the beginning when meeting a challenging situation you may not feel confident enough to assert yourself. The problem is that you may be looking for a quick fix or sudden resolution in a situation that will actually require the tenacity and discipline of a warrior. Small Restraint is a message about surrender. You can achieve the object of your desire if you do not attempt to exert the will but move gently and resolutely forward.

Line 2 Penetration under the bed, priests and magicians are used in great number = good fortune without blame. Changes to (53) Development. There are elements in this situation which have roots in your beliefs. Sometimes consulting others who can be more objective will allow you to penetrate more deeply into why you find yourself hitting a wall. Both Penetration and Development suggest digging below the superficial surface aspects to understand your or another's fear projections.

Line 3 Repeated penetration = humiliation. Changes to (59) Dispersion. You may be going over the details of this situation over and over but are failing to understand the deeper dynamics. The solution is tied to your willingness to look objectively at new possibilities you hadn't considered. At the same time, indecisiveness can be born from spending too much time thinking and not enough time doing something to change it. Dispersion is a message to release and go with the flow. Action is required in a gentle and open minded manner.

Line 4 Remorse vanishes = during the hunt, three kinds of game are caught. Changes to (44) Coming to Meet. Penetration allows you to understand the part you play in any type of difficulty. Coming to Meet suggests taking responsibility for your Shadow projections with modesty, honor and action. In this way you can obtain your objectives because of your willingness to see all sides of the situation. The three kinds of game can represent how you see yourself, how you see others and how you see yourself through interaction with others.

Line 5 Perseverance brings good fortune, remorse vanishes and nothing that does not further = no beginning but an end with three days before and after the change. Changes to (18) Decay. This can be a difficult situation that requires time before it can resolve itself. While you may initially want to fall back into an unfulfilling routine, you are asked to step back and be patient. Deterioration is at play and the necessary change will result in better conditions. Three days before and after change are a message about thoughtful action after careful consideration.

Line 6 Penetration under the bed, losing property and an ax = perseverance brings misfortune. Changes to (48) The Well. By trying too hard or too quickly to apply change to the situation you may actually lose it. The Well suggests how a situation appears to change when in actuality it does not. By looking too deeply at the situation or sacrificing too much, you can lose your identity and your power. All of your searching is not getting you anywhere so it is better to make a decision and move forward with it.

Hexagram #58
Tui (Joy)

Action: Encourage

Hu Gua (secondary influence) 37 Family: Support

Zong Gua: (underlying cause) 52 Keeping Still: Meditate

Received as 2nd Hexagram: Treat others as you would be treated and remember that life always brings opposite energies together to achieve balance.

Take aim at your heart
and release your passion.

*If you would hit the mark, you must aim a little above it; every arrow that flies, feels the attraction of the earth. –
Longfellow*

Reading at a Glance: The type of Joy that follows the hexagram of Penetration shows a sense of arrival. However, more often than not it was an inner opening rather than the effort or movement to change outer events that has led to your current Joy. Often we feel the opposite of Joy in the form of unhappiness and see it as something negative. Unhappiness is the hunger pain for change so how can it be bad? The saying, "if you never fail, you will always succeed" means that if failure is taken in stride as a prerequisite to success it isn't really failure. This accepting outlook leads to joyousness on the journey. The secondary influence of Family shows how we find purpose and meaning by offering encouragement to others. The Zong Gua of Keeping Still showed the focus on the Self. Now we must understand our relationship to what unfolds and our interactions with others to facilitate Joy. This is an excellent hexagram for artistic ventures and relationships. Where the hexagram of Innocence teaches about being at the threshold of experience without judgment and Grace shows how we experience life's benevolence, Joy is the outcome when we apply both to each and every experience. *"Content in your circumstances and genuine in kindness, you are the expression of the love that renews all things."* A change in attitude shows us that while we can do little to change the events that unfold around us, a change in perspective can magically change everything. Be Joyous in thought and action and celebrate others. Since life is your mirror it will reflect joyousness back to you.

Unhappiness
is the hunger pain
for change.
Joy -
its constant companion.

"Once you have penetrated something, you rejoice." When experience is no longer separated by 'in here' and 'out there,' you can be *"active everywhere, but are not carried away; in your knowledge of grace, you are free of care. Content in your circumstances and genuine in kindness, you are the expression of the love that renews all things."* Just as *"spring never fails in its task,"* life will never let you down.

Joyous of heart and content in thought, *"you can determine good fortune and misfortune on earth, and bring to perfection everything you see."* Good fortune is merely a pathway where nothing needs to be 'undone.'

Being content in knowing how life is leading you will allow you to discover more and suffer less. This is the sublimity of how nature brings perfection to the earth. The master said: *"If you would have a thing laid aside, you must first set it up."* You are given the opportunity to block this joy or receive it, because it resides perpetually in your heart. Only you can set it free.

To lay aside your barriers, you must first 'set them up' or come to understand how you block your ability to be joyful. Cultivating a sense of joy that you carry wherever you go can become a way of living. Although you must sometimes aim high, knowing that failure will always pull a little on your accomplishments.

One who meets all experience as a growth opportunity, never fails and always succeeds. *"Life is the refuge for the myriad creatures. It is that by which the good man protects; it is that by which, the bad is protected. Even if a man is not good, why should he be abandoned?"* In the image of someone speaking and making things equal, Tui shows how life excels on bestowing because it is always productive.

Accessing the transformative power of nature that resides within you, contentment or discontentment is simply the measure of your joy in following. *"Rid the self of expectations to find the accidental environment where joy is manifesting."*

Unchanging: Self sufficiency leads to isolation = encouragement is infectious. We sometimes become so self sufficient that we cut ourselves off from the joy of sharing our experiences with others. People who give us gifts get pleasure from doing so and we deny them that pleasure if we are not able to receive. In the same way, we can experience more joy in life by giving to others without any thought of what we get in return. If you are gentle and accepting of others, recognizing their divine suchness, you can celebrate all of life. If you are feeling judged, it is because you are probably judging others. Joy in its unchanging form can be a message of encouragement to see beyond the obvious where joy might exist. At the same time, you may be hoping for something that is not really right for you and might understand this later. You might be called to encourage others even when they are not able to ask for your support. Exchanging information, opening and letting go of resentments can be at play. Someone around you

408

may need encouragement. Like the sun, rise each day activating your subtle power of expansion to set off a chain reaction of abundance. Be the light of joy for others in their times of darkness.

Line 1 Contented joyousness = good fortune. Changes to (47) Oppression/Exhaustion. You may feel like you are confined or oppressed but you may be learning about the quiet joy of contentment. You may need to see beyond good and bad with your normal judgment to see that everything is perfect. This is a great learning opportunity that the sages call tranquility in disturbance. If you can step back and not engage you will find that your inner being can fortify itself. Sometimes silence is the perfect answer that can teach you about contented joyousness.

Line 2 Sincere joyousness, good fortune = remorse disappears. Changes to (17) Following. There is no greater pathway to joy than to understand your own sincerity. We follow others and often become lost. Life tests our sincerity so that we discover what we really want and what is right for us. However, after a misunderstanding, you may need to trust in following another's initiative even when the way seems foreign. Joy experienced by trusting or discovering sincerity of the heart is true joyousness.

Line 3 Coming joyousness = misfortune. Changes to (43) Determination. If you place your ability to know joyousness on outer circumstances, when it is not forthcoming, you lose your joy. It is better not to force or manipulate events for a desired outcome but to allow life to unfold on its own terms. The breakthrough associated with Determination can show either pushing too hard to force events or the breakthrough in thinking that returns you to acceptance of the moment. In that place, joyousness can remain perpetual. True joy must spring from within.

Line 4 Joyousness that is weighed is not at peace = after ridding yourself of this mistake, you have joy. Changes to (60) Limitation. When you live too much in the mind, analyzing every response of lack of response, you lose your joyousness. Judgment and measuring give and take behavior never leads to joy, only a sense of compensation. To give unconditionally or to accept unconditionally leads to joy. Once you recognize this limiting behavior joyousness returns to all you do.

Line 5 Sincerity toward what is disintegrating = dangerous. Changes to (54) Propriety. You may be placing your faith and trust in something or someone who finds no value in what you offer. The danger is the suffering, hurt feelings and a lack of joy you experience. Propriety or subordination shows that you are in a lesser position. However, if you can remove the threat of danger and acknowledge the difference between reality and illusion, you can avoid interacting with negative people or elements that can only bring you down. This line shows the fine line between perpetual inner joy and fantasy. When it is time for something to disintegrate for renewal, you must be open to the change.

Line 6 Seductive joyousness = leads one astray. Changes to (10) Treading. When joyousness reaches this upmost place, situations can trend toward Dispersion in the following hexagram. Treading shows a person focusing on their footsteps and the path to discover more meaning in life. However, this outward searching can be overdone and we can wander away from being centered in joy. Too much looking around to reinforce our sense of worth or self esteem leads to vanity and instant gratification. You may need to balance a sense of discovering meaning in unfolding events with the power of being sincere in joy. We are only seduced when we have lost self love, self respect or our connection to our internal compass.

Hexagram #59
Huan (Dispersion)

Action: Flow
Hu Gua (secondary influence) 27 Nourishing Vision: Nurture
Zong Gua: (underlying cause) 55 Abundance: Fulfill
Received as 2nd Hexagram: Life unloosens bindings so that we can find our true home.

There is a thing confusedly formed
and it is an all or nothing equation.

There is a destiny that makes us brothers,
no one goes his way alone;
All that we send into the lives of others
comes back into our own. – Edwin Markham

Reading at a Glance: Dispersion focuses on the interdependency of life and your connection to all you see. If you are feeling isolated or cut off from others, examine the defenses or walls that make you feel uncomfortable opening up to others. When a landscape becomes hardened because of a lack of rain, dust storms scatter the soil and the winds can actually create the storms that rise up to renew the parched environment. All things are supple when alive and are only hard when dead. Dispersion is nature's tendency toward renewal so when events appear like a storm, open your soul to the rain. In this situation there can be a hardness in thinking or response that is leading you to encounter hardness in the situations you face. We join groups because of the ways we are alike and grow uncomfortable because of our differences. But it is our differences that make us the unique creation that nature intended. There will never be anyone like you and only you know what it means to be fearlessly yourself. Dispersion is a snapshot of the way that nature finds harmony even while it honors differences. The secondary influence of Nourishing Vision asks you to take responsibility for how your outlook effects what you experience. If you want to experience union, seek to unite. If you want joy, be joyous. The Zong Gua of Abundance showed a sense of recognizing your potential and shining alone, but now it is time to share who and what you are with others. If you are in a situation that appears to be dissolving, know that behind any hardness your emotions are being reinvigorated much like the rain. Don't be afraid to allow the truth to come to light because something can only be corrected by admitting that correction or healing is needed.

Life scatters to reunite
in seeds upon the wind.
Be lifted up
by the unknown.

"After joy, comes dispersal. Dispersion means scattering." As a child, perhaps you played with dandelion pods, blowing their white, billowing seeds into the wind. Little did you realize the enormous complexity of a life form that harnesses the wind in its pursuit of regeneration. Scattering is a message about sharing your unique gifts and releasing any boundaries that separate you from others.

Over 100,000 species of mammals, insects and birds go about their daily routines, inadvertently transferring seeds or pollen grains from the male variety of one plant to the female variety of another. Why would nature devise such a complicated system of reproduction? If you were to view life as one giant organism, you would discover many checks and balances that seem to amount to an all or nothing equation.

The wellness of nature's individual parts relies on the well-being of the whole. The master said: *"If this was not the most divine thing on the earth, how could it do this?"* The sublime complexity of nature creates communities where each species thrives in each other's presence. Herbivores need plants; carnivores depend on herbivores, and predation keeps a natural balance. Without scavengers like bacteria, waste could not be regenerated into plants. Without the carbon consuming oceans and rainforests, the animals would be deprived of oxygen. At the same time that life is broken up, you can observe how it is regenerated through a reuniting. In the image of how life scatters to expand, *"there is a thing confusedly formed."*

When you open to life's interconnectivity, you can observe nature performing at its best. *"How do we know what life wants of us? It embraces and benefits all. How do we know that it embraces all? Because it holds all in its possession and bestows all creatures with the gift of food."* Although you may take this simple benevolence for granted, it is actually quite profound. This is not a time for limitations and self imposed barriers in your thought processes.

When we observe the interdependency inherent in the natural world, we must wonder if we too, are scattered to reunite in some way that we have yet to understand.

The master said: *"My Way has one string which threads it all together."*

"The Firm comes and does not exhaust itself; the Yielding receives and what is above is in harmony with it." One who can appreciate nature's profound power for renewal, and would explore 'harmony in one's greater relationship to life' will find a profound level of initiation on a pathway of environmental work. *"Whatever we do to the web, we do to ourselves."* To become a steward of just one small portion of life will create a chain reaction that reverberates across the entire tapestry, which always returns to make you stronger.

"Who can be muddy and yet, settling slowly come to life? Who can be at rest and yet, stirring slowly come to life? One who holds fast to Tao."

Undefined and yet, complex; interdependent and inspired to drive each thing to be unique, life finds harmony, even while it honors diversity. Observing this complicated chain of sustenance reveals that nature is not only your teacher, it is also your redeemer. It suggests how you must sometimes let something go in order to discover if it is real for you. Nothing real can be threatened because if it is real it will remain. Open to the ways you are connected to others and don't be afraid to share everything you are in all of your quirkyness. Whether a hardened outlook needs to soften or a relationship has reached an impasse, when you discover and open to your profound connection to everything around you, Dispersion is the only way home.

Unchanging: The inner landscape is like a garden = time is the wind that keeps it renewed. While you may find yourself at an impasse with another, there is a gentle and penetrating influence stirring deep emotional reflection. In the image of wind blowing over the water any hardness that might lead to dissolution will dissipate. Barriers that are preventing you from the object of your desire need to be addressed. This is not the time for limitations and defenses. You need to flow more. You may feel disconnected from others or feeling out of place but dispersing suggests that you begin to understand how you rely on others. The only thing stopping you from deeper interaction is your own fear of being real. With Abundance as the Zong Gua, you may be holding onto what you possess without realizing that sharing can lead to deeper fulfillment. The Gentle Wind moves slowly so you may need to give the situation time to develop. The deep waters can suggest spiritual, emotional or a creative rebirth that is brought about by opening.

Line 1 Bringing help with the strength of a horse = good fortune. Changes to (61) Inner Truth. If there is an obstacle to union, it is good to address it immediately. The strength of a horse can represent controlling the will in a way that makes you able to follow another's initiative without losing your Inner Truth. Perhaps the situation will allow for a deeper connection of shared trust. The good fortune comes from following a natural course that allows for an amicable relationship of sharing.

Line 2 It is dissolving, rush to what supports you = remorse disappears. Changes to (20) Contemplation. When feel alienated from others, introspection is required in order to see that we are misjudging others. Observing what is supportive and not supportive, we can't just take a selfish view. In most cases those that challenge us are helping us to grow. Pride or arrogance will not connect you to others. Try to be objective in seeing how your relationships provide more support than you realize. If you can change how you are viewing others in a mistaken way you can avoid suffering and achieve harmony.

Line 3 One dissolves the self = no remorse. Changes to (57) Penetration. When we are focused too much on our individual needs or are busy defending our opinions and fears, we become alienated from others. To dissolve the self is like the saying: to overcome others we have power but to overcome ourselves we are strong. We find freedom when we are strong enough to control the ego and its fears and tame our mind. While there may initially be hard feelings in this situation, it can turn around with a simple movement away from selfish aims.

Line 4 Dissolving with the group leads to accumulation = good fortune from an innovative approach. Changes to (6) Conflict. When relationships run their course sometimes we feel only the loss without recognizing how this leads us toward experiences more appropriate to what we are becoming. At the same time, staying in cliques can keep us from meeting new and innovative friends. It is important to stay open to the flow, knowing that closing ourselves off to those we meet can keep us from growing. Since most meetings are propitious, seeing strangers as new friends can lead to great good fortune.

Line 5 Loud cries dissolve like sweat = dispersion, but the one in charge stays put. Changes to (4) Youthful Folly. The message from Youthful Folly is to keep trying. There may be a lot of emotion and opposition, but the situation is leading to the dispersion of defenses. After much arguing and trying to hold onto the past, the situation softens into union. Perhaps you realize that all the fuss just brings you back to where you started and it is not so bad after all. There can be a power play going on that causes friction only while holding power is the aim. Someone may require an unusual amount of emotional stroking due to insecurity and can be behaving a little childishly. Perhaps you or they are testing their desire to go or your desire to stay the course as a type of loyalty is proven over time. Dispersion makes all things equal because we see the relationship as being more important than our individual needs. In this way we learn how to listen, share and move to a deeper level. The one acting childishly has a knack for staying in charge.

Line 6 Dissolving in blood, departing and keeping a distance = without blame. Changes to (29) Abyss. A situation undergoing dissolution can become dangerous if we keep reacting and pushing each other's button. The fear of loss and the pain of being misunderstood is what we defend at such times. This is a perfect situation where seeking to understand is more important than seeking to be understood, or where listening is more important than defending a position. Abyss teaches us to relinquish control. Dispersion can reunite but it can also lead to disunion. Your position or stance is what will determine the outcome.

Hexagram #60
Jie (Limitation)

Action: Regulate
Hu Gua (secondary influence) 27 Nourishing Vision: Nurture
Zong Gua: (underlying cause) 56 The Wanderer: Explore
Received as 2nd Hexagram: The need for boundaries is at play so whatever is limiting you needs to be respected.

Adaptation prods you to harmonize with the changes. Everything you will ever need can be found within.

Follow effective action with quiet reflection. From the quiet reflection will come even more effective action. – James Levin

Reading at a Glance: Following the hexagram of Dispersion which teaches us about not creating boundaries or barriers from others in our thinking, Jie or Limitation provides the opposite message. More often than not the idea of Limitation is the reason we make changes in life. In nature, limitations are the breeding ground that allow for the development of strengths and diversity. Both Dispersion and Limitation share the same nuclear hexagram or secondary influence of Nourishing Vision so both emphasize thought processes. In Dispersion we are coached not to create boundaries in our thinking when understanding the role we play in relationship to the world around us. In Limitation, we must honor the restrictions we inevitably face as guidelines or roadmaps that lead us to transform. The Zong Gua of the Wanderer was a time to disconnect and wander into the unknown to explore how to move beyond limitations in thinking. Now the situation calls for clear communication, agreements and guidelines so that relationships can function optimally. Limitations can resemble an obstacle to forward progress but the obstacle is really an opportunity to change how we view obstacles. Seedlings encounter rocks in the soil but the rocks keep the soil at the root where it is needed. Rather than opening to what is inexhaustible we now must focus on containment. You may have to work with the idea of 'no' to discover how to make changes in your approach. You may need to clarify something prior to gaining the support you are seeking from others. The greatest lesson Limitation teaches us is that while we might fight against the flow in terms of disappointment, we would do far better to recognize the reason for the limitations we face and how they serve our well being. In fact it may just be your preconceived ideas that lead you to experience walls. Something runs out, an unwanted change is thrust upon you, someone says no or you suddenly have to make do with less. There is a reason for all of this and you must step back to see how the Limitation is actually corralling you in a more appropriate direction. The idea of Limitations can stop you in your tracks but stopping and establishing structures, goals, business plans, agreements or a well thought out plan of action is in order.

Limitations
are the
breeding ground
for
nature's strength.

"Things cannot be forever separate. Therefore follows limitation." The Abysmal Water over the Joyous Lake is an image of something inexhaustible being contained for use. Limitation portrays how you can access an inexhaustible source within and yet, are able to give each experience definition. There is a danger that these

definitions can come to limit your ability to grow. Somewhere in the middle is a perspective that respects limitations as necessary for developing structure, definition and agreements. However, we must not assume we can classify an idea and put it away forever. Nature is about change and our path will always be about change.

The process of adaptation demonstrates how limitations force creatures to harmonize with a changing world. Opportunistic adaptation appears in the Yellow Jacket variety of wasps, which have come to resemble honeybees. Once their insect diet disappears in late summer, they often raid honeycombs to feed their appetite for sweets. Ravens too, have developed an opportunistic relationship with wolves. They will cry out to alert wolves to potential prey, so that they too, can eat.

Limitations activate the adaptive response, which transformed the scales of some dinosaurs into feathers. We tend to associate feathers with flight, although there are many birds that do not fly. While flight does aid survival, feathers developed as an evolved way of regulating body heat. Many reptiles still rely on shade and the warmth of the sun to adjust their temperature. The power of nature reveals how limitations drive the engine of evolution. Although you may grow frustrated with restrictions, limitations not only make you stronger, they also shape your forward growth.

"Once, a farmer of sheep lived beside a man who owned hunting dogs. Every night the dogs broke through the farmer's fence and killed several of his sheep. The farmer complained to the neighbor on several occasions, although the situation never changed. In great frustration, he sought the advice of a judge who told the farmer that he could solve his problem, but only if the farmer promised to do what he suggested. The farmer agreed, but the judge told him to give the neighbor two of his best sheep! The farmer was outraged. Since he was a man of his word, he returned home and offered his neighbor two of his best sheep. The neighbor received this unexpected gift with suspicion. Knowing that the farmer was a man of his word, he thanked him and assumed that it was in return for his incessant complaining. The next morning, the farmer expected to find the usual broken fence and missing sheep, but all was well on his farm. Because the neighbor now had sheep to protect, he had built a fine enclosure for his hunting dogs.

When you adapt to another's point of view, you will begin to see how harmony already exists in all discord. The imbalance needs to be addressed. To harmonize with the changes, a shift in perspective makes what appears difficult, easy. Do not approach limitations as barriers, but see them as a springboard for discovery and innovation.

Nature uses limitations as a creative treasure trove to explore endless variations. Accessing the power of nature, you can rise to meet each challenge with the same innovative vision of growth.

Although you may find yourself in an environment of limitations, recognize how you might develop a side of you that remains unexplored. Just as your environment develops new characteristics within you, your limitations will always be intrinsically tied to the development of your strengths.

Unchanging: Limitations lead to success = but only if you have a plan of action. When Limitations appears in its unchanging form the message is that the situation will not correct itself until a healthy respect for boundaries is acknowledged. If you have a disagreement with someone, guidelines and clear communication can address it. Ensure that everyone understands exactly what is being agreed upon to avoid further conflict. You may need to set boundaries in your relationships so that your own needs are being addressed. You will face a period of Limitation because you may need to develop clearer focus. In business, you need an actionable business plan. In relation to health you may need to enact more discipline if you are not moderate or exercising. Limitations allows you to achieve more and to stay healthy and balanced.

Line 1 Not going out of the door into the courtyard = without blame. Changes to (29) Abyss. In this situation Limitations are explored because someone feels it may be dangerous to proceed without them. Not going out of the door shows a type of retreat that allows you to fortify a clear plan of action. When disorder appears, words can lead to order. Maintain your silence until you can approach the situation with an objective plan

424

that serves all parties. The Abyss teaches us to relinquish control so you may need to give someone the space to establish their own boundaries.

Line 2 Not going out of the gate into the courtyard = brings misfortune. Changes to (3) Difficult Beginnings. The time calls for action not retreat or hiding. Difficult Beginnings shows a type of fear when meeting a challenge, however all new endeavors can be challenging. By limiting yourself too much you miss important opportunities. Don't cut yourself off from others who are able to support you. Don't be afraid to make a commitment or to take a first step. The situation cannot improve if you don't open the gate and go out to seek improvement.

Line 3 Not knowing limitation gives cause to lament = no blame. Changes to (5) Waiting. Because you do not understand why Limitations have been thrust upon you, you may be feeling disenchanted. Don't give up because by Waiting for the right time to act you can still achieve success. Because boundaries or limits are not being respected others can feel invaded or threatened. Step back and allow the situation to develop before making any assumptions. A period of Waiting is required to understand how to approach the Limitations you face.

Line 4 Contented limitation = success. Changes to (58) Joy. Sometimes the pursuit of joy or pleasure leads us to abandon any sense of limitations. Overdoing and extravagance always leads us to a place of scarcity.

However, enjoying oneself while clearly aware of a need for Limitation allows for a sense of abundance that is enduring. Being content with limitations not only allows you to experience more but also ensures that stability endures. When you are content with the Limitations you do not waste energy and are able to achieve great things. You understand completely that everything is unfolding exactly as it should. The path to Joy requires that you understand the saying: those who follow find contentment.

Line 5 Sweet limitation brings good fortune = going brings esteem. Change to (19) Approach. The best teacher knows that they must teach by example even if nobody follows you initially. Operating within limitations with a sense of discipline is a way to show others that limitations are the breeding ground for success. In this situation the limitations are pleasantly accepted and all are in accord. Approach is a message about being an example to others so that our skills are sought out. Going shows the effort of moving forward as opposed to coming which shows retreat.

Line 6 Galling limitation, perseverance brings misfortune = remorse disappears. Changes to (61) Inner Truth. You may need to look deeper into this situation to explore whether it is a good fit. Limitations and discipline which are too severe or too restrictive cannot be maintained over the long haul. There is a fine line between how Limitation can lead to success and how it can create resentment. Sometimes we can be pushed too far and the limitations imposed upon us force us to re-evaluate what we are doing. Even if you have to give up and move on, over time any disappointment will fade away. If you have the opportunity to stop being demanding or to lighten up, take it.

Hexagram #61
Zhong Fu (Inner Truth)

Action: Trust

Hu Gua (secondary influence) 27 Nourishing Vision: Nurture

Zong Gua: (underlying cause) 62 Small Exceeding: Conserve

Received as 2nd Hexagram: The truth may not follow popular consensus or your expectations but it is the truth nonetheless.

**Do not seek to follow
in the footsteps of the wise,
seek what they sought.**

*Nature never says one thing
and wisdom another.* —Decimus Junius Juvenalis

Reading at a Glance: As one of the last principles in the
Book of Changes, the development of Inner Truth is
perhaps its core message. We are told to treat each
principle as our parents, learn from nature and discover
the part of us that is unchanging and already alive
within. Tao active in the individual is called Te. It is like
a blueprint we were born with that we will evolve to
become. In fact, much of life is an opportunity to peel
away the layers of conformity that keep us from being
who we are meant to be. Inner Truth can be the
perspective we seek where we stand upon the firm soil
of our unique nature and observe events for how they
are coaxing our inner nature forward. We move into life
and are buffeted about by the activity, following others,
misreading the signs and casting judgment. At some
point we can become lost. What will it take to return
you to your authenticity? What is needed to allow you
to quiet the mind of worry and see the beauty of Grace
unfolding in each moment? One word: Experience. The
Zong Gua of Small Exceeding suggested flying under
the radar, tending to the small things and reducing
visibility. But now it is time to go out and test your
vision while interacting with others. Experience seems
to be a measure of what is needed at different times to
reveal us to ourselves. If you are centered in Te and
observant but not reactive, life seems to flow more
gently. If you believe you must be like others, life will
prod you back upon your path which can feel
uncomfortable if you are unwilling to go there.

Nourishing Vision as the secondary influence appears in many of the hexagrams because we must go forward and we must also take time to turn within. This is what happens when we dream. We have experiences and place judgments upon them that are sometimes incorrect. Ego would have us constantly avoiding any threat to how it upholds the status quo or its constant pursuit of comfort and stroking. If you observe nature you will see that finding protection to remain stagnant is not an option. All things in life are growing and all things are evolving from the blueprint or seed within. No matter what is unfolding around you, take time out to ensure that you are being true to yourself. React less and simply be responsive. Find this solid perspective within your unique nature and hold to it as your center while going out into the world.

> *Throw the rock -*
> *the water ripples.*
> *Life's energy flows*
> *through you in waves.*
> *Reverberate to your center.*

"Through being limited, things are made dependable. Hence follows the image of inner truth." The Wind blows over the Lake, while the Mountain and Thunder are stirring within. Chung Fu offers a message about achieving steady and Joyous movement even while you open yourself to every possibility for renewal.

Chung Fu has two open lines within, which are surrounded by firm lines. This openness at the center reveals great power because *"a heart that remains open can be guided by inner truth."* Difficulty is always transformed, once you can approach it like a question rather than an obstacle. *"A heart that is free of prejudice in meeting adversity will discover only favorable circumstances."*

To activate nature's transformative power within, you must remain objective in meeting the necessary tension that keeps you evolving. Do not fall prey to the illusion that when you reach the height of your inner truth, circumstances will not continue to further shape you. *"Be not sad,"* tension is the driving force of evolution.

However, you can begin to see tension as evolving peace, where peace must then give way to further transformations. Moving Joyfully through life's fluctuating movement in harmony, allows you to find comfort in the way of change.

Life continuously shakes you free from any stagnant way of thinking. You may give in after a long struggle or endless defeat, and this 'giving in' reveals how the pathway could not have been otherwise. Forced to make minor changes, these changes become significant to your success. This small shift in acceptance goes a long way in reducing anxiety. It is no simple thing to say: *"know contentment and you are rich."*

"Wind over the Lake: the image of inner truth." You may remember throwing stones into the Lake to observe how it moved in circular waves that rippled outward toward the shore. Even if you were to throw a

rectangular block into the water, the waves would still move in perfect circles. This is because the 'fabric' of water is not what it appears to be. Its horizontal movement is an illusion; its molecules spin vertically and remain where they are. As each molecule spins, the water crests in waves, although the molecules do not move. It is merely *energy*, which is moving through the medium of water molecules.

Observing people sitting in the bleachers at a football game, to create the 'wave,' each one stands and throws their arms into the air in succession. Like the water molecule, they remain where they are, while the energy moves from one to another across the stadium.

Like the center of the molecule, Chung is the center out of which you evolve. Fu is how you hold to it, regardless of where the changes lead you. The energy of change can move you in different ways, although the core of who you are *becoming* remains stationary. This center can be awakened by the changes, but it cannot be abandoned. You can observe your emotions as the waves or response to the movement of energy flowing through you.

The center you hold to gives shape to your unique destiny. Buffeted by events, you remain true to this center. Regardless of what you do, when you keep doing it, your actions will define your character. The force that keeps you connected to this center is your philosophy or *inner truth*.

"In the pursuit of learning, one knows more every day; in the pursuit of following life, one does less every day. One does less and less until one does nothing at all, and when one does nothing at all there is nothing that is undone." Chung Fu is an image of an arrow at the center of a target, with a bird's claw encircling a hatchling. It offers the idea of both, capture and protection.

"When your discernment penetrates the four quarters, are you capable of not knowing anything?" Chung Fu is the subtle way that you merely hold to your center and always hit the mark. The great claw becomes the image of how life protects you and holds you to this center.

Unchanging: You know the answer = it is the truth you run from, speak your mind. The message of Inner Truth unchanging is that you may already know the answer even while you continue to search for it. You have made your truth known and it really doesn't matter what the response is. Getting to the truth was perhaps the most valuable lesson you could learn from the situation. You may be rushing to judgment or being overly emotional without giving consideration to the truth of the matter. Trust your gut instincts and stay true to yourself. You may have asked a question and the answer would be: yes, you are right…you know the truth already so act on it.

Line 1 Being prepared brings good fortune = if there are secret designs, it is disquieting. Changes to (59) Dispersion. This lines begins the tying together of all that was learned from previous hexagrams. At the

threshold of experience we are innocent and remain
without judgments in the sense of being prepared. In
this situation you may have ideas of what should be
happening that are keeping you from seeing what *is*
happening. Dispersion is about letting go and if we
don't learn to follow the flow, it is disquieting. The
hexagram of Inner Truth always reveals how events
unfold as a reflection of whether or not we are being
authentically in the moment. Whatever your question, it
is leading you into deeper discovery of your Inner
Truth. Be open.

Line 2 A crane calls from the shade and its young
answer = I have a goblet of wine and together we will
share it. Changes to (42) Increase. After the preparation
of innocence we begin to explore our relationship to
others. From the heart we share our story and it
resonates outward to those of kindred spirit. The story
grows larger as we inspire, learn from each other and
weave individual pieces together into a shared whole.
Even when we are not visibly together we remain
connected. The situation is one of kindred spirits in this
way. Confucius spoke of the caution necessary in word
and action because their effects can be felt thousands of
miles away. If our words are from the heart they bring
honor even if we stand alone. If our words are spoken
merely for attention and selfish vanity, they have no
substance even when surrounded by others. Speak from
the heart.

Line 3 He finds a comrade. Now he beats the drum,
now he stops = now he sobs, now he sings. Changes to

433

(9) Small Restraint. After preparation in an outlook
without judgment and integrity in expression we move
deeper into our relationships with others. We can
declare this one is our friend and that one our enemy as
if we can really know the propitious way Tao brings us
together. Others opinions or responses can make or
break our day if we have no Inner Truth. In this
situation you are being told to stop allowing others to
be the center of who you are. When your center of
gravity is not in the Self, you will only be buffeted
about between joy and sorrow. Get centered.

Line 4 The moon is nearly full but the team of horses go
astray = no blame. Changes to (10) Treading. This line is
usually the line that can make or break how you adhere
to the principles of the hexagrams. When the team of
horses go astray, you lose your focus and your Inner
Truth. The situation is challenging but don't give up.
You may have enormous respect and admiration for
another that is breaking your forward stride and Inner
Truth. Tread carefully. Be humble but don't abandon
who you are.

Line 5 One possesses truth, which links together = no
blame. Changes to (41) Decrease. There are times when
we must hold to our Inner Truth regardless of the
ramifications. However, in understanding and honoring
another's point of view we can make concessions or
decrease our need to be right in a way that brings
union. While we may not agree we can agree to move
forward to learn about synthesis. In this situation there
may be no concrete answer except that parting or

retreating is not a satisfying option. Decrease the idea of right and wrong and be accepting of others.

Line 6 Cockcrow penetrating to heaven = perseverance brings misfortune. Changes to (60) Limitation. The situation can be one of exaggeration where what you are saying isn't actually what you are feeling. Inner Truth is the combination of expression and authentic feeling. Any limitations that you are experiencing are teaching you to combine expression with authenticity. Expressing emotion is not the same as expressing your truth. Give the situation time so that you can continue to explore what it is teaching you about authentic feeling and expression.

Hexagram #62
Xiao Guo (Small Exceeding)

Action: Conserve
Hu Gua (secondary influence) 28 Critical Mass: Adjust
Zong Gua: (underlying cause) 61 Inner Truth: Trust
Received as 2nd Hexagram: Pay attention to the small or insignificant details as they are important in this situation

The weak force is more powerful than gravity, and the smallest of life forms are the most successful. Appreciating what is small is called enlightenment.

I once had a sparrow alight on my shoulder for a moment
while I was hoeing in a village garden,
and I felt that I was more distinguished
by that circumstance
than I should have been by any epaulet
I could have worn. – Thoreau

Reading at a Glance: In Small Exceeding the flying bird brings you the message: "it is not well to strive upward, it is well to remain below. Great good fortune." If you are able to keep a low profile and stick to simplicity you will succeed. Since small lines surround the two yang lines there is not a lot you can do in this situation except concentrate on small matters and wait before making your move. Wu Wei, the principle of non action is a lesson about succeeding without striving. The secondary influence of Critical Mass also shows a type of instability that is going through transition where adjustments are required. Inner Truth as the Zong Gua was a time to test your vision and ability to be centered in interactions with others. It was a time to learn about establishing trust. Now you are called to step out of your normal routine of pushing your way out into to the world to stand beside yourself as a witness to unfolding events. The good fortune comes from witnessing the small things that are normally missed.

You might volunteer your time through charity or make a sacrifice in a lowly position to arrive where you would like to be later. Don't think about where you are going – look around you now to see where you are. Not striving means not trying but simply doing. It means not looking so far ahead that you miss what is unfolding for you now. "Striving upward is rebellion, striving downward is devotion." Devote yourself to the work and the rewards will come in time.

When the heart
soars like a bird,
and the mind tumbles
in endless curiosity -
the small exceeds itself.

"When one has the trust of the creatures, one sets them in motion. Therefore, follows the overwhelming of the small." In the same way that spiders pursue only what lands in their web, millions of tiny jellyfish ride the ocean currents to trap plankton wherever they are led. Observing nature's smallest manifestations, you can emulate how they do not strive, yet still find success.

As one of the last principles in the *Book of Changes*, it is interesting that it focuses on the little things in life. There is always a turning of events when anything exceeds the mean, and you are given a snapshot of a transitional state that arises from extraordinary conditions. *"Overwhelming of the Small signifies a transition."* Hsiao Kuo offers a message about the enormous power that arises from what appears to be insignificant.

The multi-cellular kingdom of plants demonstrate the overwhelming power of the small. As the most prolific of all life forms, they offer a picture of the great industry taking place at a micro level. The ocean too, is covered in green algae and plankton, although algae sits just below the surface and does not reflect the vibration of green. The ocean may appear blue to the masses, although *"in the perception of the smallest is the secret of correct vision."*

Your contribution is made in the small things that you are doing. In the things you fail to see - life guides you the most. Life pushes ever-onward toward its goal: *to release the potential energy that can become locked within stagnation."* You can continue on a pathway of success by keeping a low profile.

Life's smallest creatures reveal a type of success that is not always obvious. Those that travel the least teach will teach you the most about existing *just so* where your character develops. This principle resembles a bird, and suggests a type of transition that warns you of losing your sense of being grounded. *"The small bird brings the message: it is not well to strive upward. It is well to remain below."*

The master said: *"Striving upward is rebellion, striving downward is devotion."* Striving downward allows you to cultivate your character. Traveling little helps you to strengthen your ability to follow. Not striving 'out there' allows you to develop strength 'in here.'

As the opposite of Inner Truth, there is a warning that striving upward can disconnect you from your Inner Truth. You push upward to break through barriers, although at times you must *"bow down for preservation."* You are reminded of the flight of the bird and how it must return to the earth for sustenance out of necessity.

The longevity and flexibility of the insect world and plant kingdom can teach you about adaptability. Seeds find life in the most inhospitable environments. Some grow by oxygen alone, while others hitchhike on animal fur or on the wind to find a home. It is not where they are going, but how they get there that defines their unique nature. You travel in a circle that brings you back to your center so your purpose can take wing.

Seeds offer a lesson about blossoming because of the conditions that unfold. Yet, everything you will ever become grows from within. Cyclically, plants shed their growth and *"bow down to be preserved."* In this, you are reminded that life is not a constant flowering.

The idea of restraint might seem negative, but King Wen, imprisoned by the tyrant Chou Hsin, used his time in confinement to focus on the small matters that gave birth to his understanding of these sixty-four principles. Overwhelming of the Great suggested a beam that was excessive in weight and required support. Overwhelming of the Small prepares a solid foundation. In this way, restraint can lead to greater power.

"If the mind is not overlaid with wind and waves, you will always be living among blue mountains and green trees." Observing the power of the small, the master said: *"this is why I know the benefit of resorting to no action; the Way shows no favoritism."*

Like the plant, something profound takes root within, called forward by what takes place without. You might not recognize how you are following, although you can be certain that you are being led.

Success is assured when you realize how nature fortifies cyclical flowering. *"The great relic that existed before birth enters the heart one day."* Bowing down and not striving, you will discover the purpose of the great vessel within.

Unchanging: Take a different approach = less is more. The message of Small Exceeding unchanging is to not impose your will or try to sell anybody on anything. Step back and follow another's lead and ensure that you are paying close attention to the subtleties in the situation. It is the little things that matter not the big picture and sometimes releasing the pressure and stepping back allows another to process their fears and respond in their own time. The saying "less is more" is underscored in this situation. If you are asking about taking action the answer would suggest patience but if an opportunity presents itself you may need to take the road less traveled and act fast. Because of your willingness to open to the unusual you will gain a great deal.

Line 1 The bird meets with misfortune = through flying. Changes to (55) Abundance. The core message of Small Exceeding is to stop striving or pushing. Perhaps you are impatient or attempting too much too soon. The first step toward attempting to make changes through small efforts can fail if you are overly concerned with the outcome or what you will get. Remember that only small things can be achieved at this time.

Line 2 Passing by the grandfather and meeting the grandmother = not reaching the prince but meeting an official, no blame. Changes to (32) Duration. The situation isn't following the formalities which you are expecting. In meeting the grandfather or prince, one would gain recognition or be given a seal of approval to advance toward one's desire. With this line, one associates or gains assistance by showing sensitivity or coddling. This grandmotherly type of behavior is necessary to ensure that Duration and commitment is achieved. It isn't about formalities but tenderness and an awareness of the subtle nuances that are required to achieve your goal.

Line 3 If one is not extremely careful somebody may strike from behind = misfortune. Changes to (16) Enthusiasm. In your enthusiasm to achieve your aim, caution is advised. Self confidence can make you

441

unprepared to meet the challenge presented in what you may dismiss as insignificant. You may need to protect yourself from just blindly following another's lead. You are warned about the mysterious elements that are in the details should you not attend to them. Enthusiasm can run away with you, but you will be left holding the bag.

Line 4 Without blame, one does not pass the danger but meets it = be on guard and constantly persevering. Changes to (15) Authenticity. Rather than avoid the difficulty you choose to face it head on which is not a mistake. However, it is important to watch the situation carefully and be on guard for further disruption. The test of your character rests in being authentic and not just accommodating. Any mistakes made are simply an opportunity to discover more about yourself.

Line 5 Dense clouds, no rain from our western territory = the prince shoots and hits what is in the cave. Changes to (31) Influence/Wooing. Rather than force your will on the situation, examine how 'wooing' or the law of attraction might serve you better. You can't rely on what worked in the past and may need to come up with an innovative approach. This can be a time when results or responses are not forthcoming so you may need to just focus on getting your basic needs met. In order to obtain the object of your desire you may need to face your fear or weather a period of darkness or uncertainty. Don't give up.

Line 6 Passing by and ignoring the flying bird, bad luck and injury = misfortune. Changes to (56) The Wanderer. Because of your inability to establish a foundation through wandering, you are missing opportunities. Perhaps you are seeking greener pastures and not enjoying the opportunity that is right in front of you. The message of this line is to stop and examine the simple joys of life to prevent any further lack of fulfillment.

Hexagram #63
Chi Chi (After Completion)

Action: Renew
Hu Gua (secondary influence) 64 Before Completion: Prepare
Zong Gua: (underlying cause) 64 Before Completion: Prepare
Received as 2nd Hexagram: The situation is complete and over so there may be no choice but to move on.

**Equilibrium is the great foundation of life,
and harmony its universal path.**

Voyager, there are no bridges;
one builds them as one walks. – Gloria Anzaldua

Reading at a Glance: Many people find it odd that After Completion is a principle that precedes Before Completion in the Book of Changes. Perhaps the hexagrams were arranged in this way to remind us that nothing ever comes to an end. The message of Chi Chi is that while the situation appears to be stable and in order, you need to plan for inevitable changes that will continue to occur. When anything in nature achieves its highest expression or stability it moves toward regeneration. It may be that what you are inquiring about has reached a state of finality or completion as the hexagram is also called Already Across. The secondary influence of Before Completion suggests that you examine where you are, but plan for the future. This same hexagram shows up as the Zong Gua which is another message to prepare. You may think that the situation is never going to change but it will. You may think that you can rest on your laurels and enjoy complacency but you can't. It is important that you understand that in nature everything is in a state of renewal. While everything is in order and you can feel a sense of success or arrival, you are urged to remain cautious. Anything that reaches a climax will begin to move in the opposite direction. While the situation appears to be complete, a new goal or a need for further growth and expansion opportunities will ensure that it doesn't become stagnant. Water over Fire means that you must tend to it so the water doesn't burn out or evaporate. All things require care and attention to

444

continue in a constant state of wellness. The individual lines in this hexagram address the different stages one will encounter when going from completion to renewal.

Order, chaos
then order again.
Such is the way
of the great
untangling.

"One who stands above things, brings them to completion. Water over fire: the condition after completion." There is an obvious threat that the Water can extinguish the Fire, or that the flame can cause the water to evaporate. Water always moves downward; fire always burns upward. As an image of necessary balance, Chi Chi offers a message about becoming either overly confident, or too complacent.

While the current situation suggests a high degree of order, life's pursuit of change means that in time, disorder will emerge. After Completion is like a kettle of water over a fire. Too much heat and it boils over, extinguishes the fire or the water evaporates. The sage understands the small relationships existing between elements and guards against misfortune by not growing complacent.

Like the adaptive variations that remain dormant until we need them, knowing the condition that might arise after, life prepares us for the condition before it comes. The master said: *"Thus the sage takes thought of misfortune*

445

to arm against it in advance." You will be armed against misfortune by your willingness *"to see the eternity in the end."* This is the perpetual thread that reveals how nothing in nature comes to completion; it moves toward renewal. Nothing in nature comes to a standstill; it always transforms.

Approaching the conclusion to the Book of Changes, one immediately notices how the last two principles appear to be backwards. It would seem that After Completion should follow Before Completion. However, this principle describes both the certainty and uncertainty that arises after each ending.

Perhaps the principles were organized in this way to remind us that life is not linear, but is moving back and forth in an endless cycle of renewal. *"First good order prevails and in the end disorder."* This is simply the how life moves toward harmony or dissolution, but the power of nature is always productive. Chi Chi takes shape as the only principle where all the lines are in their proper places, although it is also the image where Peace or oblivion might lead to Standstill.

It is inevitable that when order reaches its peak, it will dissolve into disorder. The master said: *"Do not make plans. Do not be absorbed by activities. Do not think that you know. Be aware of all that is, and dwell in the infinite. Wander where there is no path. Be empty, that is all."*

"If one stands still at the end, disorder arises, because the Way comes to an end." The old way may come to an end, but life moves ever onward. Keeping the fire burning

446

without allowing the water to evaporate takes great skill and perseverance.

Transcending a sense of opposites suggests the creative power inherent in each paradox. Don't be too quick to judge the situation hastily. Perhaps what you thought was complete is just the beginning.

Unchanging: Already done, already decided = open to the changes. Chi Chi unchanging can have a message that the situation has reached a state of completion that won't change. However, all things change so you too will find your way forward into something new. Explore this situation from the standpoint of renewal because the past is the past and a new cycle will inevitably follow. While you can continue to fund energy into believing you can hold to the status quo, your time would be better spent examining the ways you can reinvigorate renewal. If everything is as you would like it to be, then Chi Chi unchanging can have a positive message about arrival. Since its hidden messages have to do with preparation, you are still reminded to actively ensure that renewal and a fresh perspective are continuously applied.

Line 1 Breaking the wagon wheels the tail gets wet = no blame. Changes to (39) Obstruction. During any transition from completion to renewal the way forward can appear confusing. Change is often accompanied by mistakes or missteps. You can think that you are on cruise control and suddenly get a flat tire that stops you in your tracks. There is not any real harm, but you are warned that the path you were on is changing. Any obstacles you meet are simply slowing you down so that you can examine the proper way forward.

Line 2 Losing the carriage screen, do not run after it = on the seventh day you will retrieve it. Changes to (5) Waiting. A carriage screen is meant to keep you hidden so losing it can mean you are exposed in some way. You may need to be more truthful about who you are rather than pretending to be someone you are not. Your 'real' face is exposed during a transition so there is no need to go searching for an old Persona. A period of waiting allows you to grow into a new way of expressing yourself.

Line 3 The Illustrious Ancestor approaches the Devil's Country and after 3 years conquers it = ordinary people should not be employed. Changes to (3) Difficult Beginnings. The message of this line is that completion will come after a period of hard work and dedication. Difficult Beginnings is a message to expect trials rather than an easy push forward. The reference to the Devil's Country can also suggest how this situation will test you and allow you to overcome your insecurities and demons. If you persevere toward your goal with unwavering caution you will succeed.

Line 4 Fine clothes turn into rags = be careful all day long. Changes to (49) Molting/Revolution. Appearances can be deceiving and the situation shows signs of decay. While everything appears stable, remain on guard because it can deteriorate very rapidly. Molting is the natural way animals and reptiles change their outer skin at cyclical times of the year and can portray inevitable change. Revolution can suggest how on the surface all can be calm but underneath an uprising is in the making. Examine the situation to ensure that all parties are feeling served and that there are no hard feelings rumbling below the surface.

Line 5 The eastern neighbor sacrifices an ox = it is not equal to the western neighbor's small sacrifice. Changes to (36) Brightness Hiding. It may seem that you have made great sacrifices to achieve your desire but it is what resides in the heart of giving that matters in this situation. A simple sacrifice offered with sincerity is far more powerful than grand displays of giving that are centered on what you get in return. The situation won't change until you examine what you are offering and whether it is given generously without an expected outcome. Timing can also be important. You may be still wrapped up in what was required in the past and are not acknowledging what needs to be sacrificed to the present.

Line 6 The head gets wet = danger. Changes to (37) Family. After moving forward diligently, in the sense of crossing the great stream, there is always an opportunity to turn back and gloat at your accomplishment. This would be dangerous so going forward is the only option to avoid danger. Getting the head wet is the idea of patting yourself on the back or getting too emotional when clear thinking and action is required. As the top line of a hexagram that talks about completion the answer can be to move on. What's done is done and the old situation will no longer serve you.

Hexagram #64
Wei Chi (Before Completion)

Action: Prepare
Hu Gua (secondary influence) 63 After Completion: Renew
Zong Gua: (underlying cause) 63 After Completion: Renew
Received as 2nd Hexagram: You may think that a situation is over but there is still an opportunity to make it work for you.

You are always on the threshold of change; how you approach it will determine your success.

We sometimes get all of the information, but we refuse to get the message. –Cullen Hightower

Reading at a Glance: Murphy's Law states that anything that can go wrong will go wrong and your current situation can feel much like this. The word entropy is Murphy's Law from a universal perspective and it is very much a way of life. Human beings are self organizing systems like all other things observed in nature. We are constantly attempting to make sense out of chaos. We prefer to classify what we see in terms of the past and this tendency can lead to a rude awakening. When we hear that the universe is moving toward entropy or disorganization this makes us uncomfortable. However, molecules moving inside of a box randomly are more dynamic than molecules locked in perfect order. Disorder increases energy and innovation. In Chi Chi, the situation had reached completion and order became apparent. In Wei Chi, the situation is in a state of disorganization or chaos but order will inevitably come. Better yet, because of the disorganization or unknown aspects of the situation, you will probably achieve more than you had originally set out to do. Such is the way of nature that it uses uncertainty to test all possible outcomes. You may need to live with the uncertainty because the situation is still in a state of evolution. Chi Chi as both the Zong Gua and the secondary influence guarantee that order is on the horizon no matter how unsettling things appear now. In Before Completion disorder or a lack of security and ease can become quite pronounced but given time, energy will dissipate and uncertainties will gel into a clear picture of the way forward. We can say anything that can go wrong will go wrong but just as easily say that anything that can go right will go right. The Book of Changes is always teaching us that what we experience is a matter of perspective. The rules of the

451

game that we can measure are what is observable in nature. Since disorder and uncertainty are its thrust into a purposeful future – trust that all is unfolding perfectly.

> **When the end**
> **is near,**
> **open**
> **to the new**
> **beginning.**

"Things cannot exhaust themselves. Hence, follows at the end, the principle of before completion." In Chi Chi or *After Completion,* the highest order inevitably led to the onset of disorder, symbolized by the highest display of summer that transforms into swirling winds of autumn. Wei Chi embodies the opposite condition where disorder will lead back to order. Like the chaotic storms of early spring, the landscape of spring is being composed.

Disorder can suggest how circumstance appears beyond your ability to control. Left to develop as it will, life always works out. While uncomfortable not knowing where the changes are leading, disorder is the letting go, like leaves during autumn, which always precedes the springtime of your blossoming.

Within disorder, is a dormant seed, which will inevitably lead back to order. Where complacency often leads to stagnation, the tension of change is already at play and it is better to follow where the changes might lead you. There is great power in knowing how situations evolve, moving back and forth.

The master said: *"Nature does not give up the winter because people dislike the cold."* In Wei Chi, you are standing at the threshold of change and have the opportunity to learn from the past. How you approach the changes will determine your success.

Chi Chi presented Water over Fire, and as its opposite, Wei Chi portrays Fire over Water. It would seem that since Fire burns upward and Water flows downward, there will be no connection between the two and the situation is hopeless. The fact that these two elements are moving in opposite directions is what makes the situation interesting and new. Anytime opposites appear, there will be a transformation.

The image of Fire moving upward portrays how you can lose your sense of connectivity to your current situation, looking for answers in the skies, as if your fate is in the hands of something arbitrary. Since the Abysmal is releasing its profound wisdom below, observe how life is speaking to you daily, in a thousand different ways.

The master said: *"How do we know that what we call heaven is not actually man, and that what we call man is not actually heaven?"*

Fire below gets water moving energetically yet, even without heat, water will still form itself into perfect crystals. In life, at some degree, everything is in continual motion. Wei Chi is the image of outward disorder that can lead to a sense of hopelessness, yet within it, you can already see how order is pre-arranging itself out of apparent chaos.

Regardless of the form that chaos takes, life has a special predisposition for generating disorder; it is a prerequisite in its pursuit of a better way. At the same time, it has a fondness for generating order from disorder. Perhaps that is why everything always seems to work itself out, *whether you choose to worry about it or not.*

"Although the lines are not in their proper places, the firm and yielding correspond." Like electricity, the firm or positive energy and the yielding or negative energy interact in force and fields that binds atoms, generate molecules and animate life. At all levels, life is regenerating itself from the chaotic dance of what appears to be disorder.

"Be not sad." Since nothing can reach completion, the trend moves toward the opposite condition: *renewal.* Life reveals its enormous power to sustain and strengthen its creatures to those who would follow its ways. Although disorder ends the Book of Changes, we know that it is a necessary pathway to renewal.

As the transition arrives, we see the image of the tree before it begins to branch. In between the stagnation of winter and the great fullness of summer is spring: a rebirth. It comes from *'nowhere,'* although we know it will come again, because it has come before.

The situation is strange and new, the past is a world away, and you are ripe for a transformation. Once things reach the end, you can approach the opportunity to blossom anew.

Unchanging: No expectations, go with the flow = nothing is ever complete. When we think about the chaos presented in Wei Chi we recognize that disorder is the only way that the future can be built from growth and innovation. When you receive this hexagram unchanging you are too focused on the present and perhaps are not giving the situation enough time or freedom to develop into its highest potential. You are being asked to flow the way nature wants you to flow – without expectations and without the need to classify or think of completion. They say that the journey is far more important than the destination and this is the case in your present situation. If you can recognize that Before Completion is a message to go with the flow the way will be much easier.

Line 1 Getting the tail in the water = humiliating. Changes to (38) Opposition. Although you may feel compelled to do something to set events in order, this is not the proper time to rush ahead. You are anxious for a tangible result but something about this situation is still in an evolutionary stage. Opposition can show events that stop you in your tracks and the purpose is to slow you down. Moving forward too hastily can only lead to humiliation.

Line 2 Braking the wheels = perseverance brings good fortune. Changes to (35) Progress. Because you realize that the situation requires a bit more time to gel it is good that you have put the brakes on moving anxiously forward. Progress can be achieved whether or not you are applying pressure or action. Periods of pausing to allow events to unfold naturally will lead to good fortune. It is important to be persevering in moving in step with how the situation is unfolding. Don't rush.

Line 3 Before completion, attack brings misfortune = it furthers one to cross the great water. Changes to (50) Cauldron. Crossing the great water is a message to do things differently or take the road less traveled. You may be nearing your goal and believe that an all out attack will bring completion more quickly but it won't. The Cauldron is associated with allowing something to simmer or cook until it is ready. It may not be in your nature to pause when reaching the finish line but this will allow you to complete all tasks efficiently so nothing is left undone.

Line 4 Perseverance brings good fortune, remorse disappears. Shock was used to conquer the Devil's Country and in the 3rd year success. Changes to (4) Youthful Folly. A willingness to go the distance is important because success will not come quickly. Youthfully Folly is a message that we make no mistakes through trial and error. The reference to the Devil's

456

Country suggests how the closer we get to success, the more we want to give up. The trials can be exhausting but again, without trial and failure one cannot succeed. Forget each misstep and just concentrate on the goal. If you persevere in this mindset you will succeed.

Line 5 Perseverance brings good fortune, no remorse = the fire of the enlightened mind is true, good fortune. Changes to (6) Conflict. Those who take the easy path never achieve the greatness of those unafraid to be tried by fire. This line shows the apex of success that is promised for those who know that conflict merely makes us stronger. Some people meet obstacles and give up but others see them as stepping stones to success. In this situation you have learned the valuable lesson of perseverance. No remorse means that by taking everything in stride, life is a grand adventure.

Line 6 Drinking wine in genuine confidence, no blame = but if the head gets wet, truth is lost. Changes to (40) Liberation. While drinking can be a normal celebratory activity after authentic success, some use substances to achieve a false sense of confidence. In moving toward the object of your enquiry you may be too emotional or observing from a haze of illusion. The head gets wet when we are not clear headed and using all of our faculties. The reference to Liberation can be a message to move away from self defeating or self abusive tendencies. In order to reach completion in achieving your desire, you may need to look squarely at the truth of the situation. As long as you don't get carried away and know your limits, success is assured.

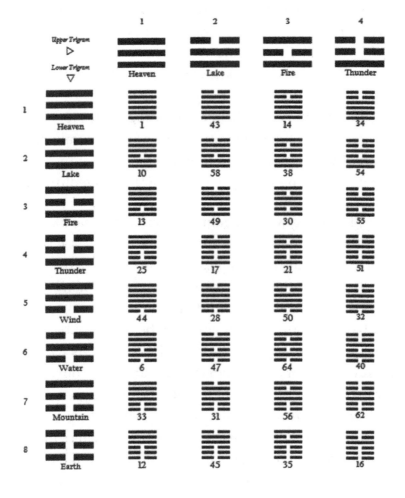

		1	**2**	**3**	**4**
Upper Trigram ▷					
Lower Trigram ▽		Heaven	Lake	Fire	Thunder
1	Heaven	1	43	14	34
2	Lake	10	58	38	54
3	Fire	13	49	30	55
4	Thunder	25	17	21	51
5	Wind	44	28	50	32
6	Water	6	47	64	40
7	Mountain	33	31	56	62
8	Earth	12	45	35	16

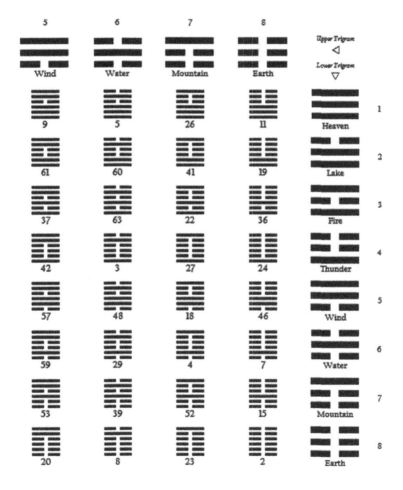

Made in the USA
Las Vegas, NV
02 January 2024